D1583859

A CALL FROM THE DARK

MIKE FISHER

authorHOUSE®

AuthorHouse™ UK
1663 Liberty Drive
Bloomington, IN 47403 USA
www.authorhouse.co.uk
Phone: UK TFN: 0800 0148641 (Toll Free inside the UK)
UK Local: 02036 956322 (+44 20 3695 6322 from outside the UK)

Published by AuthorHouse 07/27/2021

ISBN: 978-1-6655-8934-5 (sc)
ISBN: 978-1-6655-8935-2 (hc)
ISBN: 978-1-6655-8933-8 (e)

Print information available on the last page.

CHAPTER 1

THE GHOST SITTING NEXT TO THE FIREPLACE

A wood fire blazes in the hearth, the smell of pine filling the room as it burns. Faint fragrance gives comfort to the soul of the weary mind. The flames twist and swirl, dominating while being contained within the brick fireplace. They flicker in every direction, devouring the dry wood as the bursts of wood popping and swirling flames remind me of the fire's power. Visitors to the room comment on its warmth, its comfort, and the welcome respite it offers from the cold autumn day. I sit in my recliner chair no more than four feet away from the fire, dumped onto the chair by a carer who doesn't really care. Though I can enjoy the hypnotic dance of the flames and the sound of crackling wood, the warmth is denied me, as I am a tetraplegic, more commonly known as a quadriplegic, paralysed from the chest down. I have little sensation, and regardless of the heat source I have, I remain so cold that my bones hurt. I retire early for the day. At half past four in the evening I get to watch the magnificent splendour of the sun setting over the hills of Marlborough, as my bungalow is nestled in a valley of the Wiltshire countryside. I have the best seats in the house for this autumnal spectacle.

As I watch the sunset over the horizon, the sun starts its descent, reaching across the cloud-spotted sky. The clouds react with rich threads of red tangled with orange crimson strands. I'm transported from my broken, crippled body to the magnificent existence of the universe. Free of its dead body, my mind flies across the hills. I can see the full effect of

1

the autumn as the trees turn their most vibrant hues and the leaves flutter down from their branches. My escaped mind flies into the sun, emerging into the mighty universe itself. Planets float effortlessly; galaxies spin slowly like clouds gathering for a storm. Nestled inside them are bright stars resembling the fairy lights on a Christmas tree. Each galaxy seems to be orbiting a great power, slowly turning to its tune. As I float through space, I shrink and shrink to the size of an atom, and particles dart around me like crazy lovers dancing freely in the night, hidden from prying eyes.

Looking down, I see that my body has joined the dance. Though I'm now a collection of separated atoms, the crazy dancing lovers make me part of the whole. The universe exists as one entity composed of nothing but atoms that do a poor job of holding the dancing particles in line as they dart from one place to another. Everything seems random, but I can't help thinking of a greater power somehow orchestrating the dance. There is no greater power here though, how can there be a power greater than this vast architecture? Some may call this God, others quantum mechanics, others the multiverse. Personally, I see no need to name it, mainly because I feel it's so vastly majestic that no name can do it justice. This is how I have interpreted and imagined quantum physics.

My wanderings through the universe are cut short as the carer nudges me to empty my bladder with a urine bottle through a suprapubic catheter drilled into my bladder via my abdomen. They don't care about the presence of other people in the room, who I feel are as uncomfortable as I am about the spectacle of my urination. They just need to complete their timed tasks and check the boxes on their care plans. I'm nothing more than a checklist item that must be ticked off before they can finish for the day.

I attempt to contribute to the conversation that my wife, Amanda, is having with her friends. They sit on the sofas next to me. But soon it becomes apparent that my contribution isn't too significant and that I won't be missed, and I fade back into my mind again. Looking down at the table beside my chair, I see the four books that have been capturing my imagination for the past few days,a book on the history of Buddhism, one on Zen philosophies, one on quantum mechanics, and one on how modern psychology and the two thousand-year-old Zen thinking are closely related. Topics I have been tentatively reading about for years now seem more relevant. My mind has been cracked open, and I am losing the memories of my life, including past learning. Hence the books, as I try and recapture topics close to my heart. Somehow, I can't stop thinking that they are all closely related like children holding hands in a circle, each separate but together, it all makes sense as they dance around the garden sprinkler, laughing and enjoying how they have completed their circle.

In my late twenties, I escaped the fear and dogma of my Christian upbringing and vowed never to be misled like that again. So, though I have studied Buddhism, I am not a Buddhist or an adherent of any philosophies with dogma and belief. However, I do find the philosophies of Zen greatly interesting, as there's little dogma. When taken in context with modern psychology and quantum mechanics, it hits a tune with me. It fuels my imagination, creating a tune produced in my mind by a tiny ballet dancer dancing over the keys of a piano. The deeper you go into the subject, the faster and more elegantly she dances. The way I perceived oneness was based on not only Zen thinking but also science, as quantum physics also grabbed my attention. I became fascinated with atoms as the fundamental elements of matter in the whole universe. It seemed to show me that existence and the notion of us were one and the same, separated only by individual perceptions. This realisation instilled in me an even greater desire to change, as I started to see that we were all one. I couldn't help feeling excited when learning that particles, part of atoms, exist in two separate and distant places at once. It's hard to imagine, and even Einstein struggled with this theory so much so that he called it 'spooky action at a distance'. It suggests that all and everything are made of the same matter of the universe and that the millions of atoms of which we are composed are elements that bind the whole universe together as one. As I'm jumping ahead of myself, I will wrap the discussion up by simply saying that this thinking has been cultivated in me for over fourteen years, and my hospitalisation became the booster rocket that sent me across the universe into oneness and a place where I finally found some comfort.

I loo up from my pondering. It seems the sofas on which my wife and her guests are sitting have moved far into the distance. As they fade away, I wonder if I'm the one fading away. Many people feel someone near them when there's no one there. I don't feel that; rather, I feel like the ghostly presence standing next to them. I can't tell the difference between my ghost and myself anymore, each day I feel more and more transparent, more and more isolated from the world. Although I've been out of hospital for a while now, I have felt less and less connected to this world. I feel almost constantly like I'm being tugged away from life itself. Am I the one feeling the ghostly presence in the physical world, or am I the ghostly presence on some other plane?

Whichever it is, I seem to be in a dilemma that holds me in a place between two worlds—one of physical life, one of a confused spirt life. But which world do I belong to? I do have an acquired brain injury (ABI), making the brain region pertaining to hallucinations on the active side. So who knows? In the physical world, the day is in its twilight, but I still haven't solved my dilemma. What is the spiritual world? How are we all connected? I just can't stop thinking about it, as the tiny dancer moves faster and faster. I believe that I'm writing all my thoughts down in the physical world. I'm not sure what I'm trying to achieve by this. Perhaps it's just therapy; perhaps it's just to tell a story; perhaps it's to try to prove I'm real. I don't know, but one thing is for sure—I am not trying to teach anybody anything or show some great revelation. Given I'm not someone of any merit, I'm certainly incapable of offering help. That's not to say that if you come across my writing, you may not accidently find something that catches your attention or speaks to your own predicament, but that's your journey, while this is mine.

The story with which I'm wrestling begins when I was a management consultant responsible for a family of four. Though I call this my story, it's in fact the story of my wife, Amanda, and me. She, of course, can't follow me into comas or other dark places, but she will always be there like a guardian angel who can conjure up hell at a moment's notice. There's not one part of this story without Amanda in it saving my life repeatedly throughout. We were an ordinary couple head over heels in love even after twenty years of marriage. So, this is our story told from both our perspectives. When I'm unconscious, the story is Amanda's to tell. However, for now, the narrative is mine.

As normal as this story may sound, it shows how I have been trapped in this plane of existence between worlds, which is full of my dark forces and deluded beliefs of phantoms and ghosts. The question is, Am I one of the ghosts? If I am, I'm not sure when I became one. The story speaks of my self-determined giant being brought to his knees, making me face who I really am. Facades will be cracked and broken like discarded chains; reality will come pouring in to show the truth of myself. I secretly knew my life was a lie of false personas, but I just found it easier to look away, allowing the facade I called the giant to grow beyond control. The higher I rose up the career cliff, the farther I fell, exposed to the pretence of who I believed I was, as if a raw nerve had been sliced open by a reality lost in the deep dark past. The giant I imagined I had been would fall, crashing to the ground, smashing into a thousand and one pieces. To understand the psyche of my ghost, you need to know how I saw things as well as how I got there.

Who am I? Well, I am no victim, no innocent saint, no paragon of virtue. I may be a subject of pity now, but I have always known how to look after myself. Though I accept your sympathy out of necessity, I certainly don't want your pity, thanks all the same. I'm not the sort of person who mopes about, seeking sympathy. I believe in just getting on with it, pulling up my breeches to battle through—something I have always done. This attitude helped me rise up the career cliff, from a soldier to a senior management consultant. So, I didn't just arrive on the cliff a fully formed senior consultant. I do have a history. Being the youngest of three boys, I have had to compete for everything. Our parents, being of old values, held close certain ideas of how a modern nuclear family should be. My mother was and is a very religious person. She taught us that, if we weren't good, God was going to get us, while the devil was waiting for us; it all scared the hell out of me. She also taught us good values and manners and to support others in need. I think all of us three brothers have always tried to measure up to her values, standards, and expectations. Though most the time we succeeded, sometimes we failed too.

My father was a distant, aloof man. When we were children, he never interacted much with any of us. If we wanted to engage with him, we had to join him in doing tasks, such as clearing snow. I remember longing to hug him as a child, but he was not a man of public affection. However, if I looked into his eyes, I always saw love and pride staring right back at me. He was a good father. He worked hard, climbed the cliff, and provided well for his family, so much so that he was always too tired to engage with the children when he got home. When we grew up and left home, he became a surprisingly good friend, a generous man who kept us each on our feet, no matter what. Burned into my mind was how he would say 'Nonsense!' whenever you said you couldn't do something. When things got hard, I would hear him say 'Nonsense!' This would stiffen me up, and then I would just get on with it. We lost our father early in life. He was just 52 when he died. I was 22 and on the other side of the world when it happened. It was a random heart attack brought on by low blood pressure.

His death drove me to make changes in my life, as now I realised how finite life could be. The process of change still goes on, proving that, at least for me, changing oneself is a long, arduous process. It started when I lost my dad and resulted in me finding a greater awareness of myself, giving me an understanding of what I believed I should be.

This emerged when I started walking the paths of Glastonbury Festival every year for over a decade with my brother Paul, partaking in anything that expanded our minds. At the festival, we felt euphoric, open, unafraid, and accepting of and connected to everyone around us. Most others at the festival felt the same. We were in a space that allowed tremendous freedom of thought and expression. There was what I could only explain as a mass human attitude of peace for everyone, which engulfed us all. It made me look at life differently, seeing the world with softer, more accepting eyes. It also led me to study Zen Buddhism, which in turn led me to mindful meditation. However, it's important to reiterate that I'm not a Buddhist. Buddhism is steeped in dogma, with the potential of being as venomous as any other religion. However, once I got through the dogma of it all, I followed Buddhism's path through the world, discovering Chinese Chan, which encompasses Buddhism and Taoism, along with Confucianism. This, consequently, led to Japanese Zen, which led me, in my opinion, to a purer sense of mindful meditation.

The change I made in myself uncovered a darkness in me. It made me aware of my dark forces, which had been with me since being in the army. Not until my late thirties and early forties did the darkness in my mind become like a shadowy presence, following me as if it were a lost dog. It seemed harmless at first, but then it turned on me, baring its teeth. The dark phantoms in my mind were set free into the real world when I lay injured on a hospital bed slowly dying, with surgeons drilling holes in my brain. Was it them who let the phantoms out? Were the phantoms real? And how would I put them back in?

My darkness kept taking me to a shadowy place, exiling me to the deep recesses of my own mental formations. It almost appeared real, like I existed in another world, but I could not fully see. It made me feel like I was a prisoner in my own mind. The place where I was sent, I called the other world. It always smelt of burning flesh, while the sounds of firing weapons complemented the screams in the distance. One thing I knew for sure was that 'he' had been there since I was in the army—a frightening figure waiting in the dark, a phantom, who at that early point, I had never completely seen. All I knew was a dark presence existed in myself that imprisoned me. These thoughts put my mind into a spin. My fear of a darkness that was likely not real drove me to question everything, desperately trying to avoid it. As a young man, I saw the darkness as my guilt about my dark actions. I drank to run away from it, taking it out on others, acting unforgivably violent. I'm not proud of such actions. I only wish I could go back and have a word with myself. Eventually, I found a way, using meditation and calming myself, which kept the darkness at arm's length. Fighting for life and then being paralysed made me doubt myself and question my existence, allowing the darkness to come rushing back in.

The phantom was never invited and never called upon. His visits brought depression with a feeling that fear had grabbed my stomach. I felt low, which led to my self-confidence being smashed to the ground every time he visited. A lot of the time, as if he had injected me with poison, all I could think about was the darkness. Because of that, I called him Doctor Dark. His visits have never been welcome, but they've been consistent throughout my postarmy life.

The catalyst for my fall and changes in who I am come from an unseen menace—a foolish action where everyone holds some responsibility. No matter what peace I have eventually found, it's difficult to be a complete man when I'm strapped onto a wheelchair as a quadriplegic—left with a life of constant pain, uncontrollable spasms, and paralysed organs, left to shit and piss out all remaining pride and dignity.

Many parts of my brain were injured, including my sixth brain nerve. This left me with vertical/horizontal double vision, stealing both my normal vision and my depth perception. Look at this how you may. I for one have broken away from the idea of a single consciousness pointing at someone

7

saying, 'You have cancer', 'You're getting injured', 'You're going to have all the money.' No, for me, everything in this life seems random and out of anyone's control. I see no evidence of some great mind or consciousness in some way guiding or asserting power. My injury was random. How I ended up was random. How much I can recover will be random. However, I am cognisant of the possibility that the physical consequences of my injury will affect so much of my body that I'll contemplate believing in a higher existence, just so I can shout and swear at it.

There's no getting around it. My mind was broken open, with large chunks of my long-term memory disappearing, forcing a struggle upon me to retain even my personality. As time passed, my short-term memory also started to fail; perhaps that was inevitable. Left with half-confused memories, events and work places started to move around. At first, the deterioration occurred very slowly, almost unnoticeably. But it built over years until even yesterday, in my mind, becomes confused.

After holding back the darkness for so long, such an insignificant menace broke down my defences, pulling me into the other place, an apocalyptic nightmare. My battle with the darkness becomes a battle with myself. Day by day, my body failed, while I faced death, with little hope of survival. Now I'm left *crippled* and broken, and nothing will be able to comfort me until I learn the truth. The question is, without a doubt, what is the truth?

CHAPTER 2

THE FORTRESS OF SOLITUDE

Sitting at the director's table on the high peak, I quickly learnt that senior management teams were full of self-serving overconfident arrogant people who only worked together to hunt down others perceived to be in their way, like a pack of hungry dogs. They hunted down anyone who they supposed to be a threat, sometimes even turning on each other. So, I avoided them, trying not to get bitten. I never joined them. Instead, I just moved to another peak on the cliff, a different company, only to find a different pack of dogs fighting, just like the others.

The shift was admittedly a career mistake. I almost instantly regretted joining another company. They showed so much promise, so much enthusiasm for change, so much pretence that they knew what they were doing. In the end, no one was going to change. Nor did anyone really know where the whole enterprise was going. I was brought in through my old boss, who thought that, together, we could convince them to change. It was like running through treacle headfirst into a reinforced wall. The dogs of war had sharpened their teeth, ready to rip us apart flesh by bloody flesh. When my boss finally left to return to the other ledge of the career cliff, for a better role with people she knew, I was left to face the hungry dogs by myself. Bit by bit, they ripped me apart clearly, trying to find a way to throw me off their ledge. I hid myself in a project as far away from London as I could get and then just watched as they pulled me apart, replacing me with my own deputy. I endured a year of their bullshit; my stress levels went through the roof. However, I needed to make sure my family was safe, with money coming in. Let's face it. We are all only one

9

or two month's salary away from bankruptcy. I was just waiting to be sacked, so I couldn't get that thought out of my head. The stressed worry caused by the severe mauling of the angry vengeful dogs destroyed my once indestructible confidence.

As the winds of work howled around me, all I wanted to do was stand on the edge of the peak of the career cliff, fall, and then rise up above it all like a soaring bird. In the end, I settled for climbing back down the cliff to find a ledge where I felt safe. I stepped down from the position of director and joined a large company, taking up the role of senior manager consulting on organisational design. It might have seemed a strange move for the giant in my mind, but it was the best move I ever made. Working for this established business brought its own rewards, as it was one of the top four companies in the world. Plus, I loved delivery; solving organisational problems was interesting, as well as challenging. I never came to regret joining them. They were professional and caring of employees but most of all, for me, supportive of my family financially. They kept a dialogue going as I lay dying in the hospital, even though I had been employed by them for only a short time. In consideration of my experience, the proverb, 'Move and the way will open,' is particularly true.

By the time I found this great new role, the hinges of my mind had fully fallen off. Even though I felt good about my new career, as with all new jobs, I doubted my capability to do it. I had endured such a battering to my confidence at my previous workplace that it brought on a disturbed sleep, where the other world engulfed me.

The night before I started my new job, I felt very unsettled; darkness surrounded my mind, leaving me feeling pinned to the bed. I was transported to the other world. It was like a war-torn land with burning if not burnt trees everywhere. The whole place was grey, interspersed with some colour, such as that of the flames on the trees. The ground was charred, the air was thick with choking smoke. The smell of burning flesh filled the air getting right in the back of my throat. The darkness moved like black sheets blowing in the wind all around me. The black sheets brought fear—anger mixed with hatred. The feeling of anxiety I experienced when the dark wind surrounded me filling me with its dark unbeknown intent was greater than I had ever felt. The whole place made my heart beat so rapidly that it almost burst out of my chest. I felt clammy as sweat oozed from my whole body. In the darkness, I could feel its angry hatred, along with a heart-wrenching fear.

Every time I visited the other world, I was standing on a cobblestone path that stretched out to the horizon. As I walked, the uneven cobblestones caused my foot to slip, almost breaking my ankle. The sound of screams from people unseen instilled fear in me, but the intermittent sound of distant gunfire drowned out their screams, as it created thunder from the horizon. The whole place brought about despair, breaking down my resolve to keep going. It was as if I were carrying the apocalypse around inside my head. I felt a foul presence on the wind that day. As time passed, I could feel it was Doctor Dark. He seemed agitated, with a dark resolve to force dark thoughts into my head. All I could think was, *I'm not good enough. They're going to find out what a fool I will be. What will I do when they bin me? How will I pay the bills? Where will I get another job? Why am I even bothering?*

'Just stay in bed,' instructed Doctor Dark without even moving his lips. It was like his voice was in my head, but it had no form. 'You will never pull this off. You're a fake, who will be found out.' He always knew where to hit me and when to strike, like a rattlesnake disturbed from its slumber. My confidence was so battered that he easily stepped on me. He dragged depression out of my soul by punching me straight in the chest, ripping out hope like it was my heart.

He provoked me to such angry desperation that I shouted into the wind, 'Leave me alone. I deserve this. I don't need you bringing me down.'

I put so much force into shouting that I slipped on the path, injuring my ankle. So, I sat there cradling my foot as if it were a wounded child. Doctor Dark seemed angry at my outburst, but it was hard to tell, as all I could see was his eyes, his mouth, and his left hand. I could just make out that he was wearing an old-fashioned black top hat, but the darkness still covered it. His eyes flashed as if something had been turned on.

Much to my relief, the bleeping of the alarm dragged me out of the dark into the light of another day. Very keenly, I got up and showered. I felt excited yet nervous, as if it was my first day at my first job. The job was a result of my twenty years of hard slog up the cliff. Finally, there I was, off to my dream of a better working life. Suited and booted, feeling like a giant, I had used Doctor Dark's torments to stand up in defiance to my fear, breaking through the barrier of my injured confidence. I said goodbye to Amanda and our two boys, and I rushed to catch the train to London. I felt like every particle in my body was dancing around in anticipation. My hands trembled from the adrenalin rush in my body. I took some deep breaths to centre myself. I strengthened my resolve even more by thinking of a quote by Buddha. 'Each morning, we are born again. What we do today is what matters most.' I had to lay down my past to get on with life anew. Lao Tzu said, 'If you are depressed, you are living in the past. If you are anxious, you are living in the future. If you are at peace, you are living in the present.' I kept running these quotes through my head to keep myself calm, trying to enjoy the moment.

It was all I expected it to be—exciting, terrifying, and educational all at the same time. The building in which I worked was a giant glass structure on the bank of the River Thames. Inside, large escalators took you to a colourful professional-looking first floor with client reception. Behind the escalators, a series of lifts took you wherever you worked in the building. Each floor was plush with touch screens to find you a desk to work at. There were cushion-seated breakout areas with tea and coffee facilities. Surrounding the floor were identical cubicle offices for the partners.'

As a consultant, I was looking for my first client contract, for which I didn't have to wait too long. I was asked to join a team in Birmingham working for a public-sector organisation. To me, it felt like going home, as I'd been in Birmingham for two years when I had worked for a big outsourcing and consultancy firm. As a consultant, even though one works for an organisation, projects are allocated only after clearing interviews with project leads. So, when I got the role, I felt a little bit more confident about myself.

As happy as I was with my new job there was one small problem. As a management consultant, I had a working existence that focused entirely on people; so portraying that I understood people and 'enjoyed' their company was important, especially clients who wanted to feel good about using my skills and paying my fees. Yet when I closed the hotel door, the noise of people needing things, having certain sensitivities, or working on their personal agendas suddenly vanished. The silence embraced me, soothing any pains or irritations. Even taking myself to dinner to the restaurant seemed like too much work. I would risk a trip to the gym because we all had our headphones in, meaning no one wanted to talk anyway. I didn't want to have to talk to anybody or have any more interactions, as my human side was closed for business. If there was a team night out, I always went along. In many cases, I had a good time, but I would be thinking about being in my hotel room without anyone talking.

Having locked myself away, I only had one more person-related undertaking to perform—calling Amanda. I always looked forward to our call. But by the time I finished the day, all my energy for engaging with people was spent, my mind a void with my brain's gearbox crunching to a halt from the day's lunacy. I didn't want to talk about work because it was dull, and Amanda didn't want to talk about her day for the same reason. We both hated the phone—its impersonal manner, its intrusive nature. On the phone, we both felt we had lost all our visual cues, leaving us with small talk, at which I was always inept. There I was on the phone with Amanda, the person I called my life, the person I had missed all day, and we were both so tired we could hardly string two words together. When we did, the exchange was awkward and fragmented. It wasn't us; it was the mechanism of delivery. If an outsider ever witnessed our exchange, they might have been forgiven for thinking it was a relationship on the rocks. However, we both knew how in love we were. When I was home, we reverted to normal as if I had never been away. We saw the strained calls just as a blip, which we struggled through and then forgot, a sign of how much we meant to each other.

Once the day was complete, the room became my fortress of solitude, allowing me to step away from the mad hat rowdiness of family life and the stress of work. It allowed me to make sense of the stray thoughts I wrestled with daily. My creativity flourished, as I could concentrate on where all the pieces of a forming idea went. These moments of solitude were fully appreciated, as they had a profound effect on my productivity, along with my creative thinking. More importantly, they provided me with the solitude I needed to concentrate on my personal development, my change. I didn't want to emulate or become a carbon copy of anyone. I wanted to find who I was so I could build on that. Little did I know then that to truly know oneself, one first must become aware that there is no self.

My connection to my family was strong; their presence was missed, making me feel their pull home by Friday. I religiously travelled the forty miles back to see them. Nothing could stop me from getting home to Swindon. On the evening of Friday, 10 November 2014, I was, as usual, driving home at about eight in the night. The night was dark, cold, and wet, with rain coming down at a great rate as I sped through the traffic. Owing to the night mist along with the driving rain, I could hardly see. The road was busy with Friday traffic, as a lot of people were clearly trying to just get home. The whole atmosphere felt strangely ominous. My mind became unsettled, but I couldn't put my finger on what the cause was.

I had a bad cold, which was starting to kick in. Sweating, I felt hot and then cold. I fought hard to keep my eyelids open, as both the cold and the fatigue from the week of work took their toll on me. It seemed like someone was pulling a veil over me from inside. The driver of the car in front of me suddenly jammed on the brakes; his brake lights lit up in front of me like the two eyes of an angry dragon. With my eyes half shut, my mind on other things, I was slow to react. To add to that, I was driving too close to the car in front. I slammed on the brakes. My car slid as the brake crunched under my foot. Trained on a skid pan in the army, I was familiar with how to deal with such skids. I applied cadence braking, slamming the breaks on, then letting go, and then hard braking again to stop skidding in the wet. My car came to a halt at a rough stop only inches behind the car in front. Although my army driving course had proved itself useful that day, my heart still beat at a hundred miles an hour, like if it could, it would have ripped itself out of my chest and just crawled away.

After a short while, we all started moving again. I gripped the wheel tightly, carrying on with the single uncompromising thought that I must get home. The week's solitude had been nice, but all I wanted now was to hold my family close. Amanda then called me, wanting to know when I would be back. I held down the giant inside me who just wanted to shout, 'I will be back when I'm back.' Instead, I just said softly, 'I don't know, sweetheart. The traffic is quite heavy tonight.' The soft me started to emerge again as the memory of my family drove me along the road.

When the short conversation had ended, I looked down for just a second to press the hang up button. As I heard the beeping, I realised I was drifting into the middle lane. I quickly swung the car back with much effort due to the wet conditions. I slid from side to side, steering into the skid to get the car straight on the road again. Taking a deep breath to try to slow down my heart, I thanked my lucky stars and continued driving as if nothing had happened.

To occupy my mind and stay awake whilst trying to keep the thoughts about work away, I started to think about being home with Amanda and the two boys. I imagined sitting on my chair, the log burner burning, the dog lying at my feet, my family fighting over what to watch. I did miss them. I really couldn't wait to be home with them. My cold was improving, downgraded to a bit of a sniffle.

The traffic seemed to lighten up, getting moving one minute and then getting heavy again and slowing right down the next. Despite being in the car for over two hours, I was still on the M5, a bad sign for getting home in time for dinner and seeing the boys to bed All I could hear was the whoosh of the cars as they glided past me in the rain. As I passed a big lorry, the spray of rain from his wheels blinded my view. With the windscreen covered in water and the windscreen wipers just struggling unsuccessfully to clear it, it was like a dream; everything seemed to slow down as the world moved in slow motion. I finally came to my senses and slowed down but not too much, as I didn't want to get stuck in the lorry's backwash. I drove fast enough to get past the lorry but not too fast that I was blinded by all the water. Coming out of the wash, I had to apply cadence, braking again and stop on a penny. The lorry stopped as well, right beside me. I had taken a silly risk for nothing. Eventually, the traffic speeded up again, I started picking up speed. Finally, I started to drive carefully, not too fast, due to the rain and my compromised reaction time from my cold.

As I passed Cheltenham, I noticed the exit for the A419 London; my heart lifted. The route always felt like the home run back to Swindon. Even though I felt low, there was no sight of Doctor Dark or the other world. As I passed the Air Balloon pub, the traffic slowed to a crawl. It wasn't long before I traversed the mini roundabout and then started motoring up the A419 dual carriageway. The traffic had lightened, opening up a clear road ahead. *It won't be long now,* I thought. I accelerated, the speed soaring to eighty miles an hour on the dual carriage way. Looking back, I realise it was a stupid thing to do, as the rain was still heavy. To be honest, I wasn't really concentrating. The flashback of an encounter earlier in the day occupied my bored mind. I had seen a man in a wheelchair at work. He was smartly dressed; his wheelchair seemed fitted and slim as he moved effortlessly. The encounter had led me to make a very strange decision: If I were ever crippled, that was how I would want to be. As soon as I had thought of it, I dismissed it. However, for some reason, the whole encounter lingered in my mind.

Entering the outskirts of Swindon, I was really on the home stretch. I needed to concentrate even more at this point, as I was nearly home. A childhood memory of a government warning advertisement kept playing over in my mind. The advertisement showed a man flying out through his windscreen with the commentary, 'He was nearly home. He relaxed and then lost concentration.' The advertisement had stuck with me. Such crappy little advertisements probably worked, because I always slowed down, concentrating more as I neared home.

Suddenly, a car running at least at a hundred miles per hour came fast up my backside, flashing its lights. *What a wanker!* I thought, while indicating to move into the left lane. As the car speeded past me, my heart started beating wildly, and fear grabbed my stomach. I became disorientated, as the driver was Doctor Dark. Passing by, he flicked the V at me. *He might be a frightening phantom*, I thought, *but he's still a wanker.* I wondered why I was seeing him outside of my dreams, which made me realise I was half asleep. With a startled jerk, I woke myself fully up, my heart beating rapidly again.

I was driving at sixty miles an hour now, still too fast for the unfavourable weather conditions. Finally, I saw my exit and turned on the indicator. Suddenly, a white van pulled across both lanes of traffic to reach the exit. I slammed the brakes, again cadence braking to narrowly miss it, but I was on a full-on skid. Steering into the skid, I flipped into the left lane, only to see another white van driving right at me. Seeing the driver, I felt a chill run down my spine. It was Doctor Dark again, but he had transformed into a regular van driver this time. He was pissed off, but I could not have done anything to avoid it. *Surely,* I thought, *he saw what just happened.* However, he just came to a stop inches behind me and swung into the right lane, driving around me. I tried to give it no more thought, writing the Doctor Dark sighting off as just the result of stress. All this had happened in the driving rain. Not far from home at this point, I drove at thirty miles an hour all the way. Pulling up on to the driveway, I got out of my car, utterly unaware that would be my last time behind the wheel of a car.

The following Monday was a big day for me. After much effort, I had blagged a meeting with the client sponsor at work. When I woke up, I felt truly awful. My cold had developed into the flu. I didn't feel well at all. My legs kept giving way. My old back injury was acting up, something that hadn't happened since I'd had metal pins inserted in my spinal cord two years earlier after a fall. *I have always looked adversity in the eye and kept laughing, and today will be no different,* I thought. I grabbed an old walking stick I used to use when I had back issues a few years earlier. I decided to take a train to Birmingham, as I didn't feel fit enough to drive. So Amanda drove me to the train station.

When I arrived in Birmingham, I jumped into a taxi and headed straight to the client office. On arrival, I met the other team members, so we went into the meeting together. I kept running my script through my head while fighting off the terrible feeling of sickness. By then, I was burning up so badly that beads of sweat slowly slid down my face; no matter how hard I tried or how many times I shifted on my chair, I couldn't get comfortable. My agony was evident to everyone in the room. However, it was an important meeting. We really needed a go or no-go from the client. As my turn to speak arrived, I swallowed deeply, trying to disguise the pain shooting up my back, along with the strange cold feeling in my thighs. Running through my presentation, I guided the client through the new organisational design, explaining our strategy. When I looked at him, he had a blank impression almost impossible to read. Stiffening up, I thought, *Resilience! Michael, don't give up! You can bounce back from this.*

Much to my relief, he liked the design, triggering everyone agreeing on a way forward. As the meeting ended, the client bid me goodbye saying, 'Go home. You look terrible.'

Once we finished discussing plans, everyone asked me to go home. Anna, my colleague, called a taxi for me, demanding I go home and look after myself. At that point, I didn't put up a fight. I was never the one to let illness beat me, but I felt utterly terrible that day, so I went home.

Amanda, who had recently taken up a teaching assistant position, came home in the afternoon, immediately going into care mode. She ensured that I had everything and was as comfortable as possible. I struggled to sleep that night, as I twisted and turned in pain. I felt dizzy, regardless of how I rested my head on the pillow. I felt his presence all night. Doctor

Dark seemed to lurk outside the bedroom door, with the only intention of filling my soul with fear. I managed to shake him and his effect off me just for the night. This new power partly came from me feeling like burning suns had formed a dome around me. I was being burnt by a circle of fire and didn't have any energy to waste on him.

By the next morning, though, the flu symptoms had abated as if by some magical force; the pain in my legs had worsened. *Oh well*, I thought, *I can't have everything.* With the intention of going to work, I got up and showered. While in the shower, I tried to direct the hot water on to my ice-cold legs. It felt like blocks of hard ice had formed inside my leg muscles, the weight dragging me down. Nothing, not even the jet of hot water, could stop them from feeling painfully cold. As I turned off the shower, I stepped out of the bath. My legs gave way, and I collapsed, transforming into a naked, wet heap of useless flesh. Helplessly lying on the floor, I called out to Amanda. Straight away, she came running, helping me immediately to get up. With much effort, she walked me to our bed. It was no easy task, as Amanda was only five feet and nine stones, while I was six feet two inches and sixteen stones. How she achieved the feat was beyond me, but she did, like dragging someone off a battlefield.

My legs got colder, pinning me to the bed on which I was lying. 'I can't walk. What's wrong, Amanda?' I asked helplessly.

'I don't know,' she replied. 'Shall I call the GP?'

'Yes,' I shouted, more out of fear than anger.

Amanda ran downstairs, grabbed the cordless phone, and brought it up. As she started to dial the number, she stopped to ask, 'Mike, how bad is it?'

'It's terrible. My legs really hurt, with this cold feeling. I can't move them now.'

'Shall I call the GP or an ambulance?'

'What do you think?' I asked.

'I think all the GP will do is take a look at you and call an ambulance. So why delay? Let's get you straight into an ambulance.'

'OK, do it,' I barked back, starting to feel quite desperate.

Amanda immediately called for an ambulance. As the man she loved seemed to be in great distress with something seriously wrong, she was evidently feeling helpless, like she was lying at the bottom of a deep pit, her hands and legs tied, utterly unable to render me any aid. Seeing me in such distress broke her heart, while she could do nothing to help me.

I never normally allowed physical pain to bother me, but the pain I experienced at that moment wrenched at every nerve of mine. To add to that, not being able to move my body as I wanted made me feel instantly trapped. My fight or flight response was all set to fight. But the trouble was that I had nothing to fight against, except freezing cold pain; no matter how much I tried, my body was not responding to my will. The whole situation made me frustrated and angry. I lay on the bed, my face in a grimace, my skin pale and clammy to the touch. I didn't like to show pain, but I couldn't help myself. With each cry, you could tell I was consumed by pain that seemed to have no end or respite.

CHAPTER 3

NO EASY WAY

To calm me down, Amanda kept stroking my hair out of my eyes, softly telling me that everything was going to be all right. Clearly, she was trying to tell us both that. Minutes after her call, a first responder arrived. He examined me, asking me questions about how I was feeling and the symptoms so far. I was barely civil, but I tried my hardest to put a brave face on. After a brief examination, he declared, 'Don't worry. It's just sciatica.'

'No, it's not,' Amanda growled out with no compromise in her voice. 'I have sciatica, and I know my husband. That's more than just sciatica.'

Realising he wasn't going to get away with Amanda so easily, he soon buckled, saying, without hesitation, 'I will call the duty doctor.'

She stood at five feet, but she now gave the impression that she was ten feet tall and the guardian to hell itself that day. She had ripped her ties off and climbed out the pit to find the power she needed to grow to take back control from the helplessness that had made her mind captive.

It wasn't long before the first responder explained everything to the doctor and then handed me the phone.

The voice at the other end said, 'The first responder is going to stick his finger up your anus so you can tell me what you feel.'

The next minute, up it went, the first anal invasion of the hundreds more to come.

The first responder asked me if I could feel anything, to which I replied, 'No.'

'Try squeezing around his finger,' the doctor instructed to me.

20

'Yes,' I said triumphantly.

'All right, can you give the phone back to the first responder?'

Hoping for the best, I handed over the phone. Je seemed to agree with whatever the doctor said. Lying there, thinking I just had sciatica, I wondered what mode of transport I would take to work that day. Then the first responder loudly announced, 'We're going to take you in.'

He handed me the phone again, so the doctor could explain to me that I needed to be taken to the hospital, as I'd failed the anal sensation test.

During my call with the doctor, the first responder called for an ambulance. Then, turning to Amanda, he explained what was happening, along with what the examination showed, ensuring she was happy with his actions. Still struggling with the pain, I had to fight to make sense of it all. For the first time, I didn't feel in control of my life, which engendered more fear than my pain. For reassurance, I looked at Amanda. Though she looked upset and nervous, I realised that, psychologically, I had relinquished control, not to the first responder but to her. She had taken control; she was watching and listening to everything. Her silence meant she agreed with what he was doing, but I could tell that the moment he or anyone else involved with my care said or did something with which she didn't agree, the ten-foot tall Amanda would pounce all over them. For the first time in my life, I gave up control, letting her take complete charge. With that thought, the fear of losing control disappeared. I trusted Amanda completely. Though trust is abstract, my mental attitude was that she was completely dependable. I had an unwavering feeling of confidence in her, which gave me a sense of security.

It wasn't long before two paramedics came up the stairs. After a confab regarding me, the three of them spoke to me directly. 'Mike, there is no easy way to do this. Getting you down those stairs will not be easy, so we are going to bring a special chair to carry you out. We will need you to help us get you in it.'

Soon, the ten-foot tall Amanda took charge, saying in a commanding way, 'It's a wet and cold day, so let's get you wrapped up.' Amanda and the female paramedic struggled to get me into some pyjama bottoms, followed by a jumper with no shirt.

The two paramedics disappeared, quickly returning with a bright yellow metal chair, asking if I could get myself into it.

I looked around and saw Amanda, my titan, looking out for her man. She was the most important and powerful person in the room. She had transformed from a caring angel into a demigod, ensuring everyone was looking after me. Everyone in the room felt it too. I instantly felt relieved; my stress and anxiety slipped away, making me feel that I was truly going to be all right with her watching over.

With all my might, I tried to lift myself into the chair, but I failed, falling back on the bed like a dead bird falling from the sky. I was angry, not about the pain but about having failed to make it to the chair. Sheepishly, I just said, 'Sorry, I can't.'

'Don't worry. We will get you in.' The two paramedics grabbed an arm of mine on each side and threw them over their shoulders, lifting me from the bed into the chair. They buckled me in with several straps and then asked, 'Are you ready?' as if I was off on a fairground ride, which couldn't be far from the truth of the next twenty minutes.

'As I will ever be,' I replied.

I was wheeled across our landing and down the stairs. The upper half of the stairs was carpeted, while the lower half was made of polished wood. When we got to the polished steps, which were halfway down, we came to a sudden halt as if we had reached a cliff's edge but only too late. At that point, facing right down, I was looking at a Victorian-style wrought-iron radiator at the bottom. The chair and I had become one, combined and moving in unison, every bump jerking it in clumsy movements causing pain to shoot up my spine. Given that I was tightly strapped on to the chair, there was no escaping it. We soon started slipping down the stairs; now the chair and I were free rolling, bumping over each step as we went. The pain drove from my legs up my back, forcing me to shout out in agony. The female paramedic jumped in front of me and held the chair from slipping any further. Her act might not sound like much, but she had put herself in harm's way, wedging herself in between the bannisters and the chair; she had done it without a moment's thought for her own safety.

The sudden halt jarred my back, prompting me to shout out in pain and just a little fear again. The paramedics later explained that the chair was new, only being designed to run on carpet, a fact I wished I had known before my trip down the stairs. They both grabbed the chair tightly, one on the side and front and one on the back. I looked up to see Amanda peering over the bannisters, with the first responder standing next to her watching. Their faces said it all. They both looked panicked; Amanda was on the verge of breaking into tears. She would later tell me that, at that moment, she could hear her heart pounding. Her hands shook, as her heart tried its hardest to force itself out of her chest. Her vision was altered as if she was watching all this from inside a fishbowl. All she wanted to do was run away, but she would face the fires of hell to look after me even, though there nothing she could do at that moment.

I looked down again, spotting the wrought-iron radiator. 'You're going to have to be careful of that radiator.' I warned.

'Don't worry. We've got you,' a voice behind me reassured.

Though I had known these people only for a little over an hour, regardless of my predicament, I trusted their word. My trust was short-lived, as the male paramedic suddenly lost his grip, causing me to shoot forward, my head almost heading to the corner of the radiator. I stretched my arm out, which banged into the wrought iron. The female paramedic suddenly jumped toward the chair, grabbing the strap around my legs. I felt the strap tighten, as she steadied the chair with all her might, bringing it to a stop only inches away from the radiator. The paramedics couldn't stop apologising, but I was in too much pain to care by that time.

I was quickly rolled up to the ambulance and lifted onto its tailgate. The female paramedic helped me out of the chair on to the gurney. I was strapped in, covered in blankets, and given gas and air to inhale for the pain. I took full advantage of the gas and air, likely inhaling more than I needed. Looking to the back of the ambulance, I saw Doctor Dark standing by the door. Ominously, he said, 'This is not the end. It's just the beginning.' After that he just disappeared.

As he did, I noticed another figure behind him. I couldn't make out who it was. The figure was too transparent, as if it wasn't really there. I thought I recognised who it was, but I couldn't quite put my finger on it. Unlike the other phantoms, instead of fear, anger, and hatred, he had a calm sense of love, with a hint of pride.

The paramedic took my vitals, which took my mind off the strange figure. By the time I looked back, the figure was gone.

One of the paramedics asked me if I was ready, so I gave him the thumbs up, as I was inhaling the gas and air. The next second, we were off to the Great Western Hospital (GWH) in Swindon. For some reason, I felt safe; my breathing slowed down. The gas and air took its effect, making the pain seem more bearable. As we arrived, reversing into the ambulance bay, the female paramedic checked my blood pressure again. By this time, I was lying in the back of the ambulance, with a sense of safety, even comfort washing over me. The paramedics and I had been through quite a lot. They had come through for me, getting me to the hospital. Little did I know then that it wouldn't be the last time I would be in the care of paramedics. My admiration and my trust in them sprouted that day and endures to this day.

As I was slowly wheeled to the casualty department at about nine in the morning, a rough, crackling voice of despair called out from behind me. 'This is not the end. It's just the beginning.' Suddenly, my heart raced, making me grip the blankets tightly.

'It's all right, Mike. You're going to be fine,' reassured the female paramedic, who was keeping a close eye on me.

At the casualty department, a queue of patients on gurneys awaited us, like some great battle had taken place, with casualties pouring in. As in the films, only a handful of staff was around to help them. The staff couldn't cope, having to hurry from place to place. They all looked tired, with faces tensed into permanent frowns. They were trying very hard to come across as calm, ready to take on the world. That might have been the truth at the beginning of the shift, but it was a facade now. One could almost see energy draining from them, but they never stopped or broke down; instead, they just bravely did their jobs, attended as many patients as they could.

The paramedics took me to a cubicle, transferred me to a bed, and then left, telling me it wouldn't be long. Fortunately, Amanda was already there, frantic and concerned. Seeing her, I felt better, feeling myself calm down. I lay there on the bed, looking up at the fluorescent lights on the ceiling while inhaling as much gas and air as I could. At that moment, a funny comment Rob, my cousin and best friend, had made came to my mind. Once, he had been rushed to the hospital due to a suspected heart attack. As he lay looking up at the fluorescent lights on the ceiling, all he could think was that he was not going to die on the beach, looking up at a clear blue sky. Thinking about it now made me laugh, as I now knew what he meant.

Amanda was by my side, looking worried. My lower back pain was shooting up, I had a pins-and-needles sensation in my legs and my toes.

All my physical discomfort was overshadowed by the pain in my buttocks, which was radiating down my left leg. At about ten in the morning, a young doctor came in asked me some questions, while a nurse checked my vitals. They soon left, saying, 'It won't be long.'

We waited in the cubicle, listening to the hustle and bustle of the casualty department. It wasn't the best of times, as people were screaming, almost shouting; the noise, altogether, was loud, disturbing in its own way. To top it all, the woman in the next cubicle was clearly having a breakdown, as she kept singing and then shouting. It helped keep our minds off the cacophony in the casualty room.

Another doctor arrived around an hour later, giving me a more thorough examination. The doctor asked me to straighten my legs, but my left leg stayed put, no matter how much effort I put in. The pins-and-needles sensation persisted in my feet, and the pain kept battering my buttocks, as my head swam, swirling round like a whirlpool. We pressed the doctor to give us a clue about what my condition might be. At first, he was reluctant but then eventually said, 'Bilateral sciatica or, more worryingly, cauda equine syndrome. At this stage, we can't be sure.' With that, he was gone, and we were none the wiser.

An hour or so later, a nurse arrived and collected my blood for testing; she was gone as quickly as she had arrived. Unknown to us, those blood tests revealed a significant blood infection, yet we knew nothing about it nor had a clue about it until much later.

In our cubicle, Amanda was reading magazines and fighting back tears, while I was inhaling gas and air and trying to ignore the pain. Eventually, another doctor arrived at about quarter past three in the afternoon, introducing himself as an orthopaedic registrar at the hospital. We had no idea what the designation meant, but he seemed pleased with it, so we took it that he was someone important. He gave me yet another exam with pretty much the same results—pain in the lower back and buttocks, pins-and-needles sensation in my foot, weak right leg, and inability to straighten the left leg. He left quickly. Five minutes later, a nurse came in and scribbled NBM (nil by mouth) on a white board on the wall. When asked if I was going to be taken for surgery, she shrugged off the question saying, 'We don't know yet.'

We lost all track of time. I kept inhaling gas and air so much, the tank soon became empty meaning and had to be replaced. With a worried look

25

on her face, Amanda tried to engross herself in a magazine, but I could tell she wasn't taking any real notice as she angrily flicked from page to page. The pain was still biting at me, but I had consumed so much gas and air by now, it almost felt like it didn't matter. About an hour later, a nurse came in, scanned my bladder, gave me an injection for the pain, and then left. I felt the whole world slow down.

As the nurse had left the cubicle curtain open, I could see the whole of the casualty department. The staff darted from place to place, leaving streaks of themselves across the department. I could see people waiting on gurneys everywhere. I soon became transfixed by an old lady lying on a gurney in the corridor. She was frail and white as a ghost, and her loose skin created wrinkles everywhere. Crying, she was clearly in pain. In vain, I tried to wave down one of the staff. But Amanda slowly pushed my arm down and saying, 'It's all right, Mike. I promise you.'

Suddenly, the effects of the drugs wore off, and everything returned to normal. Noticing the change, Amanda looked at me in horror, triggering her to scurry off to find a doctor, closing the curtains behind her. She was probably unaware of how stoned I was from the gas and air, along with the painkillers. I must have looked awful. As she left, the smell of lavender filled the air. Standing by my bed was the old lady, by whom I had become transfixed. She put her hand on mine, saying, 'The only real fear is fear itself. The whole world is turning as it should. Nothing stops the passing of time or the phenomenon of cause and effect. This is not the end. It's just the beginning.'

The curtains swished open and closed again. Amanda had returned to the cubicle. As she entered, she muttered, 'No one is available. They're so busy that it's almost impossible to get anyone to even talk to you. When I finally did, they asked me to return to my cubicle and wait, and I guess we have to wait.'

I turned back, and the old lady was gone. I tried not to give it another thought as Amanda and I started to talk. We both agreed that not knowing was worse than how long we had been in the cubicle. We had arrived early in the morning, with daylight just taking hold of the world. It was early evening now; the sun had packed off and gone, and the night was on us, yet we were still in the same cubicle.

Eventually, a hospital porter arrived and said, 'You're being admitted to a ward, and I'm here to take you.'

26

CHAPTER 4

THE TITAN

After experiencing a painful bed transfer and then a bumpy ride, I was unamused to find myself in a ward with other people. I turned to Amanda, asking if she could try and arrange for my private medical benefit with my new company. But it was getting late; people had gone home. So, I had no choice but to share life that night with three strangers.

After an uncomfortable sleep in a hospital bed, along with a noisy morning, spine specialists examined me, ordering an MRI scan. I still had no idea what was wrong, but I just went with the flow, letting the medical team do their job. At that point, I trusted them. At about ten in the morning, over twenty-four hours after I had arrived, I was finally wheeled off to the MRI room, where my bed joined a queue of hospital beds. As I looked around, I realised no one wanted to talk. Everyone was engrossed in his or her own painful nightmare; we were all just crossing paths like burning ships in the night. I chose to ignore those unfortunate people, telling myself that, surely, I was not as ill as they were.

I soon started to feel tired, so I started fighting sleep. *Good*, I thought, *I will be asleep when they scan me, so I don't need to experience being all cooped up in that tiny cylinder of a scanner.*

As I waited in the queue of beds, a feeling of darkness overpowered me. All I could see was the dark of the night. It was so cold that my bones hurt. The smell was burning flesh mixed with sweat. The man on the bed next to me suddenly sat up and stared at me. At first, I refused to look back. I could only feel the fear, anger, and hatred brought about by his presence, but I could see him through the corner of my eye. Slowly, I moved my head, and there was Doctor Dark, his face covered in darkness. I couldn't see it fully, but I could see more of his body now. He was wearing a long, thick black coat over a grey hoody with the hood pulled up. On top of his head sat an old-fashioned black top hat. When he opened his coat, I saw syringes, full to the brim, hanging inside.

'Want something to make the pain go away?' he asked in his strangely familiar voice with an old man's crackle about it.

I stared at him, trying to see his face, but the veil of darkness still covered it.

He then nodded his head at me and snarled, 'You're going to need me. This is not the end. It's just the beginning.'

I turned away from him, trying desperately to not even see him. But he drew me in, making me slowly look around. Something was not right. He seemed only half there, like something was sucking him away. All around him was a veil of darkness. Something was wrong; he was slowly fading. Soon, it became apparent that it was me who was slowly fading, as my life ebbed away. As he spoke again, I looked at him in astonishment, thinking I had never seen so much of him. He said, 'Listen to me. When you get to the other end, you're going to need me. Like it or not, we are going to have to work together. You're going to have to open your eyes.'

This time I felt like I wanted to answer him, to tell him what I thought. 'Fuck off,' I said.

'I beg your pardon,' said an old woman's voice.

I looked away from Doctor Dark, seeing an elderly nurse wrapping a blood pressure pad around my arm. She casually said, 'I didn't hear you, my love. You have to speak up.'

When I looked back to see Doctor Dark, he was gone. There was no foul smell anymore; the place was filled with light again. *Was I just dreaming?*

'It won't be long now,' the elderly nurse reassured me.

Looking around, I saw that the number of beds in the queue had gone down, with only three remaining, two others and mine.

'OK, thanks,' I replied to the nurse, pretending to have not uttered my earlier comment, as I didn't think she'd heard what I'd said.

I waited as each patient before me was seen in turn, one by one. With the pain still running through my lower body, I did my best to steady my mind, focusing on all I had read in my books on mindfulness meditation. I tried to focus my mind on a single thought. But the pain kept distracting me, all kinds of thoughts running through my mind, as the inner monkey ran amuck.

Eventually, my turn arrived. I was wheeled to the scanning room and then transferred to the MRI bed. My ears were blocked with ear defenders. My head was secured in with a white frame. As I was moved into the MRI cylinder, the deafening noise of the machine started. My pain made me tense as the bed was locked into position with me inside the tube. At this point, as I started going in and out of consciousness, the account of the following week is mainly based on my family's perception of events, along with the doctor's report and whatever slice of memory I have. That said, I feel writing about my family's experience as well as mine is important.

I could never truly fathom the terror my family had to go through. When I awoke from my coma, they would have crossed with me to the other place but through a different route. They stiffened up, having decided not to show their true feelings in front of me. But they failed. I could see their pain. This was my beloved family. I knew their faces. They wanted to spare me their terror—the desperate fear of loss that none of them had been ready for in the slightest bit. At the point of waking from my coma, I realised how close a family I had, how supportive they were, and how much I loved them.

However, one person would prove to be my true saviour and protector, someone who was there throughout, fighting for me against all odds— Amanda. Only later did I learn from the hospital staff that Amanda had never given up on me or stopped watching over me, despite me being written off as dead a few times. We're not there yet; we're still lying in the hospital bed in Swindon. My mind flashed back to my new job.

Everyone on the project, including me, was like any other consultant— taking on more than we could chew, working hard to compensate for any shortfall in knowledge, and basically feeling like we were making it up as we went along but somehow delivering on client expectations. All the time, we were proving, probably to ourselves mostly, that we could do the job. I was at a low-level position compared to what I had been used to, but it was a good role with which to cut my teeth.

We worked hard and played hard. All of us on the edge thought we wouldn't make it, enjoying as much of the life as possible, staying in nice hotels, drinking in local bars, and learning at work all the time. I started off where I had left off in my last role, in the same hotel, the Hyatt Birmingham, which was a nice modern plush tower block right in the heart of the city. I still had points from my last long stay, so I got the best room, with complimentary wine.

After being in my new role for three months, I felt more settled and found some belief in myself again. The giant in me stood up and started his drive forward. He took over meetings, made project changes, and showed little respect to those who couldn't keep up. Work was completed quickly, and he used my main skill, my ability to break down a process or organisational structure to its basic level and simplify it so as to operate more efficiently. When I was working, I felt born again, and I really enjoyed what I did. I might not see any meaning in what I did anymore, but I was still interested in the work.

A part of my role was to travel around the country to different divisional headquarters and convince people to change. The experience felt like getting turkeys to vote for Christmas. When people used to dig their heels in and refuse to change, my job was to convince them. Looking back, I would have done a better job of influencing awkward managers if I had seen they were trying to protect both their empire and their people, who they had known for years. However, I was just trying to create the most efficient business model, and people, to me, were just required or nonrequired resources. I blamed the giant for this attitude, but I knew it was me who had created the giant in the first place.

The harder I worked, the more the giant grew. The growth of the giant had its benefits. The bigger he got, the more he seemed to be able to keep the darkness and its demons away, though not Doctor Dark so much. He came for repeated visits in the night, like he was on a mission, the objective of which I didn't know. One day, I had a hard day with a client, and my confidence took a beating. Deep insecurities and old fears of failing conjured up old dark memories in my mind, and I found myself dreaming that night that I was walking the streets of the other world. It was cold and bleak with a stench of burning flesh and the distant sounds of weapons firing. Behind me, I could hear him—Doctor Dark—stalking me. He terrified me, and I thought I woke up to see him sitting on my bedroom chair, as always, obscured in a veil of darkness. I could make out his outline, but his face was always hidden by the dark veil. Horror washed over me, and the sudden shock of seeing him made my every muscle tense. The more I saw of him, the more depressed I felt and the more my mind was tormented by the fear of darkness. He made me feel like I had entered another realm nearly devoid of all emotion, where all that was left was a feeling of numbness and fear. Doctor Dark always seemed to be there.

However, now his presence was getting stronger, as he brought fear, making the night a white-knuckle ride to get through to morning, where the day's toils distracted me from all the darkness. Though the first night and the subsequent nights, I tried not to be affected. I found myself thinking, *I'm terrible at my job. People are going to find out I'm rubbish. How embarrassing will it be when they find out?*

'Think of your suffering when all this mental formation turns on you,' warned Doctor Dark again without moving his lips.

Ignoring him and the thoughts he brought, I tried to sleep the best I could, yet the thoughts beat like the repetitive Native American drums in old Western films that sent out a message. No one knew what that message was, and they were too terrified to find out. That was how I felt. The ongoing beat would cause me anxiety, which I felt in my chest.

In the waking world, matters were different. I was slowly starting to regain my old confidence—to enjoy my new role and even own it. The giant was back, all right. As judgmental and intolerant of people's weaknesses as I was, I did love the team spirit I felt while working on a project. The team was a collection of incredibly intelligent people. Most were in their twenties or early thirties, much younger than me, a result of my having gained qualifications later in life, but I still managed to fit in. I did enjoy the consultant life, the challenging role, and the good hotels.

I missed my wife and the boys. Being away from them Monday to Thursday every week was hard. I knew I was missing out on the boys growing up and that Amanda needed my support. But my job brought in six figures and allowed my family to maintain a lifestyle that the giant believed they should have.

Secretly though, I enjoyed the solitude of living alone in a hotel room. It was a time of reflection; a chance to grow on the inside; and, in a small

31

way, a start to seeing the nature of things. Yes, I would see it from my interpretation of ideas, but to me it was beauty, and it felt right. Being alone in a hotel room might sound risky, but I loved Amanda very much and was always very loyal to her. No one ever visited my room, and I never visited theirs. The only guilt I carried was enjoying my time alone. During my free time or when not going for a meal or a quick drink with the rest of the team, I filled my evenings with work and meditation. Through sitting and being still, I worked towards mindfulness. I worked at achieving a moment-by-moment awareness of my thoughts as they passed by me like stray clouds. I also recognised my bodily sensations, the surrounding environment, and my feelings with a lens of love and compassion, even for the inner monkey.

I tried hard not to turn the TV on, as I knew that would lead to me settling in for the night. I didn't always succeed and would end up drinking the complimentary wine from the hotel while watching a programme. Following being in the forces, meditation and mindfulness were very important to me, and I practised it as much as possible. However, I was a chaotic, overcharged madman half the time, far from the calm, thoughtful person I coveted being, drawing inspiration from my books. I was a man with a giant ego who always believed he should be in charge. It always seemed like I knew a lot less than I liked to think, yet I got angry with people who didn't live up to my expectations. Let's face it. I wasn't a pleasure to be around, and though I believed in always treating people fairly, my interpretation of fair was what took predominance.

Since the injury, I had to let go of my cold ambition, even though it had dragged me up the cliff, from my days as a shopworker to a senior management consultant, with the mind of an overinflated giant. Through my mindfulness, I was starting to believe I was slowly seeing the world as it really was—to see that the darkness was a perception allowed in by my own mind, created by an unknown event, but fuelled by my own selfish behaviour—and to understand how much I needed to change. This was my last thought before I started to lose consciousness. I have little memory of things at this point, so the following is Amanda's account of events.

A doctor arrived, announcing he was the orthopaedic senior house officer (SHO) at the hospital. He told Amanda that my urine dipstick was positive for a urinary tract infection, and on the advice of microbiology specialists, he was going to start me on oral antibiotics. Amanda asked him if she could finally give me some food, perhaps a cup of tea. Giving the question little thought, he answered, 'Yes, why not?' The decision to let me eat and drink had not been discussed with the consultant who was still considering surgery.

Shortly after, another doctor arrived, announcing he was a member of the spinal team here to examine me. As he was talking, I started gaining consciousness, so was able to listen to what he was saying to Amanda. Their conversation was already halfway through. Noticing I was conscious, he asked me the usual questions that every doctor had asked us since we had arrived at the hospital. By the time he was finished, I had become unconscious again. So, he reported to Amanda exactly what had already been identified from all the other exams—pain in the lower back and buttocks, pins-and-needles sensation in his foot, weak right leg, and inability to straighten the left leg. Then he left, clearly feeling comfortable about having done a good job.

Amanda sat on a chair next to me, her angry gaze following the doctor as he left. When I regained consciousness, she told me about the doctor saying we were not getting anywhere.

I held her hand and said, with what felt like my last breath, 'Get me out of here. Call Neil, my private doctor, before this lot kills me or worse.'

Amanda scurried away and called Neil to beg him to get involved even though the insurance wasn't sorted since I had started my new job. He agreed, saying he would call them straight away. She then tried to contact our medical insurance company. But as my insurance was managed by my new employers, she didn't have the necessary account numbers to provide them. Also, my new company hadn't sent the papers across to the insurance company yet, as I had only been with them for three months. Frustrated to the point of being scared stiff, she hung up. Her only hope now was the private doctor, Neil, agreeing to call in.

The next day, he called her to tell her that the spinal consultant had carried out a meeting with a spinal surgeon and a consultant radiologist about my case. Neil, who had treated me in 2012, had been included in the discussion by telephone, at his insistence. They had reviewed the old, along with the new MRI images. At first, they had not identified anything wrong. It had been Neil who'd suggested likely changes consistent with a seeded infection in the epidural space, the unseen menace that would cause my family and I so much pain. They had considered a deep washout of the wound but agreed it would carry a significant risk of nerve damage. He had insisted they treat me aggressively with IV antibiotics and involve microbiology specialists, performing a washout if my condition deteriorated.

I need to properly introduce you to Amanda, my wife, the titan, at this point. As you already know, she is only five feet tall, but she's a force to be reckoned with. She is a phenomenal woman who can be fury itself one minute and an angel full of love the next. She was just what I needed when I was dying in the National Health Service (NHS). When I fell ill, she had health problems of her own to deal with. Only five years had passed since she had survived cancer, and anyone who has battled cancer will tell you cancer patients suffer from the side effects of the treatment even years later. Though Amanda never mentioned it, she struggled with the after-effects of radiotherapy.

Her toughness comes from her upbringing. Born in Zambia to Geordie expats, she learnt the hard truths of life early on. Her father worked in copper mines, and her mother was a policewoman. She has one brother, John. Both were packed off to boarding school at an early age, and though they were mostly apart when growing up, they are close. Amanda arrived in the United Kingdom at the age of seventeen and went to college in Cheltenham, where we met. Her friends were mainly Sloaneys, who never liked her choice of the working man, which at the time I was. So, they dropped her the moment she married her bit of rough. Believe me, it was their loss, as one couldn't ask for a better friend. She was a contradiction. On one hand, she was hard and sometimes unforgiving; on the other hand, she was sweet, thoughtful, and helpful. Owing to her unique characteristics and personality, I found her irresistible and swept her of her feet the first chance I got.

When Amanda was diagnosed with cancer, my whole being felt like it was in a boxing ring with a world heavyweight. As she fought through a hysterectomy, chemotherapy, and radiotherapy, my soul crashed into a block wall. I would find dark hidden places and start sobbing with my hand over my mouth, trying desperately not to let it all out. She was brave and strong, while I was a quivering wreck. The day came when all I wanted to do was beg for her life, bargaining my life for hers. I cried out for comfort, and there was none. I realised, perhaps a little late, with no God to hear us, we were each alone.

I am convinced that everything in the universe is random, and we have no control over life or what happens to us. Amanda's womb cancer and my brother Geoff's lymph node cancer, my paralysis, my father's early death—all of it is random. As I have mentioned, I don't believe in some God pointing at people and cursing them with diseases. If there is, then he's no one I want to meet. For me, things are just the way they are, and random things happen to random people.

Why did I think this and yet cry and call in the dark for mercy? I needed to get it out. I needed to blame someone. I needed someone to shout at. I needed someone to help. Doing so was perfectly reasonable, though in the end, it was just therapy. Once I was finished, I realised I was alone, and I just had to pick myself up, wipe the tears, and deal with this random thing that had happened to us. I personally found comfort and strength to carry on in the thought of oneness, while accepting others' beliefs. I don't know when my journey began exactly, but by this time, I was fully on my way—whether I knew it or not.

Later that day, the orthopaedic SHO visited me, telling Amanda, 'The MRI report identified a large heterogeneous, which is medical speak for not sure what but something isn't right involving the anterior epidural region, extending from L2 to S1/S2, which was particularly prominent behind the L5 vertebral body. There was compression of the cauda equina at L4/5 secondary to the collection. The epidural collection was noted as likely infected.'

Clueless about what any of that meant, she looked at me with tears in her eyes as I struggled for consciousness but was clearly losing the battle.

The following day, the orthopaedic SHO reviewed me again, this time noting that ceftriaxone antibiotics had been started. Even the casualty doctors had prescribed antibiotics the day I had arrived. However, it was not the case, as no one had checked to see if lifesaving antibiotics had been started. The pharmacy records would eventually show that I was administered antibiotics three days after I had come in. The delay would cause sepsis, blood poisoning, which caused my unconscious state and then eventually my meningitis, leading to infection of the arachnoid membrane and then eventual paralysis, something for which every medical professional involved carried some responsibility. This random event would change my life forever. As I write, I could sit here blaming all those people for being incompetent in their duty, but they were all stretched to their limits, trying their best to keep everyone alive.

Later, another doctor arrived to inform Amanda that my blood tests had identified the white blood cell count to be up, indicating the infection was rapidly progressing to sepsis (blood poisoning). He ordered a bladder scan, a bladder washout, a chest X-ray, an electrocardiogram (ECG), and repeat blood tests with an arterial-blood gas test. He also instructed the administration of IV fluids, while continuing with the antibiotics. She tried to tell him that the antibiotics had still not been given, but he took little notice as he left. He had thrown everything but the kitchen sink at me, yet he hadn't checked to see if my already prescribed treatment was being carried out.

All this time, Amanda had been left to figure out what all the numbers and measurements meant. She had stuck by me throughout, spending the day trying not to cry. Feeling helpless, as if her brain was throbbing against her skull, she wanted to let out a scream that would summon every doctor and nurse to my bedside. Instead, she was left with having to beg people to sit up and take notice. Though she was crying inside, she stayed resolute and strong; everyone around her could feel the power she wielded but hadn't unleashed yet.

About an hour later, my mother arrived with the boys. At first, they all congregated around my bed. Then my mother sat in the guest chair next to my bed, unaware of how seriously ill I was. The boys stood quietly by the end of my bed. Amanda gently swept my hair out of my face, softly calling my name. Much to her shock, I gave no reply. Instead, I just lay there, still, lifeless, my eyes fixated on the ceiling, my face ashen and my neck swollen red.

In panic, Amanda cried out, 'There's something wrong with him.'

Amanda's cry grabbed the attention of a nurse. The nurse came over and said, 'He's fine. Please don't worry.' Then she was gone as quickly as she had appeared.

Frustrated and feeling helpless, Amanda's anger grew as she started to feel that the nurses were content with their actions, even self-satisfied, unaware of her husband's growing decline. She imagined a nurse who had ignored her as she stared intently at her, walking around thinking, *I know what to do, and I'm doing it. Any problems aren't mine.* Amanda's world was rapidly changing in front of her as my condition worsened, while the nurses seemed oblivious to the decline.

My mother, unaware of the gravity of my condition, reassured Amanda that everything was fine, as the nurse had said so. Her response was also slightly self-assured, as she was secure in the belief that, by the power of prayers, I might somehow be saved. Her faith was her comfort blanket, which I am glad she had. But it was not mine or Amanda's. She got up from the seat, trying to tell Amanda not to worry.

However, Amanda's heckles were up; hell was about to be unleashed. She ignored my mother and ran over to the nurse's station, anxiously shouting, 'There's something wrong with my husband. His vitals haven't been checked; he's not looking good.'

With near contempt, the nurse at the station responded, 'Stop panicking, Mrs. Fisher. We're taking good care of your husband.'

Frustrated and ready to explode, Amanda returned to my side.

My elderly mother was now pretty much stiff with worry. Even though she couldn't see what Amanda saw, she tried to calm Amanda down, saying, 'Don't worry, dear.' What else do you say after all? Soon, she would take a good look at me, agree I didn't look right, and join in Amanda's search for help.

At my bedside, Amanda was getting more concerned. The fact that I hadn't uttered a word to my boys, whereas normally I would be chatting away with them, worried her the most. She also spotted lumps on either side of my neck; my face also seemed to be swelling. Then, I vomited a green mess, which pushed her over the edge. The ten-foot Amanda emerged, demanding of the nurses that she see a doctor *now*!

After a while, a doctor finally came. At first, she wasn't interested in doing much, arguing I was fine. After being nearly mauled by Amanda, she finally inserted a medical instrument into my wrist. As she did, a yellow fluid came out, followed by blood. Seeing this, Max, my nine-year-old, passed out. But he was keenly caught by Amanda, who, at this point, seemed to be watching everybody, from me to the kids. 'I'm going to take him to get a drink,' she said, ushering Max out the door, followed by Myles.

She soon returned with the boys, coming straight over to my bedside. My mother was anchored to the spot, guarding her son. She declared, 'It will be OK.'

Amanda, however, immediately noticed that the lumps on my neck had become bigger. She tried to talk to me, but I wasn't responsive. Turning to the doctor, who was looking more and more concerned, she said, 'He's nonresponsive. He has lumps on his neck. I'm worried this means he has fluid in his brain.'

The doctor immediately turned to the nurses and shouted, 'Clear the room.'

The doctor soon pulled a button above the bed, which set off an alarm, causing a sense of emergency. The nurses' attitudes immediately changed, as they realised something was wrong. Then on, complacency aside, the pressure was on; every medical professional carried out their role without thinking.

A nurse hurried over to Amanda, telling her to get my mother and the kids out. Amanda ushered them out and trusted the boys with my mother, knowing she would give up her own life before she let anything happen to them. As she looked back at me, she saw doctors and nurses appear from nowhere and run over to me. Ward nurses stood back and directed the doctors and nurses to my bed. Before long, I was surrounded by a team of medical staff. I had suffered a sudden collapse, and my consciousness was fading.

One might hope for a sign of faith at this point, but there was no tunnel, no flash of life, just me standing alone on the cobbled path of the other world. In front of me, a dark hole opened. I could see Doctor Dark trying to come through the hole, but the hole was too small, and he seemed to be held back by an invisible force. Everything started to fade, and soon nothing was left. I found myself standing in the dark, totally alone. In a way, I felt at peace, as this darkness was calm and soothing—with no fear, anger, or hatred to be afraid of. However, I also felt that something was very wrong. I didn't know how, but I knew my family needed me. My veins went cold, and I felt a pull backward. Then I was looking up at strangers, who were all looking down at me. I heard Doctor Dark's cracked and despairing voice, 'This is not the end. It is just the beginning.'

The doctors had injected me with naloxone, which pulled me out of the dark, and my condition started to briefly improve. As I recovered, I whispered, 'This is not the end. It is just the beginning.'

The doctors looked baffled, but they just ignored my random utterance and continued working on me.

Amanda returned after seeing my mother and the kids off, but she was kept at arm's length and not allowed to see me, covertly pinned against a wall by a nurse.

It was at this point that my brother Paul walked in, thinking, *Not another injury for Mike.*

Paul is a different beast to the rest of us. However, being only three years apart in age, we grew up together, singing to Elvis Presley, Blondie, Genesis, Black Sabbath, and others. Growing up, clad in pyjamas, we would pretend to be on stage in the living room and sing our hearts out. Progressing from that, in our thirties, we together walked the paths of Glastonbury Festival, a place that offered a myriad of psychedelic and unforgettable experiences that burned memories into my brain. I would be hard put to find any place like the festival on earth that gave me the same buzz, but then I never travelled much other than in the army and except for the odd summer holidays with the family. So, I'm sure there will be other such places on earth, just that I haven't experienced them.

Paul is a generous human being, ready to do anything to help his friends and family. When I was stationed overseas in the army, I once ended up in Dover at three in the morning, and I didn't think twice about calling him for a lift. Making no complaints or excuses, he just jumped into his car and drove hundreds of miles to pick me up. I have never doubted him, and I've always look up to him. With his quick wit and ability to make people laugh, I'd always thought he would have made a great stand-up comic. Sometimes when we get together, we laugh so much with each other that it feels like we have entered a place where there is just him and me. However, under it all, Paul has always had his own phantoms, and though we have never discussed it, we somehow have always known each other's pain.

As he walked into my ward, he thought to himself, *He's sure to be fine.*

Much to his shock, he was pushed aside by a running doctor. As I started to lose consciousness again, more doctors were called. Baffled, Paul looked up and saw Amanda being held back by nurses. Her face was as white as a ghost, and tears streamed down her face, her unbreakable air of power seemingly smashed. He watched deeply driven professionals move like clockwork with a gut-level determination and urgency to win this battle. He thought to himself, *God, someone's in trouble.* He looked at Amanda again and saw that she was going grey in front of him. She was openly crying, and her eyes were as red as rubies. The realisation that his brother was the patient in trouble hit him. He approached Amanda, and they just stared at each other, stunned and confused. One look at my bed, where a sea of medical staff was rushing with purpose, and it was obvious that something was horribly wrong. They didn't know if I was dead or alive, and nor did the doctors.

Time ticked by, and eventually the medical staff around my bed started leaving one by one. A young doctor stopped in front of Amanda and stated triumphantly, 'Well, it was touch-and-go. We did lose him briefly, but we got him back quite quickly. So for now, he's stable.'

With tears dripping down her cheeks, Amanda thanked him, and he nodded and left.

Amanda turned and looked at Paul, whose whole body was tensed up, fists clenched and eyes red. As Amanda said, 'He's OK,' Paul relaxed. He let out a sigh of relief and gave Amanda a desperate smile. Undeniably, they both were immensely relieved following the ordeal and now felt almost liberated from the previous state of pressure that had paralysed them.

They both walked over to my bed, but all I could remember was falling in and out of consciousness, feeling confused and lost in a place over which I had no control. The thought that bounced around in my head was not about being sick or dying; rather, it was about not being in control. As I fell out of consciousness, I could smell burning flesh and bad breath. My whole body went cold. I looked around and saw a massive veil of darkness in front of me and then around me, which seemed hungry to devour me. Before long, I was feeling cold and alone. The other world had returned, but I was not alone. I could see Doctor Dark walking down a path on which my bed now seemed to be. At last, I could fully see him. He stood tall, wearing a long black coat over a dirty grey hoody, a pair of worn black trousers, and an old top hat. The hood of the hoody was still up, covering his face like a cowl. All I could see of his face was his mouth, which flashed a wide smile at me, the rest of his face was covered in darkness like a shadow. As frightening as he was, he was a familiar presence, and seemingly, he was the only one who could hear me, even with Amanda and Paul right next to me. In a strange and unnatural way, he seemed like an old friend.

'Is this the end?' I asked. 'Is it approaching me? I want to die in peace with no more suffering, but I'm hardly ready.'

'No more suffering?' he scoffed in his crumbling voice, flashing a crooked smile. 'Suffering is just the reality that no one can escape from. Everyone faces death at some point. It's as certain as ageing, sickness, and loss. Life is uncertainty. Suffering is a consequence of impermanence. This whole world and everything in it are only temporary, yet you hang on to everything and try, without success, to make everything permanent. Of course you are suffering. The whole thing is rotten, yet you hold on so tightly.'

'I'm not ready to die. This can't be my time. I'm not ready,' I begged.

'I'm?' he asked with such emphasis on the 'I' that it came out as a shout. 'That's your problem. You still think of yourself as an I. There is no "self" that is independent or permanent. You can only delay or escape suffering for a while, but it is inevitable.'

'What's the point then?' I asked.

'There is no point. There is no rhyme or reason. It just is. But the magnificence of it all is that vast expanse, that ongoing existence. And all you have to do is look at it, yet it eludes you like a lost penny.'

With a tired frown on my face, I said, 'I have tried to look, but my practice has never been good enough.'

'You're a fool,' he snorted. 'You can't see it because you're hanging on to the universe you already know tightly. Let go of your perception. Recognise what a mental formation of your making is. And just see for once; just see and marvel at it.' After a moment's pause, he said, 'This is not the end. It is just the beginning.'

I blacked out then, and I couldn't remember anything until I woke up again in a different hospital, in a different town, and in a different world—the other end.

However, for Amanda and Paul, this hadn't happened yet.

The doctor who had informed Amanda and Paul that I was all right returned and said, 'We have diagnosed Mike with sepsis from urine and spinal collection, and we have decided to perform a spinal washout operation.' After that, he waited for a few seconds for a response.

41

Amanda looked stunned, and Paul remained quiet.

Considering their silence an indication to take leave, the doctor turned and started walking away. Suddenly, he stopped and looked Amanda straight in the eyes and asked, 'He keeps repeating, "It's not the end; it's just the beginning." Do you know what he's referring to?'

After a moment's silence, Amanda said, 'No, I have never heard him say that before.'

The doctor just shrugged his shoulders and walked away.

Not long after, I was wheeled off to the operation theatre and left to wait in a corridor for the theatre to become available. I was unconscious and looked like I had been inflated by a giant pump. Amanda was now sitting in the waiting room with Paul, and they were making small talk to try and keep their minds off what was happening.

A long while later, the doctor returned and said, 'Unfortunately, we have been waiting for three hours for a theatre to drain his epidural collection, but emergency bleeding patients have been correctly prioritised. At present, though he is lethargic, he is opening his eyes, communicating when prompted, and moving his lower limbs with good power. He's still muttering the same words though.'

Amanda just looked at him blankly.

He turned and walked away as if he had another pressing concern to attend.

Then a nurse approached Amanda and Paul and said, 'He's comfortable and stable. There's nothing more you can do. You may as well go home. It's 3 a.m. after all.'

Reluctantly, they both agreed. Amanda took a look at me, kissed my forehead, and hesitantly went home. She needed to get the boys ready for school, and she had to leave me, as much of a wrench it was. She returned home to find my mother asleep on the sofa and the two boys fast asleep in bed. She gently woke my mother up and saw her to her car. She gave her a big hug and softly kissed her thank you and good night. As my mother was too exhausted to say anything, she just kissed her and drove home. Amanda went inside and quietly started ironing the boy's clothes. A lot more needed to be done, but she was too tired to do anything more. So, she went to bed, and as soon as her head hit the pillow, she fell asleep. Her dreams were haunted by images of me slipping down a hill on a hospital bed, with her, Myles, and Max holding ropes tied to the bed, each hanging on for dear life. Then, she saw me sit up and quietly say, 'This is not the end. It's just the beginning. Don't let go. It's you three who are keeping me here, and I don't want to go.'

The next morning, she got up, almost forgetting that I was in the hospital but then noticed the empty cold side of the bed where I normally slept. Suffocated by a myriad of emotions, she just got on with the day. As soon as she showered and dressed, she woke the boys up and got them ready for school. While checking Myles's bag to make sure he had everything, she took a minute to finish her tea, and then she became aware of two pairs of eyes fixed on her like laser beams. She looked down and said gently, 'Daddy needs an operation, which he should get today. He's going to be all right, boys. Your dad never gives up, and nor shall we.' Out of nowhere, she said, 'Boys, this is not the end; it is just the beginning. Don't ever give up because your daddy never gives up.'

After seeing Myles off at the bus stop, she took Max to school. As soon as they reached the school, Max ran to the playground and started playing with his friends. The sight, just for a second, made Amanda feel normal, as if nothing had happened. Then the bell rang, and all the students lined up to go into the school. As she turned to leave, one of the other mothers, Linda, came up to her and gave her a big hug. At first clueless about what was going on, she soon recognised the woman as the mother of one of Max's friends and remembered she was a nurse. *She must know*, thought Amanda. She was, of course, right.

When Linda asked how I was, Amanda answered with great positivity, 'We think he will be fine. They are operating on him today.'

Visibly fighting back tears, Linda said, 'I must tell you something. I walked past a man on a gurney last night. I was with two surgical doctors, and we all took a sideways look as we walked past him. One of the doctors whispered, "Christ, he doesn't look good. He's not going to make it." "Nope," concurred the other doctor. I shook my head in agreement too. Then, it hit me that I knew the man. I stopped dead on my feet, swung around, and walked quickly back to his bed. I took a good look and recognised the man as Max's dad. Even though his whole face had become swollen, I could still recognise him.' Holding Amanda's hands, she continued, 'If he's still going, then he's still fighting, and there's still hope.

To still be alive after what we saw, he must be very strong minded. Don't give up hope. He will need you to be strong.'

Without thinking, Amanda thanked her and left. She got straight into her car and just sat there, stunned. Soon, she started crying uncontrollably, as if weeping all her power as a titan out with every tear. She felt empty inside, all that was left was her anxiety, which was beyond butterflies in her stomach rather angry wasps. Suddenly, she sat upright and almost sucked all the tears back in. She had seen the truth of her present reality—she was the only one keeping me alive, and she needed every tear of strength to get her through the ordeal. She drove straight to the hospital, her eyes red from crying and her make-up streaked from the tears. When she arrived in the ward, Paul was already there.

He turned to her and said, 'Apparently, they kept considering what to do with Mike all night, and the combined decision was to transfer him to the high-dependency unit (HDU) and drain the collection first thing this morning.'

They both immediately went looking for the HDU and finally caught up with me. At this point, I was in a coma, kept alive only by a series of machines. Too stunned to say or do anything, Amanda just sat by my side. Across from her, Paul sat, looking steely eyed and strong, yet he was crying inside and desperate for his little brother to wake up.

I was soon taken for the spinal washout. As I was rolled away, my mind was transported out of my body, and I saw a picture of myself lying in the bed with Amanda and Paul standing and watching in the HDU. The picture slowly faded away, and I saw every atom in the room and in me. Particles and electrons danced around as if they were keeping the whole of reality pulled together as one. I started to feel myself slowly break up, and the atoms in me just seemed to join all the others. Strangely, as I broke up, my mind flashed back to when I was a child.

I was never still, a rootless spirit whirling around in the dust, creating havoc. Today you might say I had attention deficit hyperactivity disorder (ADHD). But in the seventies, no such thing existed, and one would just be labelled a 'wrong'un'. Everyone, from my immediate to extended family, as well as all their friends, tolerated, bullied, ignored, blamed, disgraced, belittled, undersold, and crammed me into the form of a convulsing bull. It was all done with a smile and a laugh, but no one checked to see if I was laughing too. If they had, they would have seen not a laughing boy but a sad, lonely soul, yearning and desperate for some positive interaction.

Eventually all thoughts floated away, so now everything was happening with no thoughts or emotion at all, and it just was. Then, almost from nowhere, a picture of Amanda and the boys flickered in my slowly decaying head, which triggered the thought, *I can't leave them. They need me as much as I need them.* Concentrating my mind on the love I felt for them, I started pulling back the escaping atoms, and they immediately changed course and returned to make up my body once again. I didn't know if this was real or just another apparition. So much had happened already, and I had many visions of my inner fears. I was about to go through a period where things seemed real but were in fact hallucinations. So, who knew or could say what was real and what was not at this point? Everything went blank, and the whole vision disappeared. Unbeknown to me, the general anaesthetic for my operation had just been administered, and for all intents and purposes, my brain had just been switched off.

The doctor returned to Amanda and Paul and explained, 'We started with a midline incision on the old scar and found dissection of scar tissues down to the implant. Extensive scar tissues were found everywhere. We drilled the lower part of the lamina of L4 and removed the flavum. We found the dura and identified the nerve roots. Initially, no puss was seen, but we used a ball-tip probe to reach under the equina. Suddenly, we felt that something gave under the blunt ball-tip probe, and puss started coming out. We took and sent cultures, and now we're just waiting as he remains in a coma.' Once he delivered his message, the doctor was off.

Stunned, Amanda didn't know what to do with what she had just been told. Her legs folded, and she gently she crumpled, d onto the chair by my side. Her whole body was shaking rhythmically, and she could feel her bowels churn. 'Oh God,' she said, almost in prayer, 'don't let anything happen to him.' She sat next to me as long as she could, but the loosening of her bowels made her run to the loo.

When she returned, she noticed Paul standing by my bed. He had been there all along, but she had been so worried that she had lost sight of him. Looking at Paul, who was looking at her expectantly, she said quietly and carefully, 'I guess we wait.'

45

Slumping back into his chair, Paul stuttered, 'All right then.' His whole being felt like it had just been put on pause.

Later that day, the spinal consultant came down to the HDU and pulled Amanda away from my bedside. A few steps behind, Paul followed, keen not to get in Amanda's way or miss out on what they had to say about his brother. She was informed I had hydrocephalus, the accumulation of cerebrospinal fluid (CSF) in the brain. However, the team was unsure about the cause. She was told they wanted to refer me to the John Radcliffe Hospital (JRH), but as beds weren't available there, they were considering Bristol.

With that, the consultant was gone again, leaving Amanda and Paul to stare at each other, both lost for words. Her heart started thumping, and she could hear blood pumping through her body. Her hands trembled. Feeling unsteady on her feet, she collapsed into the chair beside me. She was hot and sweaty, and she couldn't stop her heart from pounding until it nearly burst out of her chest. She took a deep breath to try and calm herself down, but she couldn't manage more than a bird's breath. Her eyes swelled up, and it was then that she felt a hand on her shoulder that squeezed her firmly. As she looked around, she realised that it was Paul, who was trying to comfort her. He was lost for words, as he was going through his own pain, and all he could do was make some kind of physical contact. She held his hand and squeezed. Time slipped by as if there were no here and now. Day turned to night, and Amanda and Paul stayed by my side.

A doctor arrived and informed Amanda that the neurosurgery team at the JRH had called back and said they would accept me. They asked for me to be transferred directly to the neurosurgery theatres for urgent surgery, which the GWH team was considering now. Amanda and Paul didn't know, at first, what to do with the information. It seemed good news at first, but nothing here was good news.

Amanda always felt lucky that she had been referred to the Churchill Hospital in Oxford when she had cancer. Oxford was a town full of different hospitals, catering to the university's future doctors. So she thought the JRH would be as good, and she would be proven right. She, the titan, determined to never give up, decided it was time for her to speak up. Pulling her slumped body straight, with the fury of hell, she said, 'Don't consider anything. I'm making the decision. I want him transferred to the JRH right now.' She might have been temporally floored, but she had picked herself up and was raging.

As the doctor didn't know where to look or what to say, he just turned tail. Not long after, a pair of paramedics arrived to take me to the JRH. A nurse accompanied them to my bed and injected me with an antibiotic for the first time. I didn't know why they chose to start then, possibly to make sure all their boxes were ticked before I left, but who knew? The paramedics transferred me to a gurney and started wheeling me off to the ambulance.

Amanda and Paul followed me out, with the nurses from the ward smiling and nodding to say best of luck. The paramedics pushed me through a set of double doors. They then informed Amanda and Paul that they weren't allowed entry in the area, and they would meet them in Oxford. My wife and brother agreed to meet the paramedics in Oxford and quietly walked back to their cars.

After arriving at the JRH at well past midnight, I was taken straight to theatre, where I had two external ventricular drains (EVDs) inserted into each side of my head to drain the fluid from around my brain. Following the operation, the nurses tried to wake me up but couldn't get a response, as I just wasn't coming around.

Suddenly, I started convulsing uncontrollably. Thinking I was having a seizure, the doctors gave me medication to stop the convulsions and prevent another episode. I was soon sent to the JRH HDU and rigged to different machines. A junior doctor sat by me and slowly and calmly changed the settings on the machines to keep me alive.

The following afternoon, the senior neurology consultant who had operated on me, James, came to check how I was doing. Over time, he would save my life repeatedly and fight every little problem to do so.

He informed Amanda, 'The CT scan carried out the previous day at the GWH showed hydrocephalus and likely basal meningitis. I discussed the surgery of the previous day with the spinal surgeons from the GWH. As there was no evidence of CSF leak at the time of surgical drainage and in view of Mike's abrupt deterioration, I have concluded that the possible sequence of events is either bacterial translocation from the extradural to the subdural space or seeding to both these sites from an as yet unidentified source. After review with microbiology, antibiotics will be administered.

47

Owing to the amount of CSF in his brain, we will put him into a medically induced coma.'

Amanda asked solemnly, 'What are his chances? Will he be OK?'

Looking at her, James replied in a caring but clinical voice, 'I have never seen anyone with so much CSF in their brain, and Mike having made it this far is a good sign. However, Mike has both hydrocephalus and bacterial meningitis, and his brain is swimming in it. I'm afraid I don't rate his chances too positive.'

Amanda broke down into tears. Her whole body felt like it was collapsing, while something inside her felt like it wanted to burst out.

James said, 'He's a strong man, clearly with a strong mind. He's made it this far, so he has already beaten the odds. Don't give up. He will need you to be strong, and we never know until we know. There's hope, but I want you to be ready for the worst.'

Steadying herself, Amanda asked, 'What's worse? Viral or bacterial meningitis? And how the hell did he get meningitis in the first place?'

James replied empathetically, 'The viral type of meningitis is the most common. It's caused by many different viruses and can be treated quite quickly. Bacterial meningitis is less common than viral. It can occur alongside sepsis, which is blood poisoning, and sepsis can be more life threatening than bacterial meningitis itself. Mike developed sepsis from the spinal abscess. The infection got into his meninges, which are the three membranes that cover the spinal cord and brain for protection. Bacterial meningitis attacks the central nervous system. Even if Mike survives, we won't know the full extent of his infection for six to nine months. He could lose limbs or at least the use of limbs; or we could be lucky, and he may only suffer limb weakness.'

She was grateful to James, not only for keeping me alive but also for being the first doctor to explain things to her and be honest about my chances. Though she didn't realise it, she was in shock and numb, just carrying on as if nothing was happening. She felt disorientated. Her place in the world was turning upside down; her plans for the future went on instant hold; and her purpose in this life might change at any moment, making her feel she was entering a new world. Steeling herself, she told herself that she would not cry in front of me even once, and from now on, she would ensure that she was always there and was strong. True to her word, since then, she hardly cried when she was with me. But she did cry herself to sleep every night, as the feeling of pain of losing me ran through her mind over and over again, and anger swelled up inside her, prompting her to shout in her mind, *Why us?*

The following day, I was taken for a CT head scan. The scan revealed a large amount of CSF and meningitis. However, following the insertion of the EVDs, the amount of CSF was reducing.

As time went by, my family gathered around my bedside—or at least they would have if not for the strict rule restricting the number of people who could be by the bed at a time. So, they all gathered in a side room and took turns to come and see me. The only person who was absent was my brother Geoff, as he was away in Singapore on work. His wife and my sister-in-law, Caz, didn't know if she should tell him about my condition because even if she did, she knew he wouldn't be able to leave straight away, and all he could do was worry. In the end, she decided to inform him because he would never forgive her if something grave happened to me. So, one night on the phone, she quietly asked him to sit down and spelt everything out to him. Geoff worked with the government advising other countries how to detect terrorism; he couldn't just drop everything and come running home. He had no choice but to spend the next few days in Singapore finishing his job.

As Geoff left home to join the police cadets when he was 16 and I was just 9, the only childhood memory I have of him is his fleeting visits. His role in our lives was that of a deputy dad. When our father passed away, I was 22 and still in the army, and I looked, as everyone did, to Geoff for strength. He never hesitated to step in and support us all, especially our mother, and it is something he still does today. Describing Geoff is not easy. He's very black and white. To him, matters are either good or bad, right or wrong, and there are no grey areas. And he will tell you that until you get it. He's a strong unwavering man who fights hard for what he believes in. He's also a really caring person who will never let you down and will always be there for you. He and I are very different. We argue over politics, what is right and wrong. And where he's black and white, I'm very grey. I don't think anybody else like him can be friends with me. One minute, he will argue with me, and the next, he will be my best friend.

He's always been a tower of strength. Even when he was battling lymph node cancer, it was him who kept everyone positive and upbeat. When he was ill, he only took the challenge head-on, beat it, and went on with his life. He has been a lighthouse on the rocks of life, showing his strong resolve for us all to see. Steady and always standing tall in the same place, he has been a light I can always see, no matter how rough things get or how far away I drift. As different as we are, he is the person I admire the most.

He married twice. Though I always liked his first wife Mandy, I found his second wife Caz to be a beautiful soul, full of life and always upbeat and bubbly. Whenever music plays, she dances, and she is never scared to be free. Caz is always pleased to see you and always showers you with compliments, making people instantly happy. The whole time I was in hospital, she stood tall next to Geoff and supported us both. I consider her not my sister-in-law but my sister.

After Caz told him about me, each day, he called in and checked on me, but no one working with him had any clue that he was a tornado of thoughts inside. He finally returned and landed at Gatwick Airport. He got in his car and drove straight to the hospital and made his way to the HDU. He saw his wife, Caz, just as she saw him. It was obvious that she had been crying, and he gave her a long kiss and a big hug. Holding each other tightly, Geoff knew instantly that things were bad. 'OK, tell me,' he said, looking Caz in the eyes.

'Mike is in a coma, Geoff, and they said his brain is swimming in meningitis.'

Geoff's face dropped, and the rock he was crumbled around him. His face contorted in horror, and his eyes shouted, *No!* He walked into the HDU with Caz, and Amanda and Paul left so they could visit. Geoff took one good look at me lying there with a tube in my mouth and machines all around me. He let out a cry as if he had been holding it back for years. Tears poured down his face, and he grabbed Caz's hand tightly. His other hand-picked mine up and held it like a wounded bird. He didn't know which way to turn. Amanda, Paul, and my mother were watching him from the side room, and their hearts broke.

Later in the week, suspecting a possible CSF leak from the surgical wound, the doctors performed a surgery on my lower back to wash it out again. My dura, a spinal membrane, was noted as intact. A few days later, an MRI brain scan was carried out, and the result indicated extensive meningitis with associated ventriculitis, which meant my brain's ventricles were swelling up. An MRI of the spine was also carried out, and the result was consistent with severe meningitis, affecting the brain and spinal canal. The meningitis was infecting my whole nervous system, and no one knew what that might mean or how it would affect me, either in the short or long term. The news was devastating for the whole family. Having pictures of people who had their limbs amputated because of meningitis, they all feared the worse.

Each day, my family turned up and took turns standing by my bed. All of them were tearful, especially Geoff, who failed to hold back emotion no matter how hard he tried. At this point, my whole family looked forlorn, as if they had given up their independence of self and somehow formed a collective of fear. Their emotions had taken over the functioning of their entire existence. As a collective, they seemed to have worked themselves up to a point where they couldn't control anything and had lost all power to make independent decisions.

Caz would later tell me that she shuddered at what she saw when she looked at my family that had always stood strong in the face of adversity. She immediately grabbed Geoff and dragged him to a side room. She closed the door quickly but gently and turned to Geoff who was still fighting back tears. With a stern face but with the greatest care, she said, 'Geoff you're the rock of this family, yet you're falling apart. They need you back there, and you're just not there. You need to pull yourself together, suck it up, and be Geoff. I know it's hard, and I know it's not fair, but everyone looks to you to be strong and show them some strength. So, I'm going to leave you in here. Take as much time as you need. But when you come out, you need to come out as Geoff the rock.' She reached up, kissed him tenderly on the cheek. and wiped away his tears. But he looked at her, stunned and forlorn. Caz walked out and joined the family, not letting on to anyone what had just taken place.

Geoff stood perfectly still, looking out at the distance through the room window, and all he could see was an old graveyard, which did not lighten the mood. The workings of his mind were for Geoff to reveal, which meant we would never know them because they were locked away in a deep dark place in his consciousness.

After about five minutes, the door to the room opened, and Geoff walked out, somewhat taller, somehow different. He walked up to my mother, who was standing over me, put an arm around her, and asked, 'You OK, Mum?'

As she buried her head in his embrace, she started to feel safe again.

Since that day, Geoff never shed another tear, no matter how hard things got. Nor did he ever give up on me. He would go on to organise an army of visitors, making sure a single day didn't go by without someone at my side. On his shift, he would sit holding my hand while I slept. He would pace the halls as each challenge appeared, and he was the one I called when I finally believed my end was nearing and looked for someone to take care of my wife and boys. The rock was back, and he was there to stay. He was now fully focused on the whole family, treating them not as some kind of collective but as individuals. Slowly, one by one, he pulled each one out of the collective and helped them face what was happening with hope rather than fear.

While he looked after the family, Amanda looked after me, focused on the whole picture of my care. She didn't know what any of the machines did, what any of the doctors really said, but she knew me, and she was watching for any sign of life or change.

CHAPTER 5

THE NEW NORMAL

As usual, Amanda spent the evening cleaning the house, doing the laundry, cooking dinner, and taking the kids to after-school lessons and clubs. Her life wasn't her own, and she hoped for a better existence. She was too busy to be mindful and break the chains of her perception and the false mental formation we all carry. She would sit down and try her hardest to get the kids to do their homework. Myles, our oldest, was a gentle soul. Those days, he struggled to make friends, and being someone who enjoyed people's company, it was a very sad time for him. To add to his burdens, he was bullied a lot, as the bullies saw him as a soft target, something that would change dramatically as he developed his own giant, both physically and mentally. He is too much like me for comfort. However, at that point, he was still innocent. Both the boys had endured the fear of their mother almost dying, and both pushed their fears down low, ready to kick them up the arse if they popped back up. There was no stopping this when I was in the hospital dying right in front of them. They let the anger in, creating their own angry giants.

Max was a slightly different character. Liking things his way, he'd been a handful right from the start. He loved a cuddle and making a mess. As soon as Amanda tidied his room, he would mess it all up again, and then he was happy. It saddens me that the two little angels I knew have developed their own giants, changing them for life. Like all parents, I'm very proud of both my children, and I love them very much, so much so that the very love will eventually save my life and soul. You may have to forgive me for wearing rose-tinted glasses when it comes to them, especially when they're being teenagers and creating merry hell.

53

Still in the background, keeping everyone going was Amanda.

Amanda sat down for five minutes, remembering my first day at my new job and how nervous and excited I had been, which brought a smile to her face. She also remembered that, at the time, she'd recalled her past as a CEO's personal assistant. She recollected the excitement of a new job and the satisfaction of receiving a good salary for a good month's work. She felt that feeling of contentment all over again as she sat there on her own. Amanda cut off those thoughts, telling herself that such sentimental longing for the past was nothing more than a memory of the past, which she illuminated in her mind, making those good old days look better. All these thoughts were shattered as a crash came from upstairs. She ran up to investigate, only to find Max buried under piles of Lego. Also, the shelf of all the Lego models I ever built him had tipped over on top of him.

Without thinking, she quickly picked up the shelf and pulled Max out from underneath the piles of Lego. It turned out that Max had been climbing the shelfing unit, and it had fallen on top of him. When Amanda went to tidy it up, he just said, 'No, leave it. I like it.'

His reaction made Amanda want to scream. She felt all she was was a kind of machine on hand for anyone's use. The mind is a powerful thing, and what she thought, she would become. I might have seen her as the family CEO, but I had never walked a day in her shoes, so I missed her discontentment and negative mental formation. I was too wrapped up in my own world and my mental formations that I unforgivably missed this.

As she left Max's room, she checked in on Myles, who was playing with his toys. He was only thirteen and at that place where he wanted grown-up things, but he still liked his *Star Wars* toys. Caught in this fourth dimension of time, he craved both the future and the past. I had wallpapered one of his bedroom walls with music posters. He loved it because it appeared grown up to him, but he hid the fact that he was still playing *Star Wars*. He was a kind boy and gave all his toys to Max and then borrowed them back. He didn't own them, but he still had access to them. Max has always adored him and still does today. He would do anything for Myles and wanted exactly what Myles had. Myles happily took on the world to keep his little brother safe, something he couldn't do then. But as time went by, he would become a formidable defender for the entire family.

54

Amanda recalled that, on the night before that first day, she had fed the boys and gotten Max ready for bed, while Myles got himself ready, but with a lot of pushing and prodding from her. She finally sat down for the day even though a lot more was left to be done. But it seemed like there was always more to do, no matter how hard she worked. She was tired and heavy on her feet and really didn't think she could do more that day. She felt like she had weights tied to her, holding her down from just floating away. A once sharp mind had been sucked of all its powers, and now she felt lost in a world where only the kids existed. If she could only cut the ropes of the weights, she could escape such toil. But those weights were us—the two boys and me. In a strange way, she wanted to be free, but she would rather stay tethered to her love for her family.

As all this washed through her mind, I walked through the door, completely shattered and expecting a cheerful wife. Amanda gave me a big hug and a big kiss and asked me cheerfully, 'So how was your first day?' Even though she was just as shattered as me, she wanted to be enthusiastic.

Amanda felt a little tug on her heart, as she was envious momentarily. But she would never let that be known. She steadied herself with her early thoughts, *It's only nostalgia. Let it go.* She then excitedly said, 'I'm so pleased for you. Well done, Mike! You deserve this. What did they have you doing for the day?'

'Not much, just getting security badges, being shown around, and a few introduction meetings with different business partners.'

She waited for a second and then gave me a kiss.

The kids had heard me come in and were just as excited. They both ran downstairs, sat quietly on the sofa, and looked at me expectantly. Realising she was outnumbered again, Amanda squeezed my hand and quietly left to start my dinner. It didn't matter that she was tired. She wanted me and the kids to have some time together. She was the glue that kept us all going, yet I didn't ask her how her day was or give her a chance to talk about it. I sat down between the boys, both of whom gave me a hug. I told them all about the glass office.

Amanda burst into tears, all this was just a few months ago. And now here she was watching the love of her life in a coma, clinging to any hope he might recover.

In my coma, my world became confused. My mind took me back to my first days at my new job. Everyone in the family was happy that I had found my dream job. However, what I kept from them all was that the giant in me felt small, and I was very nervous about the whole thing. I might have been born again that morning. But by this time, tomorrow mattered most, not the present. I should have been happy; instead, I felt depressed, the hungry dogs of the past still haunting me. I kept thinking, *I won't be able to pull this off.* I was anxious and living in the future. The peace of the present was lacking in my heart. I had created a demon to go with all my other phantoms, and I was tired of it all.

Every day, I headed home on the train, feeling inadequate and terrified they would find me out, as if I didn't belong. Everyone in the company seemed much younger and brighter than me. I had forgotten my skills and abilities, and my self-confidence was low, though I would never show it. I didn't want to take the fear home with me, as it was my demon to conquer and not something the family should see. One day, on the trip home, I fell asleep to the gentle rocking of the train. I was so tired that sleep came easily. Even though my six-foot two-inch, sixteen-stone frame was crammed into just enough space for a ten-year-old child, I still found some comfort in the train seat. I dreamt I was woken by the train conductor, who asked me for my ticket. As I handed it to him, black waving sheets of darkness swirled around him, emitting fear and anger. The hidden image of Doctor Dark replaced that of his. He stared right into my eyes. I froze. In my mind, my thoughts became irrational, and my scattered fear of work turned into the fear of Doctor Dark. I became paralysed in the seat at the menacing sight of such a phantom crashing into what I thought was reality. I felt his cold grip tightening in my mind. As he leant over, the waving sheets of darkness started to fly around me, intensifying the feelings of fear and anger.

Suddenly, he was gone, and the conductor was back. The conductor handed me my ticket and said, 'Thank you, sir.'

When I awoke, I was visibly shaken. Thankfully, no one with direct sight of my seating area was around. I dismissed it all at first but kept thinking about my fear, which only aggravated it. To keep my mind off it, I said to myself, *It doesn't matter, as I'm getting stronger, and life is getting better. Right now, I'm going home to my family, where I always feel safe.* The

56

sight of Doctor Dark in my world made me start doubting what was real and what wasn't. Before long, I reached home, with no more visions. I kissed everyone hello, took a bath to relax, and collapsed into my chair. Then, the fear started again, and I started feeling afraid I was going to be called out as inadequate. And how I would support my family? Doctor Dark was making an impact.

That night, I read a book on Zen teachings, known as Dharma. A quote in the book by Sathya Sai Baba said, 'Mind is like a monkey jumping from branch to branch, thought to thought.'

How true! my inner voice shouted. My mind truly jumped from place to place, creating its own anxiety and problems.

Reading on, I came across another quote by Adi Da that said, 'Relax, nothing is under control.'

Again, I thought, *How true!* Nothing could be controlled when everything was so random.

I also found a quote by Jiddu Krishnamurti: 'I don't mind what happens. That is the essence of inner freedom.'

It occurred to me that I was far from such wisdom. The continual self-talk in my mind was an uncontrolled commentary, jumping from thought to thought and across all experiences. This inner voice was negative and brought on doubt and, ultimately, fear. This was my inner monkey. I still pondered from where the voice came. Was it the giant? It couldn't be, as he seemed to destroy all doubt and have me rush in where angels feared to tread. I soon realised that my ego had been damaged by the hungry dogs. My ego had become the co-architect of all my fears and unhappiness. This ghostlike entity that seemed to exist in me was fabricating inappropriate emotions. Fear wasn't some waving black sheet external to myself; it was created by me, it was played out by me, and it was only me who could turn it from what seemed real into just a painless gust of emotion. I felt surrounded by dark forces. Wherever I looked, new demons seemed to be popping up.

My mind then switched away from the past, and I found myself in a strange black-and-white world. In my mind, I had been chosen by my company for the trial of a new Ebola drug. I should mention that, prior to all this, Ebola was spreading across West Africa, and the world wasn't sure how to deal with it. Though I knew my company had nothing to do with pharmaceuticals and West Africa, nothing made sense here. In this strange place, hundreds of beds lined a large warehouse. An attendant hovered over each bed. Those on the bed were unconscious, with tubes coming out of them, reaching from their mouths to the ceiling of the room. I was shown to my bed and told to 'strip and get in'. The whole place made me feel very uneasy, and I started to worry, unsure any of it was above board. As I started to strip, I felt nervous and anxious about what was happening, and I concentrated on everything around me rather than undressing. Like a clown, I fell over, with my trousers wrapped around my ankles. I had forgotten to take off my shoes first, so I quickly resolved the problem and threw them under the bed. The activity above caught my eye. I looked up at the high windows of the building, and I sensed something was very wrong, but I couldn't put my finger on it. A wave of darkness crashed around the building. The crashing seemed deliberate, almost like something was taking its anger and frustration out on the building. Out there, somewhere, a phantom of some sort was trying to get in. I immediately thought of Doctor Dark, but I told myself the possibility was impossible.

An attendant then came up to me and asked me to hurry up and get into the bed.

I asked him, 'What's going on outside?'

'Nothing that concerns you or me,' he replied. But he was unconvincing, and his eyes looked terrified.

As I climbed into the bed, the attendant started rigging me up to machines. He gave me a shot in the arm, and I started to feel relaxed and calm. Even the phantom outside no longer worried me. He then slid a tube down my throat and flicked a switch on the machine beside me. I could feel its secret contents slowly running into my stomach. I immediately reacted and started convulsing. But that passed, and I felt like I was just sinking into the bed, whereas, in reality, I was floating up towards the ceiling. I thought, *I don't think this was such a good idea.*

Still dreaming, I was now on the dark wave as I crashed against the outside of the building. Weightless and lacking control, I violently crashed against the walls, as if the phantom was using me as a battering ram. I then saw a figure in the dark.

He was unmistakable, as he was wearing a long black coat over a hoody and a top hat. Grinning from ear to ear, he floated through the darkness. 'This is no place here for you,' he growled.

'What do you want from me?' I asked.

'I'm not here for you. Today, I have another purpose other than you.'

I immediately doubted his words. 'Why are you frightening these poor people?' I asked in a commanding tone, though I had no command of the situation whatsoever.

'The only people frightened of me are the deathmongers inside that building.' He stopped talking, and the already big smile on his face grew as if something good had just happened.

Suddenly, I was woken out of the coma by the doctors. I saw my family all around me, but I didn't really recognise them. Owing to my seizures and convulsions, the doctors decided to put me back under. I didn't really remember any of this, but I was told by Geoff that he had tried to explain to me that the doctors were going to put me under because I wasn't ready to come out. Geoff being an ex-policeman, I believed he knew all about the dream I was having, which was particularly harrowing and real. Of course, he couldn't possibly know, so he was confused when I kept winking at him.

Out of nowhere, I said, 'This is not the end. It's just the beginning.'

Geoff had no idea what I was talking about and held my hand as I was slowly induced back into a coma. As I went back in, I found myself floating above my bed, still in the large warehouse. Tubes were sticking out of me, and I was still being force-fed the secret medication. I dropped suddenly and landed on my bed. As I landed, all the tubes burst from my body, and I vomited up the one down my throat. *Shit, I think he's gotten in! Was it me? Was I his way in?*

All the attendants started running towards the exit, but the doors ahead slammed shut. I could see Doctor Dark standing in front of them, with his arms down by his side, his hands pointed outwards. The running crowd of attendants just froze out of terror. Then Doctor Dark calmly walked among them, touching each one on the shoulder, making them collapse onto the floor.

The next minute, I rose up again, while all the other test subjects dropped. As their tubes came out; loud noises of vomiting and sounds of the tube contents splattering on to the floor could be heard. I keep floating until I found myself in a giant cloud. As I rose above it, I saw people looking down at me.

Geoff was there. He spoke, but I didn't recognise him. 'Are you OK, Mike?'

As I slowly come around, I was more and more aware of people standing around my bed.

Indicating towards my mother, a doctor asked, 'Mike, do you know who this is?'

'No, I don't. Who is she?' I asked.

Pointing to Paul and Geoff, the doctor repeated, 'What about these two chaps? Do you know who they are?'

'No,' I replied again.

'What about this lady?' he asked, pointing to Amanda.

I saw her standing there, looking all worried and browbeaten, and with a big smile on my face, I said, 'That's my wife. Of course I know her.' With that, I stretched my arms up and gave her a big hug.

She hugged me back.

I pulled her onto the bed, wrapped my arms around her and declared, 'Now I'm home.'

Taking full advantage of my embrace, Amanda relaxed. Her longing for normality seemed to be almost achieved. Unfortunately, this wasn't the end; it was just the beginning.

It had been several days since I was put under. I couldn't believe what had happened during the coma had taken so long, but it was just a dream at the end of the day. Even once I was out of the coma, my family continued visiting me every day. Slowly but gradually, I started to remember them all, though things remained confusing. They asked me if I remembered anything. I just looked at Geoff and thought, *He will know all about the Ebola experiment.* I winked at him, smiled, and said, 'No nothing at all.'

Geoff, of course, still had no idea why I'd winked at him. As the days dragged on, I was confined to the bed, with tubes draining fluid from around my brain into an EVD. Every time I lifted my head above the EVD, I passed out because of the pressure, and it felt like my head had become detached from my body and was spinning off into space. I had to lower my head quickly, to prevent an escalation, which made me feel pinned to the bed. I became more and more agitated, as I felt like

Gulliver tied down on the shores of Lilliput. I was confused, my memory was fragmented, and I felt utterly vulnerable. One afternoon, noticing my mother sitting at the foot of my bed, I whispered to Amanda, 'Who's that old woman at the end of the bed?'

Amanda replied, 'That's your mother.'

The information Amanda provided me didn't matter to me. Pointing to the bed curtain rail, I said unforgivingly, 'If she doesn't leave, I'm going to break down that metal bar. Make her leave.'

My poor mother stood up and said, 'Don't worry, love. I will go.' And she walked off.

I don't remember the incident now, but I'm horrified that it happened. I have no idea what was going through my mind at the time, and it wasn't the real me.

CHAPTER 6

CONFUSED AND LOST

Later that week, things became even more confusing, as I entered a new world that seemed real. For some reason, during the night, I dreamt that all the head injury patients were taken to a hunter's shack somewhere in the woods. The shack had a big burning fire in the middle, and strange sculptures of animal heads made of twisted branches hung around the walls. We were all given a blanket and told to sleep on the floor of the living room but near to the fire to keep warm. The nurses who had brought us there looked worried and anxious about what was outside. Once I got semi-comfortable on the floor, I started to understand their anxiety. Outside, the same wave of darkness from my coma world was flying around the shack. Every now and then, it would crash into the building, making it shake, as if it was trying to get in. *Is he out there?* I wondered. *What on earth is in here that he could be unhappy about?* I never found out, as I fell asleep and didn't wake up until morning. By then, the darkness had lifted, and the sun shone brightly. As I walked outside, I saw fields of corn glistening in the sun. Hearing Amanda's voice in the wind, slowly I came back to reality. Looking up, I saw Amanda on my right, and a large window on my left, with the sun shining through.

'They have moved you into a four-person ward so they can watch you. You're in a different bed space,' Amanda informed me.

I just smiled at her and hugged her. I lay my spinning head back down with Amanda's head on my chest. No more words were needed, and they would have just spoilt the moment.

After a few nights of visiting the shack, I met the Brethren, two tall men, very thin, wrapped in brown blankets that covered their whole body, including their faces. Only their bright blue eyes could be seen, and they carried a long black pole. A man creeped up beside me and whispered in my ear, 'They're the Brethren. They protect us from the darkness.' He sounded almost reverent.

I looked around to ask questions, but the man was gone as quickly as he had arrived. When I looked back at the Brethren, we had moved to the ward corridor. A strong feeling of trust emanated from the Brethren, providing a deep sense of assurance. I didn't know what was going to happen, but I felt I would be all right with the Brethren standing tall in front of me. They stared at the bolted ward doors, as an outside force was ramming the doors. I could feel it again—the darkness—and it was back and outside. The Brethren exchanged looks between each other with cool and unconcerned eyes. Then they hopped into the air and landed effortlessly on the floor, creating no noise whatsoever. They reminded me of two Maasai warriors proudly jumping up and down to gain their rite of passage to manhood.

As the evening went by, the Brethren showed no sign of stopping or of being tired. Whatever was outside was clearly scared of them, as the banging slowly stopped, and the feeling of darkness lifted. The following few nights, they stood guard beside my bed. During the night, one of them would lie under my bed while the other would stand by my head and place one hand on my forehead. One night, I awoke, and I thought the Brethren had left my bedside. I saw them back in the ward corridor where I had suddenly appeared. I felt the darkness outside yet again and its crashing against the doors, trying to get in. Feeling a sense of dread, uneasiness, and anxiety, I looked at the Brethren, and their eyes appeared concerned. As one of them stepped forward, smoke emerged from where his mouth should be. He turned his head from side to side, and the smoke seemed to float into every nook and cranny. The other jumped up onto a medicine cabinet in a single leap and sat there like a tiger about to attack. Smoke bellowed from his mouth as he turned his head from side to side.

Before long, smoke covered everywhere, flowing out the ward doors from underneath and the cracks around the sides. The crashing stopped, and the feeling of darkness, which I never knew existed, lifted. It felt like a vacuum cleaner being turned off, as one realised the sound was present only when it stopped. I wanted to watch the Brethren all night, but my eyelids were getting heavy. Eventually, my eyes opened, and I was back in bed. Amanda was sitting next to me, grasping my hand.

The next night, I saw the Brethren standing in my bed space bay, staring at an old man on the bed opposite to mine. The old man had been having restless nights and day. He was in much distress, and he mumbled all kinds of rubbish. Clearly, he was in a worse state than me. Also, my condition had been slowly improving. The Brethren moved closer to him, almost gliding effortlessly. One climbed into bed with the old man and wrapped his arms around him. Immediately, he stopped mumbling and seemed to rest well for the first time in days. The other stood at the foot of the bed on guard like a guardsman at Buckingham Palace, his stare fixed on my bed. The night before, they had been standing guard next to me, and as I was better now; they'd moved on to someone else.

I was moved to a single-occupancy room, as my carers didn't need to keep a close watch on me anymore. I didn't know what was real and what was not. But as I lay in bed all day, every day, I started to come out of the strange dream world I'd been in and return to reality. I couldn't remember much about those first days out of the coma. Amanda told me of my madness, but I remembered the shack and the Brethren. I wasn't out of the woods yet, and I wasn't allowed to sit up, so as to keep the flow of fluid from my head balanced.

A few nights later Amanda had gone home, and I was all alone. I wanted to scream for the Brethren, as they seemed like my only salvation, and then I remembered that they were just a hallucination. Now that they were gone, I felt the darkness all around me and felt trapped. Adding to my discomfort and fear was my inability to piss. I had been given a trial without catheter (TWC), which involved removing the catheter to see if I could piss independently. Unfortunately, it didn't work for me. I was as full as a water balloon. My calls for assistance seemed to be ignored. In the room, by myself, I felt like the only person there. *Did the darkness finally get in and take everyone? Or am I just being ignored?*

After waiting for almost half an hour, a nurse finally attended me. She was in a foul mood, more than likely because she was overworked. But I just didn't care, as my bladder was about to burst. She looked at me with angry eyes and asked, 'What's wrong with you?' She spat out the words like they were venom.

'I can't pee. I'm going have to be re-catheterised,' I shouted back with a strong hint of desperation in my voice.

'Just pee,' she instructed, like I was a naughty boy holding it in out of spite. As she said it, she hit my pubic area with the back of her hand, in the very mistaken hope it would help. She kept going, and every strike forced me to want to piss more. But the problem was that my urethra pipe wasn't letting anything out, and her strikes felt like she was just swishing water around my bladder and forcing more liquid into my closed urethra. All I could do was shout out in pain. Eventually, she stopped and said, 'I think you need a new catheter.'

'Finally,' I cried.

Ignoring my cry, she walked off. Half an hour later, she came back with a catheter and went about the business of reinserting it into my penis. She then stood back in surprise as the bag instantly filled with the piss. She held up the bag and said, 'Look how full you were!' as if it was a big surprise, and I had never said a word.

Though the anger in me shot up from my soul and forced its way to my mouth, I controlled my reaction and just ignored her.

Regardless, she just stood there, repeatedly picking my catheter bag up and showing me how full it was getting. When I finally stopped pissing, she held the catheter bag high once again. It was filled to about 1300 ml, which proved my discomfort and moaning to be valid. Uncaring, she just put the catheter bag back down and left the room. I felt like my whole stomach had been drained out; the relief was incredible and the feeling after was euphoric.

Before I finally left the hospital that year, I was moved back to the main ward for observation. One minute, I was in a signal occupancy bed, quite happy with my solitude. The next minute, I was in the main ward again. I had stopped eating because the food was extremely bad, and being a vegetarian, I had limited options. Every time I tried to eat, I vomited it back up. My whole body seemed to reject the food. In the end, they fed me liquid supplements via a food pipe through my nose into my stomach. The pipe made me feel like plaster was stuck in my throat and my nostrils were blocked. Life was barely bearable. I couldn't piss, I couldn't eat, and I had to endure such discomfort. To top it all, I was back in the main ward again.

My condition made me sleep most of the time, which was a relief. The time I was awake was split between drawing the curtains and talking to my visitors. Once the visitors left, the curtains would be opened, to watch the others in my ward. Most of the patients in the ward were old men on their way out, except one who was my age. His bed was opposite mine, which was too far to talk, and he didn't talk much. Strangely, watching them was the highlight of my day. My hallucinations had mostly stopped; even Doctor Dark seemed to have gone. Lying in bed with pipes attached to my cock, nose, and head, all I could think of was my own misery. I had little to do other than watch these other people, who at first were just strangers with whom I was being forced to share a room. One day, I overheard a dying old man tell a nurse he was scared. I wanted to say something to him, but I drew a blank, as I doubted my random universe theory would either interest him or give him any comfort.

Next to me was another old chap who was always very cheerful, until he was told he had to have suppositories. He told the nurse to stick them up her own arse. She stormed off in a huff, and he lay back down with a big smile on his face, clearly pleased with what he had said and having stood up for his own dignity. He looked over at me and said, 'It's my arse. I will decide what goes up it.'

'Bloody right,' I replied. 'Don't let them get you down or up, come to that.'

He laughed and said, 'I'm Frank.'

'Hi, Frank. I'm Mike.'

We both laughed though the exchange wasn't that funny, but anything to make you smile at that place. We didn't speak much, but every time he was rude to a nurse, he would look at me and give me a cheeky wink. Don't take me the wrong way. Most nurses were kind, but some were complete witches, such as the nurse who had hit my bladder during my failed TWC.

One night, I woke up in the dark and heard someone sobbing. I immediately thought it was the dying old man opposite me, but it was Frank. I never said a word, as he clearly was using the cover of darkness to hide his tears, and I wasn't going to expose him. After that night, as I paid close attention, I realised he had no visitors, and he was alone. I wished I had talked to him more than I did.

I struck up a conversation with the old fellow opposite Frank's bed. His name was Bill. His wife had died a few years back, and he looked forward to seeing her again. Though I didn't believe one could get to see dead people again, as the universe was too random for that, I went along with him. I wasn't going to challenge his belief. He was so convinced of God in heaven that he contemplated out loud if he had done enough to reach heaven. I told him that I didn't think the entry to heaven was based on deeds but one's goodness as a man overall. He seemed content with my response, as he clearly thought himself to be a good man, and I was pleased for him. A few days later, the old chap died, and he was wheeled away.

Frank, who always had something to say about everything, was silent all day, and he didn't even talk to me.

The chap opposite me looked over around midday and simply said, 'Life is fragile. You never know when your time is up.'

That was it. I agreed, and both of us went about our own business of lying around. Though I enjoyed being in a room of my own, I was pleased that I was in the main ward. Bill's death showed the fragile grip we all shared as humans. I had known Bill for less than two days, and we had spoken for less than an hour, but his death made a profound impression on me. Even though he believed he was going to meet his wife again, he was still scared of the unknown. His wife's death had brought about a definitive separation, and there was no turning back. In Bill's case, there was no time for goodbye, though perhaps our brief little discussion about his wife was his final goodbye. From then on, I started to see that being afraid of death was harmful, and it could only stop me from enjoying the life I had left. I feared death because of the unknown. I always wanted to die having achieved some wisdom connecting all life together and having understood life's purpose. Being close to death, I wanted to live a life of meaning. I wanted to experience the here and now. I realised that the most important thing was the journey itself and not the destination.

I must have lost count of the weeks because it was late December before I knew it. My doctors wanted to keep a close eye on the infection in my back, so I was sent for a spinal MRI. Fortunately, the result indicated improvement from that of the previous MRIs.

I was back in a single-occupancy room now, and I missed the company in the ward. One day, as Amanda stroked my forehead, I was thinking of Bill and his profound effect on me. I looked into her eyes and said, 'I want to be out for Christmas. I want to see the boys' faces when they get their presents.'

Looking worried, she said, 'I don't think that's a good idea. You need to take your time.'

As we discussed it, I became more agitated, and she became increasingly concerned.

Eventually, I hardened my stare and said, 'Look at me, darling. You know I'm coming home for Christmas. So, you may as well get on board and help it happen, or I will just walk out of this place.'

She tried a few more times to convince me to not have such a target and to get it into my thick head that the hospital might not take me back if I just walked out. Eventually, she took her hand out of mine, kissed me on the forehead, and said, 'I have to go now.'

CHAPTER 7

MERRY CHRISTMAS

Amanda left and started calling everyone she could think of to get me home for Christmas, including different consultant physician assistants, microbiology specialists, and even the peripherally inserted central catheter (PICC) line team, who she'd been told would play a big part in me going home. She called and pestered whoever needed to be involved with my discharge.

After that, she drove for an hour and a half to get back to the kids and cook for them. She was worried sick about my plan to leave the hospital because she knew that, once I had decided something, I would do anything to make it happen, and she was concerned I was making a medical mistake. She would, of course, be proven right, but we will come to that later.

Once at home, after fighting with the kids to get ready for bed and making sure they were both wrapped up and comfortable, she went downstairs and started the laundry. By this time, she was absolutely drained, burning one end of the candle looking after me and the other end looking after the boys. All she wanted to do was sit down with a cup of tea and cry, which, I'm sure, was brought on by the worry of me demanding a Christmas release. However, she just had no time to spare to confront her feelings, as the house needed cleaning, school uniforms needed washing, and the ironing was piling up. She went about everything as if she was a robot following a programme, but her programmers had long disappeared. Life had become a foggy haze to her as each day merged into the next. She felt like she was tied to this world with heavy weights, and her own life force was sucking her into the ground. Regardless of how she felt or how late it was, she would inevitably tackle the ironing.

Her friend Clare, who had been around during the day, had taken the laundry back to her house, where she would work on it until early in the morning. It wasn't the first or last time during my time in the hospital that Clare would offer such a help. Amanda always knew the laundry would be returned, washed and ironed. Clare was a good friend, and Amanda and I appreciated everything about her and always felt privileged and blessed to have her as a friend. Her partner Terry was an equally good friend of ours too. Terry was a general house maintenance person. He did all our DIY, and when I was in the hospital and eventually out, he came over all the time and fixed all sorts of household problems for us. Only one other friend helped out during that time, Amanda's friend Gail. She would come and leave Marks & Spencer shopping for Amanda while she was at the hospital. It meant that when Amanda got back late at night, she would have some quality food to eat. There are others too, but they don't appear until later in the story.

That night, as usual, Amanda finally got to bed at about one in the morning, well aware she had to be up early to get the kids to school and then travel back to Oxford to be with me. When she finally fell asleep, her dreams were full of fear and anxiety. She had her own phantoms, likely fuelled by me. She was burning out, but nevertheless, she was determined to be with me as much as possible. She dreamt that a great weight of rubble was on top of her. Though she was trapped, she could see me also covered in rubble. She saw that the boys were playing on the other side of the road near to a crumbling building. She called out to them, but they didn't hear her and just kept playing. She looked around at me, and I was convulsing. She woke up calling out my name.

As always, she got up early and showered. As she was getting the boys up and in and out of the shower, Myles asked, 'When's Daddy coming home? Will he be here for Christmas?'

She looked at them both as they stood looking at her expectantly. She went down on one knee and gently said, 'Daddy and I are trying very hard to get him home for Christmas. We just don't know yet. But as soon as I know, I will tell you, OK?'

They both nodded but looked disappointed. She hurried them along, aware that her words had fallen short. She wanted to cry because she knew

I may not make it at all, not just for Christmas. She would never let the kids know that. She just got them ready for school and then phoned my mother to check if she would pick them up from school that day. As soon as both the kids were off, she just directed the car towards Oxford and drove, half in a daydream, half watching the road.

I had another operation to take out the EVDs, and it was a relief once they were gone. Though I still had a urethral catheter in, I felt a lot better, a lot more positive. The physiotherapist came in with a Zimmer frame and showed Amanda how to get me on it from a sitting position and me how to walk with it. When the physiotherapist left, Amanda and I just looked at each other and laughed.

'I can't believe I have to go home using a Zimmer frame. I will have to pull my pants up high like an old man,' I said.

Though Amanda tried to stop laughing, she couldn't and burst out, 'Don't you dare.'

Seeing her smile again felt good.

That week, I was seen by James, who was much more upbeat and told Amanda that he thought the hydrocephalus was now under control. Later that week, I was seen by the consultant who had operated on me in Swindon. He dictated to his minion, a poor junior doctor running behind him taking notes, that I was doing impressively well and was up and about, with no complaints of leg pain anymore. He suggested continuing with IV antibiotics for at least another eight weeks and adding rifampicin.

Until Christmas Eve, I remained in the JRH, where I had slowly started to recover to the extent that I was able to move with the Zimmer frame. Later that day, I was discharged under the care of a community IV team. They came to my room and inserted a PICC line into my chest. A PICC line is a long, thin, flexible tube, like a catheter, used to provide regular IV treatment straight to the heart. The nurse inserted it into a vein above the bend of my elbow. I was told it should stay in place until my treatment was over. I felt like a lab rat with all the pipes and tubes hanging out of me. They were a constant reminder of my condition, but by that time, I was too high in spirts to care.

I was going home, and this horror was nearly over—or so I thought. Amanda, assisted by a nurse, very carefully got me up with a special standing machine. I stood on a swivel plate, grabbing hold of two handles. Amanda

71

slowly turned me until my buttocks were in line with the wheelchair, and I could then slowly sit down. I wanted to leave standing up on the Zimmer frame, but the nurse insisted on me using the wheelchair. Amanda bundled me up in jumpers and blankets like a little lost bird, and she finished with a kiss, making the whole experience better. I was pushed out, with Paul carrying the Zimmer frame, and off we went to the car. We were given a banana board (a comfortable, lightweight, curved transfer board, designed to aid seated transfers of individuals between two surfaces, such as from a bed to wheelchair) to get me in. I slid into the car like a badly made jelly. I still had a lot to learn. But once inside, I was quite proud of myself and used a new phrase, which would be used a thousand times over and over. I announced, 'It's not pretty, but it's effective.'

For the first time since this ordeal had begun but not the last time, we all had a giggle and finished off the job of making me comfortable. The episode summed up how we approached my condition—mainly with astonishing care from my family and a good deal of mocking the whole stupid situation.

On arriving home, I found that Amanda had prepared a bed behind the sofa at the end of the living room so that I didn't have to climb the stairs. I headed for a chair and slowly sat down. 'Ahh ... it's good to be home!'

That night, lying alone on the bed in the living room, a darkness ascended on me. I considered calling for the Brethren, but then I remembered they were in the hospital, and I was home now. I looked outside, but I couldn't see anything. It was then that it hit me—the smell of burning flesh. I looked around, and there he was, sitting on the side of my bed. I couldn't fully see him, and he seemed more in the darkness than in my world. As Doctor Dark had nothing to say, I just ignored him and tried to get some sleep. Yet in my sleep, I dreamt of his crackling voice saying, 'This is not the end. It's just the beginning.'

On Christmas day, we all woke up in the anticipation of the festivities. I awoke feeling well. I looked forward to the day; in fact, I was really excited. All the neurons in my brain were firing, electrifying my thinking, which was focused on seeing the boys' reactions to their presents. The kids were up soon, desperate to start opening their presents and as electrified as I was. They brought Amanda and me their pillowcases, which were full of carefully wrapped boxes. On starter's orders, they looked at us both with focused anticipation.

They got the go from their mother, and they were off. One by one, they opened their little surprise boxes faster than the speed of light. We kept telling them to slow down and enjoy the experience, but they were in heaven, having the time of their life. It wasn't long before they had gone through the entire sack of presents. They happily played with their new toys, while Amanda and I were left with a heap of wrapping paper. Amanda started to clear it all, and I tried to help, but there was little I could do.

Later that morning, my mother arrived, and we all sat down for some Christmas breakfast. Halfway through breakfast, my mother announced that she must go back to check on the lamb, which was cooking for Boxing Day when the entire Fisher clan got together over Christmas. I asked her to be as quick as she could so that we could start opening all the big presents for the boys.

Finally, the time had come. We were all sitting in the living room. I was gripped with excitement, almost as much as the kids. Amanda was a lot cooler but was enjoying the buzz. She brought the adults some hot coffee and the children some orange juice. I plopped myself on the floor, dragged myself over to the tree and started to hand out the presents. I took one of the largest boxes and gave it to Max and asked him not to open it until Myles had received his present. As soon as Myles received his present, they both started ripping in. Max was the first to open his, and when he realised he had received a PlayStation 4 for Christmas, he screamed with joy. Myles looked up and realised something good was happening. He too started to open his present as quickly as he could. Then he saw his PlayStation 4 and reacted similarly to Max while fighting back tears of joy. Their reactions made all the effort to get home worth it.

It was now time for Amanda to find out what she was going to get for Christmas. I asked Myles to fetch her bicycle waiting out in the hallway. Every atom in my body tingled with excitement and joy at being home for this great event. As she saw the present, she jumped in joy, looking elated, exactly what I was hoping for. She got on the bicycle, but it was too big. I couldn't believe it. I was sure I had gotten the right size. Taking note but missing the important facts was typical of me. I deflated like a leaking balloon, my tingling excitement turning into a mass lump in my stomach. The morning had gone well, a harmony of fun and laughter, full of promise. I now sat looking at my mistake and Amanda's crushed expression though she was trying to hide it. I could see she was disappointed. I went to sip my coffee, but it had gone cold. Just like me, it was only good for pouring down the sink, and that was exactly how I felt.

I quickly searched the Internet to see if I could find another bike, the same type but smaller. Much to my horror, all I found was children's bikes, nothing Amanda would like, and I was absolutely gutted. The kids ran off to play with their PlayStation, leaving my mother, Amanda, and me together. I started to feel really sick at this point and went back to bed. The morning had all been too much for me, a disguised indication of the future.

Soon I started to vomit violently and started to feel dizzy. In my confused state, I accidentally pulled my PICC line half out, rendering any attempt to give me an IV antibiotic impossible. Now over the disappointment of her Christmas present, Amanda called the hospital and was told to bring me in. Half an hour later, I was sitting in an NHS wheelchair at the GWH casualty. I was a pathetic sight, doubled over in the wheelchair, wearing a large tartan blanket on top of me. Half my hair had been shaven because of all the operations, and I was struggling to even keep my head up. No matter how bad I looked, we still had to join the queue of people waiting to see a doctor. As far as I could see, the worst casualty in front of me was a bad hand. However, we waited our turn quietly and uncomplainingly. Eventually, we ended up in a treatment room, where a nurse decided that the best course of action was to leave the PICC line for the specialised team and give me my antibiotics through a cannula in my arm. A doctor came in and agreed with the nurse and her course of action. I was finally given an IV antibiotic, not through the PICC line but a cannula in my arm. Now, all I had to do was just lay there and wait for the antibiotics to go in.

When we finally returned home, I felt pretty sick, so I went back to bed. This feeling lasted through the day and into Boxing Day, by which time I felt like my whole colon was trying to escape through my mouth. My stomach was churning like a washing machine, and my head felt like a thousand evil pixies had got inside my brain and were chipping my brain cells with tiny hammers. My mother came over and said the whole family was at her house, and we should join them for Boxing Day dinner. I tried to explain to her I was feeling far too sick but didn't have the words or energy to explain how bad my condition was. She kissed me on the head and quietly left. She couldn't possibly know how bad I felt, and she left disappointed and perhaps feeling I was being a killjoy. Amanda asked me later if my brothers could come over to quickly wish me Merry Christmas, but even that felt too much for me. For the rest of the day and evening, I just lay in bed, feeling like death and wanting to vomit rotten carcasses.

The next day, I felt considerably better. My antibiotics were administered by a district nurse into the arm while at home. However, the following day was a day from hell. My bowel became blocked, and my catheter stopped working. The district nurse came over in the evening and tried to help me. She had to remove my catheter and manually empty my bladder by shaking my penis. This was followed by yet another anal invasion. In the end, with her finger up my anus to help me empty my bowel and shaking my penis at the same time, I experienced the most humiliating moment and one of the most uncomfortable moments of my life.

Not long after, the nurse called the paramedics, and I was whisked back to the casualty, which was, as usual, like a war zone. In a queue of gurneys, I waited for five hours. Eventually, a nurse called my name and put me in a cubicle. After yet another five-hour wait, I had started shaking, and my blood pressure had gone through the roof.

Seeing my condition, Amanda started sobbing and grabbed a nurse. 'You need to help my husband, please!' cried Amanda.

The nurse replied, 'I'm sorry. I can't help.'

Amanda the titan wasn't having that. She grabbed the nurse by the arm again and said, 'No! He needs help now!'

The nurse followed Amanda back to where I was lying, took my blood pressure, and started to panic.

Amanda shot the nurse a menacing look and said, 'He is going into autonomic dysreflexia.' AD was something she had been told about when I'd been discharged from the hospital.

Confused, the nurse said in a shaking voice, 'I don't know what that is.'

Amanda, without hesitation, gave her a sharp lesson in spinal injury medicine. 'Autonomic dysreflexia is a condition in which your involuntary

75

nervous system overreacts to external or bodily stimulus. The reaction causes a dangerous spike in blood pressure, constriction of blood vessels, and eventually heart failure. People with spinal cord injuries and who have suffered meningitis, like my husband, are very prone to the problem.'

'What do you want me to do?' asked the nurse, clearly feeling the power of the titan.

Like a fed-up school mistress, Amanda replied through her teeth, 'Empty his bladder now!'

'I haven't done a catheter for a while. If you're all right with that, I will give it a go.'

Amanda jumped at the offer, and the nurse finally inserted a new and working catheter, which drained my bladder. I immediately stopped shaking, my blood pressure returned to normal, and I started to look better. The nurse had taken a big career risk to do what she'd done. However, she'd done what every good nurse should do—put the patient first.

We waited a couple of hours until I was finally taken upstairs to the minor surgery ward. I waited there for another hour to be seen by a doctor, who simply checked whether I had a catheter in and sent me home.

The following day, the PICC nurse arrived and inserted a new PICC line. I could finally receive IV treatment through the line straight to my heart again. We discussed the fact that I had been off rifampicin over Christmas and was not keen to try it again but afraid of increasing risk of relapse. I was booked into the BIU OPAT clinic in Oxford that Wednesday to discuss this further.

As Wednesday approached, I had begun to experience worsening double vision, which the community nurses recorded as 'diplopia'. At the same time, they noted that the rifampicin had been stopped due to nausea.

On Wednesday, Amanda and I travelled to Oxford to the BIU OPAT clinic. A CT head scan showed that my ventricles were 'largely unchanged' but did not find the cause of the diplopia. I was seen by a doctor in the bone infection unit for a review of my antibiotics. The doctor and the Home IV Clinic team made a plan that I complete the remainder of the six-week IV ceftriaxone at home and for me to be seen on 14 January for a review at the end of the period. The rifampicin was neither restarted nor substituted with other oral antibiotics. We went home, as always, not really knowing what was going on.

On 7 January 2015, I was taken again to the casualty at the GWH, this time with back pain, abdominal pain, and constipation. I was discharged once the pain had subsided. The following week, I spoke to my GP for the first time over the telephone, as he was too busy to see me. He noted that I might be suffering from left-sided weakness, as I was walking with a Zimmer frame and sleeping downstairs. While on the phone with him, I requested a private referral to urology and colorectal, as I had failed four trials without catheters and was also struggling with constipation, despite taking laxatives. The GP agreed to the private referrals and rushed off the phone.

I remained unwell at home, and my condition deteriorated by mid-January. We rang up the PICC team, who immediately had me seen at the Oxford Bone Infection Service. When we arrived, Amanda struggled to get me into a hospital wheelchair and push me into the hospital. When we were finally seen, I required Amanda's assistance for the transfer from my wheelchair to the bed so that I could be examined by the doctor. The infection specialist I saw was so concerned about my lack of strength that she gave me a full examination. The results of the examination increased her concern, as she suspected possible cord compression. She immediately telephoned a neurosurgical registrar at the JRH, who confirmed the need for an inpatient assessment. That day, I was transferred by ambulance to the JRH, where I underwent an MRI. The scan showed a severe leptomeningeal enhancement extending from the cranial cervical junction to the sacrum, which was caused by severe spinal meningitis.

They admitted me immediately to the hospital, which marked the start of days and days of lying in bed, slowly fading away. The doctors would come and say they had no idea how I would be affected, and there was nothing to be done but wait and see what would happen. The meningitis was still in my system, and I was in a severe state.

Amanda was right. I should have never left the hospital for Christmas though I would have happily traded my life to see the boys' faces and reactions on that Christmas day. It was the last time the magic of Christmas would visit us. By the time I got out of hospital, Amanda and the boys would have gone through hell, and the boys would have left childhood and childish things behind to deal with my decline.

For weeks, I just lay in a hospital bed as the meningitis did its damage. It was slowly destroying my body and would bring me close to death. My whole body felt weaker and weaker, like I was getting lighter and lighter, and the only thing that stopped me from floating away was the bedsheets. My life was now confined to the four walls of the room, and the only event in my life was being administered various shots in the arm by blue angels.

Amanda would visit, but it felt like she was on the other side of a glass wall. I couldn't explain how I felt, and I was desperate to smash the wall down. There was, of course, more to my existence than just the room and the angels. Every day, I would vomit, and health assistants of all sorts of nationalities would come in and clean up for me. I wanted to talk to each one of them. What a chance, so much diversity! I wanted to ask them where they were from and what it was like, but they too were on the wrong side of the glass wall.

One morning, as I was pinned to the bed as usual, I started drifting off, helped by a painkiller injected into me by a blue angel. I could just hear the TV through the dark tunnel of sleep and faintly made out that the conversation was about people with Alzheimer's. As I listened to a lady who suffered from the disease talking, her words rang a bell somewhere inside me. She said dwelling on the condition or being depressed or feeling angry was pointless because you just lost another day of being happy, and I realised I would rather be happy than down and depressed. She sounded very strong and brave, so much so that I admired her. At first, the words were just words, lost in a sea of words uttered with the best of intentions. Slowly and surely, throughout the coming ordeal, they became louder and louder. And in the end, I couldn't ignore them anymore. I would use those words to keep my spirits up and stay as positive as I could.

Later that week, I started to feel a bit stronger, and the glass wall had fallen away. I was visited by a microbiology consultant, who suggested the IV ceftriaxone be stopped and changed to oral clindamycin. And I would need six months of oral treatment and a follow-up with the spinal team in three to four weeks. I was discharged back to the care of the GWH in Swindon.

I ended up in a gastro disorder ward. Why? I had no idea. No one there could understand or help me with the fact that my limbs seemed to be failing, which was a real concern to me. After about a week, in a ward with no provisions to treat me for walking difficulties, I managed to pass the local physiotherapist test. It wasn't hard, as all that was required of me was to climb some makeshift stairs and walk on a Zimmer frame down the corridor. On the way back to bed, I had a very humiliating experience, as while walking down the ward corridor on my Zimmer frame, I had defecated, leaving a trail right across the floor. I was told not to worry and put back to bed. I know now that the loss of control of my bowels should have been a sign of spinal damage to a trained spinal professional. However, it was missed, and I was discharged home.

The family and I tried to act as if nothing were wrong, and we went on a trip to Marlborough. The kids pushed me about in an old folding wheelchair that Amanda had purchased from a second-hand shop. The ride over the cobbled streets and uneven pavements was difficult, and when we finally landed in a tea shop, everyone was glad of the rest. On the way back, we stopped at a walking stick shop. I tried out different sticks and eventually picked two, which I foolishly thought I could use instead of the Zimmer frame. By the time I got home, I was exhausted and had a piercing headache. I soon fell into a deep sleep.

In my sleep, I saw my body to be haemorrhaging light. All the atoms in my body seemed to be escaping. I saw a little ballet dancer dancing and spinning around in the light, and she too was floating away from me. Looking around, I was floating in space. I could see planets circling a dent in space made by the sun. My light was dissipating into the universe, and I could do nothing. Once the little dancer had gone, there was no more dancing, not even by the hidden lovers, the particles. Everything seemed still and totally silent, and my body was almost gone.

'Michael … Michael … Michael!' Amanda woke me up to have some toast and coffee.

At that moment, I knew she hadn't really done much but wake me from a dream, but I was grateful to her, once again feeling like the titan had saved me. She sat me up in bed so that I could drink and eat my breakfast. I looked around and saw I was back in the living room. I drank the coffee, ate the toast, and made small talk with her, not telling her about my dream. Then, by accident, I vomited all over her.

After feeling down and heavy for days on end, I was readmitted to the JRH. A CT scan identified a persisting infection and acute hydrocephalus, and I needed a permanent shunt to drain the CSF.

79

CHAPTER 8

FACING THE ABYSS

To insert the shunt, James drilled a hole through my skull; inserted an inflow catheter into the centre of my brain; and fitted a programmable valve, which could be turned up or down depending on the need. This part of the process was almost painless, but the pain came when they fed the outflow pipe under my skin and muscle, which led to my stomach, where my body could reabsorb the CSF. To do this, they had to make an incision in my abdomen. I was, of course, under general anaesthetic, my brain switched off, devoid of dreams, thoughts. The pain started the moment I gained consciousness, shooting through my shoulders like I had been knifed right through the muscle. I couldn't sleep or get comfortable after the operation. Despite the absence of EVDs, the pain in my shoulders was almost unbearable. All I could do was lie there and suffer the pain.

Turning to James, Amanda asked, 'How is he doing?'

Looking strong but sympathetic, James replied, 'There's still a long way to go. He still has a lot of CSF fluid in his brain and his central nervous system is being attacked by the meningitis. He is strong and has made it this far with little or no significant injury. He must be very strong to keep going like this.'

'Is he out of the woods though?' Amanda asked.

James took a breath and said, 'Not until I can get the hydrocephalus under control.'

Many more general anaesthetics were to come, over thirty if you include all the procedures performed after I finally left the hospital in December 2015, a year after all this started. There were times when all

I could smell or taste was anaesthetics. After every op, I would be rolled back to my bed space, and Amanda would be there.

CT scans showed a likely entrapped fourth ventricle, which had been missed before. Later that day, a second shunt was inserted into my head to drain the ventricle in yet another surgery. My world had become a dazed existence of pain. I shouted in vain, 'Who do I cry to? Who do I beg for this to stop? Why have I been left like this?'

I knew no one was going to answer any of my cries. It was all random, but I needed someone or something to shout at and to beg for mercy. My cries didn't mean I had started to believe in a God; instead, I needed answers that no human could give. Later, when I reflected on this time, I understood more about people's need for a God and how nice that might be. As I looked up at the fluorescent lights, I started to believe that it was to be my final view. I was staring into the abyss, and it was staring right back at me. My whole existence seemed irrelevant and almost pointless. Dark thoughts of death penetrated my whole being, and I felt like I was floating through the dark, which went on and on.

I was moved to the main ward for observation. The nurse in charge that night was split across two wards, so we hardly saw her.

Geoff, who had come to visit, was sitting next to me. I desperately tried to focus on him and our conversation, but my focus kept fading in and out. Each time I lost focus, I would find myself in a tunnel, with no sound and no movement, just a still calm with a hint of panic. I tried to tell him how I was feeling, but all I could tell him was I couldn't focus no matter how hard I tried, and the pain of the operation was unbearable.

Not long after, Amanda arrived. He took her into the corridor and explained that I was losing focus, I was in pain, the nurse was nowhere to be seen, and she had to sort it out. She was a little taken aback by the order, but he knew what he was doing, summoning the titan, and he succeeded. The moment she saw me, she grew ten feet tall and went off to create a sense of urgency.

The nurse came running back, checked my vitals, and stated nothing was wrong, and I was fine. The nurse's assessment wasn't good enough for Geoff or Amanda, who demanded James come and examine me.

James appeared quickly, examined me, took some blood samples, and said he would return soon. About an hour later, he came back and said that the blood sample was showing that the shunt may be infected, so he was going to have to go back in. I was rushed away and taken to the operation theatre. Both my shunts were found to be infected—so much that they were both removed, and EVDs were installed.

I faded in and out of consciousness. When I was conscious, I was confused and agitated. Finding the source of my pain—a pipe on the side of my head—I somehow pulled the EVD out. Nobody came to check on me, and I just lay there in a mess.

Amanda found me hanging half out of bed, my face collapsed, drooling saliva onto the floor. She lifted me up and tried to bring me around, but all I could do was grunt at her. The titan appeared, and before long, nurses and doctors were rushing towards me. The temporary EVDs were not inserted correctly, which meant I was taken back to theatre to have them re-sited. From then on, I was given intrathecal vancomycin through both EVDs, which continued for almost three weeks. I was reviewed by the consultant microbiologist and neurosurgeons, who carried out further CT scans to monitor the infection.

As March arrived, the shunts were reinserted into my head to drain the fluid out of my brain without EVDs. Though I had been intubated in preparation for the operation, I wasn't extubated until five days later, as they couldn't wake me after inserting the new shunts. I also had fluid in my chest, which prompted them to insert a clearing pipe down through my throat into my lungs and transfer me to the HDU.

In my mind, I was transported to yet another world. Though I could walk normally, I and everyone around me had pipes down our throats, which reached up to the sky and off into the distance. I slowly became aware that we were all being controlled by a new East European bloc that somehow had taken control of the West. Then, I bumped into Doctor Dark, and I soon realised the danger, as he also had a tube down his throat. Having not recognised me, he just walked past me without a word, and I never felt any fear, hate, or anger. Not long after, the Brethren walked by with pipes down their throats, clueless about what was going on. I knew something was wrong and what needed to be done. I had to escape from the mind-controlling pipe down my throat, and I decided it was coming out if I survived. I wanted to help the others, but if I couldn't and I died, then better dead than being under such control. Luckily, following that decision, I woke up and saw my whole family waiting for me, looking more and more worried.

Seeing me, Caz burst into tears. She couldn't watch me in such discomfort, so she walked away, crying.

Though I was awake, I couldn't cough up the spit tube that was down my throat. They tried everything to get it out, but, in the end, they just said I would have to cough it up naturally.

The HDU nurse picked up Max and put him on the bed with me, who cuddled in straight away. Myles, who was sitting on the other side, picked up my hand and held it tightly. He was too big to get in the bed with me, but I could see in his eyes that he longed to. A feeling of complete calm came over me. Comprehending the love for your children was hard, as it was not quantifiable, and if it was, then no number could be an adequate measure. Though I lay there with a tube hanging from my throat, the company of my two boys brought about some contentment for the first time in months. My two boys were the best things that ever happened to me. Though Amanda had put in most of the effort, giving birth to them, enduring physical pain, even nurturing and moulding them, I was their dad, and the strength of that feeling alone made me feel like the greatest man on earth.

Minutes later, I had become so relaxed and calm in the company of the boys that I coughed the pipe up naturally. The HDU nurse took the pipe away and cleaned me up. She knew exactly what she was doing. She somehow knew that just sitting there quietly with my boys would relax me enough to cough up the pipe. Once she cleaned me up, she walked away, like Willy Wonka in his chocolate factory, knowing it all seemed strange, but she knew what was going on. That moment with the boys sealed the deal—I realised I would survive this ordeal no matter how hard it was. And no matter how I ended up, the little boys needed their dad, and their dad needed them.

Amanda came in to see if we were all right. Seeing Amanda, I realised I had another reason for not leaving. The presence of the three of them overwhelmed me. In my mind, I heard a scream, and all fear seemed to leave my body. However, this thinking would be challenged many times over.

Geoff and Caz had cancelled their holiday because they didn't want to be away when I was ill. They spent days sitting by my side even when I was asleep. Geoff and I held hands; it was still hard for both of us to let go. With a smile on his face, he said, 'We might be holding hands now because you're this sick, but when you get better, this hand holding stops. You got it?'

I laughed out loud and replied, 'I knew it was making you uncomfortable, big old softy!'

For a few days after, I would wake up in the shared ward to see the curtains drawn around me and Geoff or Caz reading the paper and keeping an eye on me as I slept. It made me feel calm and, in some way, safe. Though I was sorry they'd had to cancel their holiday and stay, I was glad they had.

Five days later, I was reviewed by the neurosurgeons. They confirmed the shunts were now working, but they had found that the bilateral sixth and fourth cranial nerves were being paralysed due to increased intracranial pressure. My double vision, both horizontal and vertical, became worse. As the whole world became skewed and distorted, I could hardly see. My eyes were so badly affected that all I saw was a kaleidoscope of images. Nothing made any sense. I might as well have been blind. In a way, having to endure darkness seemed less torturous than a mess of visual information that would give me a massive headache and almost tease me that I could see.

An ophthalmologist called John Ellis took an interest in my case. At that time, he was close to retirement and about to leave the NHS. I was lucky to be assigned to him, and when he did leave the NHS and go private, Amanda tracked him down, and he stayed my eye doctor for good. I was a rare case by all accounts. For someone to have both vertical and horizontal double vision was unusual at best. He found something else interesting too. I never asked what it was, and I didn't know why. When he made me look up, the whole world start jumping up and down, which would excite him. Whatever it was that got him excited was shared with every ophthalmology student, and they flocked to my room to see the wonder. Having been told they might never see such serious nerve damage again, they were keen to pay me a visit. In the end, I had to ask the nurse to only let one or two in a day, as the constant visits became wearing, though I now felt like a part of the furniture, and these visits seemed normal.

I felt like I was fighting a losing battle. I had no strength, and again I was vomiting up any food I ate, though the word *food* overstates what the hospital served.

When James came to see me, my condition shocked him. He quietly had a go at the nurses and ordered that I be put in a room with an ICU nurse who wasn't to leave me. That night was a blur and confusion. I didn't know why it was any different from any other. I later learnt from Amanda that I had slipped into such a critical state that it was uncertain whether I would survive the night. Every time I moved my head, the whole world seemed to get sucked into a small hole in my mind. I pinned myself to the bed and grabbed onto the sheets as if the hole was real and I was fighting not to fall in completely. Doctor Dark sat at the end of my bed, just staring at me. Though I felt fear, hatred, and anger, I was too weak to be affected by my feelings.

I felt sweat dripping down my face, and my breathing became shallow and irregular. Amanda had to endure the night with the knowledge that I was dying and would likely not make it to the next morning. Even then she wasn't allowed to stay; I was dying of infection, so I had to be held in a sterile room. She wasn't even allowed to kiss me. All she could do was leave, crying and wishing she had made more time for me, a wish that couldn't be granted because of all the other responsibilities she had.

I saw life as a form of atoms, and though my body seemed unchanged, my mind was moving on. Physical and mental energies that made up my consciousness started to break down. My body was being reduced as the atoms left me. My soul, if there was such a thing, was leaving, yet I still couldn't identify an 'I'. Who was 'I'? And if there wasn't an 'I', then who was asking these questions? The breakdown of my mind seemed to cause ripples in the fabric of space. The impression was that this fabric seemed to be a wave of consciousness, and my mind seemed to just contribute to the great ripple in the wave. As I started leaving, I saw my body reduced to a number of physical organs, one of which was my brain, still struggling to make decisions as if its programme hadn't been shut down yet. It was working freely and independently of my mind, yet the two had a thin line of attachment as if the brain wasn't quite ready to let the mind go. Or was it the other way around? Somehow, I found the strength to pull the two back together as one. At that moment, I realised that the 'I' I'd been looking for never existed. What I believed to be the 'I' was just a part of the ripple through the fabric of space. To identify an 'I' was a falsehood, as 'I' represented one individual, where we seemed to be part of one unimaginable ripple through space. I was everywhere and everyone all at once.

The nurse kept adjusting the drips and taking my vitals, reacting to whatever she found in the physical world, where my body and brain still existed. For the first time, I felt safe in someone's hands and eventually relaxed and fell asleep. Doctor Dark had moved on. As he left, he patted me on the foot and said, 'Your "I" is dead. Now you have to find the truth.'

Clearly, my life hadn't come to an end yet. The next morning, covered in sweat, I suffered the headache of all headaches. The nurses gave me a bed bath and dressed me. I soon felt a lot better than I had the night before. I was then moved again, this time to a four-person ward so they could keep an eye on me. That night, I fell asleep, and when the whole ward was dark, I hallucinated I was at home and my living room had been turned into a computer games room. Wherever I looked, I saw TVs with PlayStations linked to them. The ward doors were left open, and as people walked by, I kept thinking I was at home and a gang of people, who seemed threatening, were talking outside. I started to call for Myles, as only he could have set up such an elaborate games room, though the truth was I wanted his protection from the people outside.

As I woke up, my bed was surrounded by nurses, all looking at me. One asked, 'Myles, isn't that your son?'

'Yes,' I replied. As I came back to reality, I started to realise where I was and what was going on. I apologised to the nurses, rolled over, and fell asleep.

The next night, I was more guarded about what I saw or heard, so much so that, until now, I always thought the following had come from the guy in the bed next to me. It was probably me with my mind still swimming in hydrocephalus and meningitis. The guy next to me was a farmer called Mick who had fallen from his tractor and hit his head. He had a few nights before deciding wrongly that the chap opposite us was his brother. One night, he woke me up to say his brother was covered in snakes. I told him they weren't snakes but tubes and not to worry. He calmed down and went back to sleep. On the night in question, either he woke me up, or I imagined that he did. He or the imagined him was worried because he had bought a rainbow from a salesman and he had promised to build at the end of the rainbow a pond and raise carp. He said he was worried because he knew nothing about carp, how to build a pond, or rainbows. Either way, one of us was hallucinating. Four people were in the ward, all hallucinating. And who knew who said what to whom?

Soon after, James came to check on me. He was a nice chap and had worked hard to keep me alive. Two doctors and Geoff were around me. The consultant said he was happy with my progress, but I was an unusual case. Hearing it, I felt a bit fed up and said half-jokingly, 'I'm sick of being called an unusual case.'

James shot a look at me as if to say, *How dare you?* For a moment half his face seemed to be that of Doctor Dark's, as I felt the tension stiffen and started feeling insecure. Even now, my reality seemed broken, though I wasn't going to tell James that. Glaring at me, James said, 'OK, let's put it this way. It's unusual you're still alive, Mr Fisher. Your brain has been swimming in meningitis. I have never known anybody to survive that much of an injury to the brain and still be here. Every day is a gift, but we are working our hardest to keep you alive.'

For courtesy's sake, I replied, 'Thanks, doctor. I really appreciate it.'

As I lay there considering my situation, I lost sight of my former decision regarding staying alive for the sake of my family. I started to think there was little point in going on, and now I needed to think of a way to end it all. One thing was sure; I needed to do it in the hospital. Better to be found by a nurse and not one of my family. After an hour, I was in the same place, contemplating suicide.

Soon Amanda returned and sat on the bed with visibly red eyes, a consequence of crying for hours. She held my hand tightly, and I fell asleep, thinking, *I can't kill myself. Think what it will do to Amanda.* At this point, I was so conflicted I didn't know what to think and fell asleep once again with dark thoughts.

I awoke, or at least I thought I did, on the floor of a dark misty forest. The smell of burning flesh pervaded everywhere, and I could hear weapons' fire in the distance.

Doctor Dark glided through the woods and the mist towards me. He was much clearer now, though his face was still in white cracking paint. He knelt beside me and asked, 'Can you feel it?'

'Feel what?' I asked.

'The dark embrace, the cold feeling of steel passing through your brain and piercing your reality.'

I didn't answer him with words. Rather, I just looked at him, as it dawned on me that he had brought me here.

'When will you accept things as they are and not as you hope or already think you know?' he growled.

I growled back, 'I don't know what you mean.'

He looked at me as I did, with suspicion. He pulled himself closer and said, 'Before you wanted to know if you were dying. You felt like you weren't ready because you were still suffering. That was wrong thinking. It is you who causes the suffering. Your purpose in life is to find your purpose and give your whole heart and soul to it. Yet you know you have not.' After a pause, he continued, 'Fear will come until I do. The only way out is for you to take control and recognise the functions of the brain. Fear is merely a function, not your whole existence. Look at you! You have lost all your power over this crazy anxiety cooked up in your own head. It's pitiful. Take control and mandate the emotion away. It's your mind. Demand a solution before the fear makes you self-destruct and take your family with you. Remember, you created a world of suffering for yourself and others, simply by believing there was an "I". How bloody arrogant are you? You think I am the dark, yet I am merely a gateway to the dark. Listen to me, and your fall may not be that bad.'

He seemed to be talking about the conversation I'd had with him back in November when I was close to death and scared.

The horrible growl continued as he said, 'Holding on to anger is like grasping a hot coal with the intent of throwing it at someone else. You are the one who gets burned.'

'What are you saying? That's me?' I asked.

Like an exhausted teacher with a hopeless student, he looked at me and said, 'Those who consider the unessential to be essential and see the essential as unessential fail to reach the essential, living in a field of wrong intention.'

'I don't know what you're talking about,' I replied.

Angrily, he looked at me and said, 'You will. Oh, you will.' Then he inched closer to me and whispered, 'Don't you feel it? That dark embrace, that presence of emptiness? Why will you not wake up and see the need of the fall of your own facade? You once asked me if you were going to die. I tell you now that you already have, and you know it. Your body may have survived, but what you believe of yourself is dead. You have been just waiting for the next moment, forgetting the moment you're in.'

Amazingly, I started to comprehend him, and the forest wasn't his doing; it was mine. In the here and now, I had a wonderful loving family, yet all I craved was my selfish solace and abhorrent ambition, always seeking the future. I had willed some part of me to die. How could one go through what I had and not have a part of oneself readjust, change, or die? I was asked for a sacrifice, and I chose the giant. That would be a battle for sure.

Staying positive in the days to come was a struggle, and every day was a fight to stay sane. One day, as I lay on the bed, staring up at the ceiling, washed, shaved, and fully clothed, the same as every day for the past few weeks, I was surrounded by sound—the music from my iPad, as well as the sound of the busy corridor as nurses rushed from one place to another. It was strangely hypnotic to listen to. It was accompanied by the constant ringing of people's call alarms going off across the ward. I held a sense of pride about one of those alarms not being from me, as I only called the nurses in dire need, or at least I liked to think so.

Lying there, I couldn't help but indulge myself in some self-pity. I thought about my death and my belief *I thought about my death and how nearing it affected my belief—making me have an open mind about the random universe.*

. I experienced twice my almost death, with atoms decaying into a ripple throughout space. Or did I just have more hallucinations? Who could tell? Though I didn't believe in a godhead, a man about to judge me for all my misdeeds or reward me for my bravery, I found my belief change from a resolute certainty of the random universe to being willing to accept anything. I just didn't know yet, so I had to wait and see. In the end, I found the most comforting thought was that existence and the universe were so vast that I couldn't rule anything out. However, still no one was there to pray to. And right now, I could do with a good prayer. But what was the point if there was nothing or nobody to hear me or answer me or help me?

89

Though open minded to possibilities, I still found most comfort in believing that everything happened randomly and not by design. I might die randomly, or I might live randomly. I just didn't know. Things seemed very bad—the pain, the confusion, the weakness, the unexplained slow loss of movement in my legs. I didn't think survival was a safe bet. I went back to my life, hoping to find some solace, but all I felt was pain. Slowly, I was letting the darkness in, and my state of mind was desperate at best.

The days to come seemed to drift into one another, and each night was a bare-knuckle fight with the darkness in my mind. The mind-numbing monotony was interrupted with brain surgery of one type or another.

After a few weeks, James appeared and repeated that he was sorry, as he could do nothing more. Things got incredibly dark at this point, yet there was no sign of Doctor Dark. It felt like my body was doing the work for him, and he didn't need to turn up anymore. At that point, my despair was such that all I could see was the darkness. Everything seemed so hopeless. One night, as I lay in a single-occupancy room, waiting for more surgeries, the pain in my head became so incredibly bad that I felt like my head was being split into two. With every move I made, pain that felt like an electric shock shot through my brain.

In a moment of despair, I even called my brother Geoff and begged him to look out for my boys when I died. At first, he didn't want to say yes, as he wanted me to stop thinking in such a dark way. His voice cracked, and he begged me to stop talking about death. I pressed him to promise me to look after my boys.

'Yes, of course,' he said in a broken-hearted way.

Once again, he begged me to hang on and keep fighting. I said goodbye and hung up on him, as I couldn't hear my big brother sound like that.

A nurse kept popping in to check on me and tell me that my surgery spot had been taken by an emergency. Every time she came in to check on me, I would ask her when my operation was happening, and each time she would say she didn't know. I was wrapped in darkness and sure of death. I didn't ring Amanda up, as I didn't want to burden her with my pain or give her the smallest of hints that I had given up. *Where is Doctor Dark?* I thought, as even his presence would have been a welcome distraction.

I finally fell asleep, only to end up in the other world. The smell chocked my throat as the heavy air pinned me to the ground. I could still feel the pain cutting through my head. I heard a voice from behind me. I looked around and saw a man emerging from the distance. It was me, not the me now but the me when I had been in the army—a young fearless man full of confidence, with a look that suggested he would do anything required of him. He walked past me like a ghost disappearing into the cloud of ash. As he faded away, another man emerged from the same place. It was me again, wearing nothing but a black plastic bag around my waist, a muddy pair of boots and an African kente kufi hat. It was the Glastonbury me, unashamed and free. He smiled at me as he passed and then faded into the cloud of ash. Looking back into the distance, I saw a crowd of people emerging. They were all me, led by the me from work, clad in a smart suit and looking overconfident, like he had the answer to a difficult question. Just like the others, he walked past me, fading away into the cloud. Before I could do anything about it, the crowd of people who were all different versions of me started advancing. This time, they didn't walk past me; instead, they walked over me, trampling on me and then walking into the cloud of ash fading away.

When I eventually woke up, I was glad. I lay in bed, the dark of the night strangely soothing me. Hot and sweating, I lay there thinking about my dream. It had been so real that I couldn't help thinking it meant something. I probably had built up so many personas to deal with the situations in which I found myself that I had never stayed true to myself. I thought about the march of the personas that crushed me under foot. The real me was deep inside my psyche. I had to find myself before I did anything else. Over the years, I had started wearing ethnic beaded necklaces and bracelets, bohemian clothes bought from the festival, and listening to music that I wasn't too sure about. At that moment, I vowed that, if I survived, I would drop all these ways and concentrate on the search for the real me. This thought kept running through my mind until I fell asleep again but, this time, peacefully.

Suddenly, the bedroom door swung open, and standing in the doorway was my brother Paul. After pausing for a moment, possibly for a comic dramatic effect, he entered the room. Sitting down by my bed, he looked at me and said, 'What's all this shit about death? If you go, can I have your car?'

Even though I was in massive pain, he made me laugh. Just one look from Paul was enough to make me laugh. Laughter was the cure. And that all the three brothers understood very well. Paul would never know how much he encouraged me to fight that night.

I was finally taken down to surgery. When I awoke, whatever they had done, which was fix my shunt, had made the pain go. At the time, I felt a bit foolish about my call to Geoff. However, when I looked back at it, I had been dying, and every operation of mine had been a shot in the dark to keep me alive. Every day, I would lie in bed as my body failed me, and in the end, I actually hoped for death to come and take me. My respite from the ordeal was the constant flow of visitors, thanks to Geoff. My favourite visitor was, of course, Amanda, whose very presence calmed me down. Doctors and nurses came in over the days and nights. One by one, they came, but none came with any good news. The nurses checked my vitals. The different doctors on duty just seemed to come in, shoot meaningless questions, give no real answers, and rush out to do the same to the next patient.

I was still staring into the abyss, and it was still staring right back at me. Something had penetrated my soul, and the darkness of the abyss seemed to be slowly swallowing me up. Fear would grab me and make me see the horror of life and the hopelessness of the abyss. It was nothing but a deep dark void, where nothing seemed to live. But something was in there—something that was not alive. I could feel it scrutinising me. I could feel its anger and fearful intent. It wasn't Doctor Dark. It was something else, another phantom, a darkness I did not want to face.

'It's your choice, but staring into the abyss will only destroy your hope!'

I looked around, and lying in bed with me, his hands locked together on his chest, was Doctor Dark. As usual, he had brought his own foreboding fear. Strangely, I found strength in defying him now. And though he still instilled fear in me, I fought against it over and over, like a tennis ball bouncing back after a hit against a wall.

'It's time to let it go. Let the giant fall and die. It's your only option.' His voice crackled.

'I'm the giant. I'm in charge of him, not the other way around. To kill him is to kill myself.'

'You have never been the giant. If you think the only way to kill him is to kill yourself, then go ahead. If your mind is not filled with desires, then you still feel fear. Do not depend on others, especially those created to protect you from a world brought on by your own thought.'

'I have all I want,' I said, meaning Amanda and the boys. 'What else would I desire?'

'Your giant is full of desire, making you full of desire.' Shooting me an annoyed glare, Doctor Dark said, 'If you won't listen to me, then you might listen to him.' And he vanished, leaving no room for any follow-up questions about who him was.

CHAPTER 9

THE LONG DECAY

As I lay on my bed looking up at the ceiling, my face distorted out of shape and my vision affected by both horizontal and vertical double vision, the days kept merging into one another. Even so at this point, my mind seemed empty of thoughts. My body was slowly breaking down. Every time a thought came into my mind, I instantly dismissed it, thinking, There's no point.

Eventually, I took in a deep breath with the intent of starting to meditate. My mind, perhaps resistant to meditation, dwelled on the thought of me slowly losing the use of my legs. When ten doctors in a row came to visit me one after the other, all in one day, they all told me about the possibility of never walking again. In a single day, they had come to my room, one visitor after the other, each avoiding a conversation and just spitting out that I faced the danger of being completely paralysed in the legs and confined to a wheelchair for the rest of my life. One doctor said he didn't know what level of paralysis I could end up with. I purposely mentioned this detail in passing because that was how they all told me the same, casually visiting and talking as if it could be a forgone conclusion. At the same time, no one committed to anything—in a medical textbook matter-of-fact way.

All hell was let lose in my mind. My inner monkey hopped from one horrible consequence to another. My heart was pumping and ready to burst, while the sound of call buzzers going off and off and off drove me to despair.

When the last doctor entered the room, I was determined I wouldn't let him go until I got some answers. He couldn't even look at me as he said, 'You have damaged the nerve that controls your legs, and it looks like the damage may be moving all the way to the nerve that controls your arms.'

As he got up and walked towards the door, I shouted to him, 'Which nerves have been damaged?'

Without even bothering to halt his exit, he just turned his head and said in a very annoyed, dismissive manner, 'Oh, T4, T5.'

One didn't need to be an expert to know that he would have said just about anything to get out of there. I didn't know what the hell he was talking about. I lay back on my bed, feeling stupid for asking, and just buried my head into the pillow. I have since learnt that the spine is made up of thirty-three bones:

- In the cervical region, seven vertebrae (C1 to C7), which are the neck bones, along with a C8 nerve cluster
- In the thoracic region, twelve vertebrae (T1 to T12), which is the main spine
- In the lumbar region, five vertebrae (L1 to L5)
- In the sacral region, five vertebrae
- In the coccygeal region, four vertebrae.

Meningitis had caused damage to my spinal cord at the C7–C8 level, which was totally different from what the doctor had said. His attitude and the situation made me feel like going to sleep and never waking up again. The following day, I awoke feeling totally empty, contemplating my slow slip into the darkness of my future—death or paralysis. I neither felt good nor bad, just numb.

One thought now occupied my mind: If I became paralysed, I would be a burden on my family. I didn't think it was fair. Perhaps I should have died. Maybe it was not too late. I still had a bag of saved-up pills just in case. I planned many different ways of doing it just in bed. I could be found too early and then be saved. I would be found in the morning, but that wouldn't be fair to the cleaner. There was always the loo, but what a way to go to 'the toilet'!

The days kept merging into one another, and my mind kept dismissing all thoughts, keeping it void of life. The darkness of the other world surrounded me and dragged my mood lower and lower. Though there was no sign of Doctor Dark, depression took hold of me, and I stopped caring about everything. I just couldn't shake off the sadness in me. I had changed from a fun-loving man to a man who found no enjoyment in life anymore. Feeling empty inside, I lay on my bed day after day.

I was finally discharged on 25 March 2015 back to the care of the staff at the GWH. I was recorded to have mild bilateral leg weakness, though no detailed neurological assessment was undertaken at the time. As the paramedics rolled me out of the ward to the lifts, a young but senior doctor from Scotland called Ravy exclaimed, 'Mr Fisher is going! I have to see him out.' He walked beside my gurney and wished me the best of luck. He was one of the good ones.

Back at the GWH, I was admitted in a ward with two elderly gents and a man with whom I felt incredibly uneasy at just one look. However, he did say hello and introduced himself as Bob. One morning, I woke up to hear his visiting sons laughing about how they had chucked some poor guy out of his wheelchair and given it to their father, though he didn't need a wheelchair. From that day on, he continued to get around in one. I couldn't help feeling incredibly sorry for the man whose wheelchair they had nicked. Imagine your whole living environment being stolen and you being abandoned on the ground in the middle of nowhere.

A few days later, as only Bob and I were in the ward and I didn't want to talk to him, I was pretending to be asleep. I overheard him on the phone to the council complaining about the state of his council flat and how he didn't have long to live and now needed a new one. As far as I could tell, nothing was wrong with him.

On 1 April 2015, my legs started to give way. My every attempt to use the standing machine failed, and I continuously collapsed onto the floor. I was finally reviewed by a doctor because of an altered sensation on my abdomen and both feet. I suffered from incontinence and complained of reduced power in my legs. On examination, the doctor found my upper limb function to be normal, but I had reduced power in my lower limbs, altered sensation, and reduced anal tone. The doctor noted my symptoms were supratentorial, code for saying that the symptoms were psychological in nature and not due to physical or pathological changes. This was subsequently proven not to be the case. The next day, during another review, on my forty-fifth birthday, it was discovered I had sensory loss to the torso and lower limbs and reduced perianal sensation. Further, I had bowel incontinence.

The doctor who had first seen me and operated on me, a Greek fella very confident of himself, came to see me with something that no other doctor had seemed to bother with—my MRI scans. He was surrounded by students and junior doctors. They pulled the curtains around me as if to create a private space.

He sat on the end of my bed and said, 'Now look here, what was all this you were telling the doctor yesterday?' Before I could answer, he just continued, 'You have a damaged nerve in the cervical, which means you're not going to walk again. All what's happening to you now is that damage taking hold, and there's nothing we can do about it.'

I took a deep breath and said, 'Are you saying I will truly never walk again? I have always maintained hope that I would, as no one has ever been absolute in such a diagnosis.'

'I'm afraid there is no hope here,' he answered.

Amanda was sitting next to me holding my hand. Her hand tightened on mine, and she began to rub my arm reassuringly.

The silence was broken by the doctor. 'So you understand all these symptoms are because your spinal column is being slowly crushed by the damage?'

'I understand and thank you for being straight with me,' I replied. 'Can the crushing of my spine kill me?'

He just looked at me and said, 'We're not ruling it out at this point.'

I thanked him again while fighting back the urge to shout, 'Piss off, you fucking twat!'

He and his gang of doctors then drew the curtains and left.

Stunned and speechless, Amanda and I just sat there. At that point, for yet another time in my life, I saw Doctor Dark in the waking world. He was standing opposite my bed, looking at me. His eyes pierced my soul, and without words, he told me there was still a way out.

Amanda leant over and said, 'Mike, a lot of people are waiting to wish you happy birthday in Costa downstairs. It was meant to be a nice birthday surprise. Do you want me to tell them to leave?'

97

'No! It's my birthday, and they have all made the effort to come. Let's go down there, heads up, look them in the eye, just like nothing's happened.'

Amanda leant over, gave me a kiss, and said, 'OK, no one needs to know right now.' After a minute, she said, 'But the boys are down there, and I think we should tell them alone and later.'

'All right,' I said. 'Let's fake it as if nothing has happened.'

She held my hand, and we both cried quietly. Then she wrapped me up in the wheelchair, and off we went and got in the lift. As the lift descended, not a word was exchanged between us, and the only contact we had was Amanda slowly rubbing my neck with her hand. Both of us fought back tears, trying not to scream in anger. As I saw my reflection in the lift mirror, I realised I looked like a Japanese prisoner of war who had just been released. I was thin and gaunt. Most my hair had been shaven off, and my face looked like that of a ghost, with big black eyes and a look of despair.

As the lift door opened, we both took a deep breath. Without saying a word to each other, we both stiffened up, ready for the friends awaiting us. Amanda pushed my wheelchair into Costa and sitting there were all my family and our good friends. Amanda went to get coffee while I was subjected to the normal 'How are you?'

I avoided the question by asking everyone how they had got here.

A birthday cake was presented to me, and everyone tried to make it feel like a birthday party, though it was actually more like a wake. As everyone slowly made their excuses to leave and my mother took the boys home, we used the time to talk to our friends from Wales.

Amanda squeezed my hand and whispered in my ear, 'Shall we tell them?'

I smiled at her and said, 'OK.'

'So, guys, before we came down, we got some bad news,' I started off, oblivious to what my announcement must have sounded like.

They sat there, stunned and pinned to their chairs, waiting for my next words.

'I'm never going to walk again.'

A look of relief appeared in their eyes, as I hadn't said, 'I'm going to die.' If only they knew. The relief soon turned to grief as they digested what I had just said.

'Oh, Mike, I'm sorry,' they said, followed by a string of questions that, quite frankly, I wished I had asked the doctor myself.

When they left, Amanda and I made our way back to the ward. We spent the rest of the day in silence. except for Amanda's occasional muttering under her breath, 'Fucking doctors!'

The next day, I was informed I needed to go back to Oxford and take an MRI scan. The news was music to my ears, and I soon started to hatch my plan to escape the GWH and get myself transferred back to the JRH.

On 4 April, two paramedics arrived, dragging a gurney behind them. 'Mike Fisher?' they asked.

'Yep, that's me,' I replied.

As the standing machine was no longer an option for me, looking forlorn, I said to the paramedic, 'Sorry, I can't stand. You will need to move me.'

'Don't worry,' he replied, and they busily prepared me for my transfer.

Not long after, I was secured into the gurney and the paramedics were rolling me out. I bid goodbye to the guy in the bed next to me as if I wasn't coming back. I did so mainly because I had no intention of returning. My plan was to get to Oxford, have the MRI scan, and make a fuss. I rolled past the guy opposite and gave him a nod and said, 'See ya,' which was all I could muster.

The uneventful trip to Oxford gave me ample time to take yet another nap. When I arrived at Oxford, I was transferred to a bed. Without a long wait, I was wheeled off, bed and all, to the MRI room. The procedure was the same as always—a quick transfer over to a thin stiff bed, securing my head in place, and then the wait for an hour-long ordeal sealed in a coffin-like tube.

I was rolled in and pushed up to the MRI machine. The radiographers were so practised at the routine that they just spouted reassuring words that I had heard a thousand times. Once inside the machine, I decided to try some mindfulness and concentrate just on my breathing to combat my claustrophobia. I meditated for what seemed like the first time in ages. As I counted each breath, I struggled with the claustrophobia. Every time I opened my eyes, I felt like I was sealed into my own coffin, just like I had every time before. 'One … two … three.' I counted my breath again. My mind firmly concentrated on the air passing through my nostrils. After a while, I calmed down and became settled as the *knock, knock, knock* of the MRI machine went on around me. Before long, my eyes became heavy, and I fell asleep. In what seemed like the next minute, but actually thirty minutes later, I was being rolled out of the machine, thanking God it was over.

'First part, all done. Mike, now we have to inject you with the contrast.'

'Oh right,' I replied, 'of course.'

Though I tried to maintain a calm exterior, I was screaming *noooooo* on the inside. Once the contrast was administered, the bed juddered and pushed me back into the coffin, making me feel like I was being buried alive. I counted my breath. 'One … two … three … four.' Eventually, my heartbeat slowed down. I focused on the air passing through my nostrils, ignoring the knocks and bangs of the MRI. A feeling of calm descended over me, and just for the glimpse of a moment, I felt like I had no more worries. My whole body relaxed, and I felt serene. I felt I was lying on a mountain, and my thoughts were clouds drifting past. As I lay there, I could see the thoughts, but I didn't grab out to any of them, just letting them float by. Strangely, I could have laid there forever, but finally they pulled me out and started stripping off the head clamp.

'All done,' they said with a smile, giving no indication of what they had found or making no mention of whether the results were all right, just a routine and well-rehearsed chorus of care.

I can't blame them. They're just doing their job, I told myself.

I was transferred back to the ward and wheeled off to a single bedroom. After just a three-hour wait, I was transferred back into the bed and tucked in.

By the time James arrived, I was bored out of my mind, just staring intently at the fluorescent lights on the ceiling. As James entered the room, I was filled with anticipation about what he was going to tell me. *He's kept me going this long,* I thought. Instead of preparing myself for bad news, I convinced myself he was going to tell me an operation would bring the function of my legs back.

'Hi there,' he greeted me as he entered the room.

'Hi, doctor,' I replied, knowing he should be called Mr but unable to bring myself to do it.

'We think you have a cyst positioned on your C7 and C8 vertebra, and it's pushing your spinal cord out of shape, causing paralysis. It's hiding behind a large area of scarring, which is like a spiderweb. It's known as arachnoid scarring because of its spiderweb qualities.'

'Can it be removed?' I naturally asked.

'I'm not sure, but I'm going to have a telephone conference with some colleagues later tonight, one of whom was a specialist in this field. I will know more then.

'What I can say is the scan shows significant new changes that were the cause of your deterioration, predominantly in the cervical spine. There's kinking and distortion of the spinal cord at that level, with evidence of arachnoiditis with cyst formation and consequent kinking of the cord in the lower cervical spine.'

'OK, I guess there's not much to do but wait until after that call then.'

'Not really, no,' he said. After a pause, he asked, 'Are you comfortable?'

'Yep, I'm fine,' I replied.

The slow, long wait began. At this point, I was still upbeat. *They will find a way. And after a quick operation, this will all be over,* I thought. A feeling of relief came over me as the thought of not being in Swindon came to my mind. All in all, I was all right. Or at least that was what I told myself as I stared at the fluorescent ceiling lights. Time seemed to drag on slowly in my mind; I kept thinking how the Swindon doctors had told me I would never walk again. *What rubbish! I'm back in Oxford now. It's all going to be all right.*

The night created a pitch-black screen at the windows, which reflected everything back into the room. I stared out of them for a while until I realised I was just staring at myself. I quickly looked back up at the fluorescent lights, and the night went on.

The door finally opened, and James entered the room. He looked tired and sympathetic. He put his hand on the bed rail as if to hold my hand.

'It's not good news I'm afraid,' he started. 'The cyst is under a thick layer of arachnoid scarring, and no one on the conference call, including the specialist, thinks it will be a good idea to operate, as it will only make things worse. I'm sorry.'

'What do you mean?' I asked. 'You can't fix my legs?'

'No, your arms will also become paralysed with time.'

'What? I won't be able to use my arms?' I asked in a quivering, panic-stricken voice. 'What does that mean?'

'It means that, over time, your hands and your arms will stop working. You will become a tetraplegic. Or you may have heard it said as quadriplegic. Mike, I have to tell you that we can't rule out this being fatal. If the scarring keeps progressing, it could crush a nerve coming from your brain.'

I was pinned to the bed. My heart started pounding, and thoughts of just being a head in a bed ran through my mind. At that moment, I ceased hearing absolutely anything. The room seemed to have become silent, and nothing existed other than James's face. I looked for any sign of him saying 'though' and they could fix it, but his face remained the same. I caught my breath as my stomach started to do somersaults. I started to cry inside. Sucking back the tears and keeping an exterior look of stiff upper lip, I asked, 'What now?'

'You will need some physiotherapy. Plus, we're still tracking that infection.'

'Look,' I said, 'please don't send me back to Swindon. They don't know what to do with me. No one knew what was wrong with me or what to do.'

'Don't worry,' he said reassuringly. 'We will find you a bed here. Is there anything else you want to know?'

Looking directly at him, I choked out the words 'How long until my arms go?'

'We don't know,' he answered. 'It could be within the week or it could be months.'

'OK, thanks,' I said dismissively.

'If you need anything, let me know.' Then he was gone as if the whole thing were a bad dream.

Every muscle in my working body became tense, and I just lay in bed, looking up at the fluorescent lights. I didn't know how long I lay there, motionless and pinned to the bed. I thought I should call Amanda, but I wasn't ready to talk yet. Then the smell of burning flesh and sweat hit me straight in the face. My whole body shivered as the room temperature dropped. The room now seemed to be blanketed in a black sheet waving in the wind. A black, waving mass of darkness entered the room. Staring at it, I was transfixed by how sleekly it moved. As it moved closer to me, I could see a figure in the darkness. I couldn't see the face as normal, but I knew it was him—Doctor Dark. A voice came from the darkness: 'Well, I told you so. And now we're going to get to know each other much better.'

'Fuck off! I'm not in the mood,' I spat at him.

'I know, I know.' His voice sounded rough and gravelly. 'You're going to be a cripple, a vegetable, nothing more than a head in a bed.'

'I said I'm not in the mood,' I shouted.

'You know there's a way out of this, don't you?'

I remained silent and just looked upwards.

'Don't ignore me. You're going to be trapped in your head with just you to keep you company. It sounds awful,' he growled. 'Death will be your only release. Why wait and go through all that agony?

'Just kill yourself,' he hissed at me, like the snake in the Garden of Eden tempting me.

'How? I can't get out of bed because my legs don't work.'

'I don't care how you do it. Just do it,' he ordered.

The mass of waving darkness appeared to get thicker and more active, and a face seemed to emerge. 'Kill yourself!'

'How?' I asked again, knowing I would get no answer.

Doctor Dark took a deep breath and said, 'Caring for the lives of the people all around you is more important than prolonging or extending your suffering life when death is imminent.'

Each demanding shout seemed to get louder and louder. 'Kill yourself. You're not there anyway.'

'Leave me alone,' I shouted back, which had no effect.

'Killing yourself is your best option. Death is a natural part of life. It's inevitable.'

Covering my eyes with my arms, I attempted to ignore him. But his voice penetrated my every thought. I then found myself rummaging inside the bedside cabinet, my hands desperately perusing my meagre belongings, hoping beyond hope that I would find the little bag of pills I had saved up. But my search was to no avail, as it seemed the nurses had taken them away when I was transferred.

What a waste, I thought. *It took me weeks to save those. Now I want them, and they're gone.*

'Kill yourself and be done, Michael!'

The utterance 'kill yourself' was all I could hear as the dark mass now seemed to hover over me and surround my whole body. I felt like a giant rock had grabbed hold of me, and I was being dragged to the bottom of a deep, dark lake. I gasped for air, but all I could muster was a few short breaths, each tasting foul and bitter.

'Kill yourself. Death is just a pathway,' was the last thing I heard before losing consciousness. My head was swimming in pain, and I fell asleep.

My sleep was interrupted constantly by his insistence that I should kill myself. Tears welled up in my eyes, but I fought them back and allowed the horribly interrupted sleep to take hold. As I woke up the next morning, I could feel the sun shining on my face. Both the dark mass and he had gone. As light flooded into the room, I somehow felt a little better. It was past nine. I grabbed my phone and rang Amanda. As the phone rang, I took a breath and thought about what to say. *What will she say?*

'Hello, sweetheart! How are you?' answered Amanda.

Wow! How do I answer that? My head was still throbbing from my experience last night, even though I couldn't tell what that was. All I knew was I felt like I had been drowning all night, and I had somehow made it ashore by morning.

'I'm not good, sweetheart,' I said in a slow, deliberate voice. 'I had an MRI, and the doctor told me they can't operate to save my legs.'

'Sweetheart, don't worry. We'll find a way,' replied Amanda.

'That's not all,' I replied sharply. 'He also told me I was going to lose the use of my arms.'

'Oh, darling, no! What does that mean?'

'It means that, over a period of a week or months, my arms and hands will become slowly paralysed. I'm going to be nothing more than a head in a bed.'

'No, you're not, Mikey. At least, you still have your mind.' Her voice shuddered as she tried to reassure me. 'I should be there with you. I'm coming up now.'

We ended the call with the promise of her coming to be with me and a chorus of I love you.

Eventually, I got a visit from someone with something to offer. It wasn't much, but it was the first slice of hope I'd had in days. The ward physiotherapist came to visit me with two large green elasticated bands, which he called resistance bands. He told me that a way to keep my arms from completely failing was to keep them moving. So he tied one band to each side of my bed and told me to keep pulling them, as the nerves might find a way to keep working. As days passed, I lay on the hospital bed, pulling my resistance bands and listening to all the sounds outside—the crashing of trays, the calling of nurses, and the constant buzzing of people's help buttons going off in an unstoppable chorus.

Life hadn't finished with me yet. Many sunny mornings later, I awoke feeling sick as usual. I requested the nurse for some anti-sickness medicine. The staff was busy that day, and by the time someone came back with an injection, Amanda had arrived, and I was out of bed. Pedro, the nurse gave me the injection. He was in a rush, so he injected it quickly. I had secretly hoped for that, as when they injected it quickly, I would get a really nice high. When they did it slowly, I didn't.

Just as the medicine was kicking in, the physiotherapist arrived and told me she was taking me to the gym for movement practice. Before I knew it, I was wheeled off to the gym for a workout. The high of the medicine was very fragile, and I lost it with the sudden activity. When we got to the gym, I was met by more physiotherapists, who only had half an hour for my exercises. Wasting no time, they got me on to a plinth and started my workout. As they did, I felt a strange feeling in my head. Dizziness took over my reality, and I felt sick. I decided to ignore it because I always enjoyed physiotherapy, as it gave me hope that I might get better. As the exercises got more difficult, the dizziness increased. I felt like my whole face was being dragged down, and my head was swimming. I told the physiotherapists that I was having a funny turn, and I might need to go back to my room. They agreed and got me back into the wheelchair. As I was pushed back, I found myself fighting to keep my face from falling off. Or at least that was how I felt. I was rushed back to bed, and Pedro arrived, looking worried and concerned. He was a good nurse, and he genuinely cared about me. After checking my vitals, he got me comfortable in my bed.

The pain in my head started to scream at me, and my fight to keep my face in place failed. My head hit the pillow, and the last thing I heard was Pedro saying he would get a doctor. I was woken up immediately to see the doctor. He soon started a series of tests to look for a stroke. As I was being taken away by the orderlies, I overheard the doctor telling Amanda that he didn't think I'd had a stroke, but they wanted to CT scan me just to make sure. I was put through a scanner and put back to bed so quickly

105

that it felt like it had never happened. The doctor returned and told us the scan hadn't revealed anything. He couldn't explain what was going on. Strangely, he left the matter and moved on to the next patient.

The left side of my face had now dropped. My eye was pointed inwards, making my sight even worse. And I couldn't move my mouth. I tried to kiss Amanda, but my lips couldn't pucker up a kiss, and all we could do was touch our lips together. I broke down and nearly cried, 'What's the point if I can't kiss my Amanda!'

Both Amanda and I welled up with tears, and we held hands tightly. Amanda fought back the tears and said, 'Please don't be like this. Just keep fighting, please.'

I looked at her face and held her hand more tightly.

A nurse came in and asked Amanda to leave, as it was lunchtime. Amanda got up to leave and told me she would be back as soon as I was finished eating. I was helped out of bed and pulled up to the table to eat. The nursing assistant asked me if I needed any help eating. I looked at him and said in a muffled voice, slurring all my words, 'I can't grasp anything. My face is paralysed, and I can't close my mouth. So yes please, mate'.

He nodded his head and walked out to inform the nurses he was going to help me eat. Once he returned, he had to hold my back, as I couldn't sit up without help. Slowly and carefully, he scooped up my food and put it in my mouth. Much to my shock, my mouth had become paralysed and couldn't hold food long enough for me to chew it, making it all fall out. Despite many attempts, we made no progress.

With tears in my eyes and desperation in my voice, I turned to the nursing assistant and said, 'What's the fucking point if I can't even eat?'

The nursing assistant just looked at me and asked if I wanted any more. I told him there was no point to anything, and he might as well get back to help the others. He left me looking like he had just been told someone was dying.

As he left, I heard Pedro ask him, 'So how's Mike? All right?'

'No, not really. In fact, not at all,' replied the nursing assistant.

As each day passed, my face continued to droop on one side. I couldn't talk, so people couldn't understand me. I feared the drooping face was just a sign of the disease progressing, which would kill me in the end. Or worse, I was going to be the same for the rest of my life. I had plenty of time to consider the possibilities as I lay in my room. The walls in my room were blank and bluish grey. Posters once hung on the wall had left marks all over, and there were cracks all along the top of the plaster. The room needed a fresh coat of paint, probably three years before. But clearly no one felt that was a priority. I was left with an old and dreary room.

As I lay there, one day I wondered, *What the hell can I do with all this time?*

No answer seemed to come, and no bedridden activity interested me. My mind was unoccupied and bored, leaving me to contemplate my situation.

In desperation, I cried out, 'Oh my God, I have lost my legs. And now I'm going to lose my arms.' Though I said the words out loud, they still seemed unreal. I had been through so much—fluid in the brain, head taps, operations, infections, brain shunts, hallucinations, degrading procedures, embarrassing accidents, paralysis, and much more. Yet I was still suffering the overbearing pressure of waiting for my arms to fail.

The nights were no better. The call buzzers settled down, but then the poor souls with serious head injuries shouted out all sorts of things. The worst were the people crying for help, even when the nurse stood right in front of them. The truth was nothing could help them, and all they could do was shout for help. Sometimes, they would fight with the nurse, and I would hear the screams of both sides. I would put my earphones in and try to sleep. But the moment I closed my eyes, my mind started its rambling. *I'm paralysed. I'm not going to walk again. I'm going to lose my arms. I can feel them going. I know I can. I haven't told anyone, yet I'm finding it harder and harder to pick things up and grip things. What use will I be to anyone now? Is it even worth still living?*

Every night, these thoughts would run through my mind. And when I reached the question, Is it even worth living? I would answer, *'No?.'* At that point, I would feel like the doors had swung open and a cold draft was drifting in the room. No position in bed felt comfortable, and my head only tossed and turned. The smell of burning flesh and sweat would fill the room, and then I would feel his presence. A dark mass and an almost figure of a man with a look of pain and pity would appear, and I would silently beg him to leave me alone.

'How will you do it?' he asked me.

'I don't know,' I answered, starting a conversation we'd had a hundred times.

'Yes, you do. Stop lying.'

'Why can't you leave me alone?'

'I'm here to help you make the journey.'

'What journey?'

'You know—the one where you finally feel no pain.'

'You mean my death?'

Then silence would descend upon us, as if he was tired of the question. After a few moments of silence, he would start on again. 'How are you going to do it?'

Too weak to argue, I said, 'Save up my pain meds, and when I have enough, wheel off to a secluded part of the hospital where no one can find me or stop me.'

'Yes,' he replied.

At this point, I would usually pull myself awake to a silent and dark room, and all I could hear was the chatting of the nurses outside. Though being awake seemed better, dark thoughts still ran through my head. I would imagine collecting drugs and consider which secluded place to go. At first, the possibility would seem frightening, but then it would feel like the only thing I could do. So, each day I lay there, looking up at the ceiling, and each night I lay there, struggling with the plan of suicide.

From time to time, I allowed myself a little giggle and imagined funny scenarios about my impending death. As the old saying went, 'If life is a joke, then death delivers the punchline.' I would stop that line of thinking because I found myself answering my questions. *Talking to yourself is OK. Answering back is risky. Oh, I'm bored.* I will think to myself. At one point, I remembered the quote, 'Being bored is an insult to oneself.' It was probably by Jules Renard. I didn't know why I remembered the quote, but I just did. Each night, I would be in a fight to stay alive and stop myself from wheeling off to a secluded place. Every day, the same question would trouble me. *Surely, I can think of something to relieve this hell?* Just lying there every day looking up at the ceiling wasn't just boring; it was lazy. I had no answer to this, no quick response, probably because of the dangers of answering oneself.

As the days marched on, my arms became weaker and weaker and my grip looser and looser, as I slowly succumbed to the tetraplegia. Each time I felt the weakness, I would exercise my arms with the resistance bands until my hands blistered. Each pull meant pain, as the resistance bands cut into my skin. This eventually wasn't a problem, as I lost all sensory feeling in my hands. When resting, I would touch my thumb with my other fingers to try and keep my fingers from stopping working. Once I felt rested, I would pick up the resistance bands again, wrap them around my hands, and start pulling all over again.

The fear of losing my arms was immense. My stomach was knotted like an old dry rope, my heart rate seemed to rush blood through my body, my mind would become numb, and no other thought seemed to make sense. Only the thought of suicide persisted. My mind kept thinking my plan was simple; all I needed to do was take the stash of painkillers I'd been stockpiling bit by bit each day. I had accumulated the painkillers with great effort. When the nurses looked over to check, I would pretend to swallow the pills and hold them behind my teeth. Once they'd leave, I would stash one away in a bag at the back of my side cabinet and take the other. As for somewhere to go, come night-time, I thought I would ask to be put in my chair as I couldn't sleep. Then I'd wheel myself over to the main hospital and find an empty room. That way, no one could stop me, and I would be found by people used to dead bodies. Each time I thought it through, it seemed like a perfect plan. The thought of carrying out this act calmed me and would bring about a strange, serene feeling, and my breathing would slow down.

I had all this time on my hands. Yet I didn't read a single book. I had loads of books, mainly on Buddhism, mindfulness, and meditation, but I had lost all interest.

Lunch would arrive, yet again, and would be laid out on the bedside table in front of me. I would just lie there, staring at it, wondering, *How the hell am I going to eat that?* I still tried to eat, but my attempt was only a balancing act of trying to keep the food on the fork and then trying to get it into and keep it in my paralysed mouth. I was so depressed at this point that I saw asking for help from a nurse as humiliating. If I was lucky, Amanda would turn up. She would have none of my rubbish and would feed me in a dignified and caring way so that I almost forgot that, as a forty-five-year-old man, I was having to be fed.

One morning I lay on the bed as usual—washed, shaved, fully clothed and staring up at the ceiling. I smelled, as always, the horrible odour of sweat and bad breath. My mind just kept skipping from place to place. I still wasn't able to achieve mindfulness and one-pointedness of the mind. So, I took in a deep breath yet again with the intent of starting to meditate. My mind just dwelled on my condition—having completely paralysed legs and being confined to a wheelchair for the rest of my life. At that point, all hell let lose as my mind hopped from one place to another.

For the first time since the ordeal started, I was actually giving the idea of killing myself, before I became a burden, real thought. *He's right. I may be about to make Amanda and the boys' life utter hell.* All I could think about was the same question over and over: *Isn't it better to go while I still can?*

As these words flowed through my mind, Doctor Dark seemed to just walk out of the wall, which was now like a dark veil blowing in the wind. As he appeared, he said, 'It's human nature to avoid suffering. How you do remain is the question. In terms of the view, one way to look at suicide is to understand that suicide comes from your own wild case of mistaken identity. In life, there are two fundamental levels of identity—the relative and the absolute. The relative level is the false level that comes from identifying with the contents of your mind—your thoughts and emotions. When you enter a genuine path that transcends the false and embraces the absolute, this is the only level of identity that exists.'

The idea was crazy, but I knew what he was talking about. My study of Zen philosophy had taught me that our world was based on preconceived mental formations. So, though the physical world existed, it existed as a perception created by our own mind. I had read a quantum physics theory that stated we were a wave of potentiality, which was full of atoms, with electrons and protons jumping around and creating our physical world. So, I couldn't deny the existence of the physical world. And everyone had his or her own perception of the world though similar. People's own mental perceptions determined how they felt about different objects, people, and life itself, which created their own personal universe. No wonder we all found it difficult to relate to others 100 percent. Quantum physics also accepted its limitations. For instance, there were three layers of perception in the universe. First was the perception of the self and existing in the physical world. Second was the solar system, which we seemed bound to; yet this was another whole perception based on how we all saw distance and imagined planets. Third was the perception of the universe itself, something so vast and dynamic that we could hardly comprehend it. Yet, in science, an admission existed that there had to be a world beyond the universe, for which Doctors had no answers.

After breaking free from my childhood indoctrination of religion, I always believed that when I would die, my light would just go off, and my consciousness would end. I realised it really was only a theory in itself. *What is the beyond? Is there a godhead there? Is it a collective consciousness that perhaps we transcend to when we die?*

There were many different religions in this world, all with different beliefs, including the beliefs of reincarnation and a transcending soul. Could one of those hold some truth? Though we were connected to a single consciousness, we couldn't comprehend its meaning.

With a look of almost sympathy in his eyes, Doctor Dark said, 'You must make the decision to live by yourself. I offer you only the darkest view. I'm begging you to make the decision. Once you have, you will be absolute on your path. This is not my path or anyone else's path. It's yours. If you decide to die, then you must summon the strength to do it. If you choose life, then I can promise you much more of you must die in order for you to survive. But only you can face that dilemma. No one will hear your screams or your begging for help. You will find only emptiness. Life is a lonely existence. Choosing to end it is a brave solution. Choosing to live for whatever reason is even braver, especially for you.'

He then just vanished, as if he was never there. I thought about what he had said and was taken by surprise how sincere he had been at the end and how much his words had actually spoken to me. Since breaking free of someone else's preconceived idea of life or the existence of a godhead, I had felt a level of emptiness. To me, calling out in prayer felt like just getting things off my chest and instilling some hope in myself. I yearned to pray for mercy, to stop the paralysis, yet all I got was my mind's own method of dealing with depression—a conception I called Doctor Dark. As his words echoed in my head, they strangely gave me some comfort. I remembered what I had learnt from Zen and physics, and it occurred to me that my preconceived idea of what happened after death was just one possible outcome, making death less fearful, while at the same time giving me some way to deal with the perception of what was happening to me. All of this led to what at the time seemed the inevitable—my 'death' either by the attack of my nervous system or the damage to my brain after swimming in meningitis for such a long time or me ending it all for the sake of my family. I kept asking, perhaps to take my mind off the brutal truth, a big question: *What is consciousness? Does it live on after death? If so, where does it go?* I would spend my days lying in my hospital bed, trying to understand and perhaps answer my questions.

To this day, I still don't have an answer, but I do have, perhaps, a theory. The brain has eighty-six billion neurons constantly interacting with each other. Through this activity, the brain makes many different decisions based on its flight or fight core thinking. Studies by Karl Jung, Sigmund Freud, and William Marston have shown that we react almost automatically to different external stimuli but in different ways. Now, regardless of whether you agree with them, one thing has always been demonstrated as a constant to me. All people react to their world either objectively, engagingly, socially, or analytically. I'm sure of this because I've studied it and worked in the field for many years. So, I came to the popular conclusion that our brain operates our body and reacts to the world in an almost automatic way. The consciousness seems to come from different parts of the mind and acts as an overseer of what the brain is doing. When a big or complex decision needs to be made, then the consciousness takes control and makes an independent decision based on its own perception of the world, built up by mental formations, which themselves have been distorted by preconceived thoughts and perceptions.

Describing the mind in this scientific way leads my mind to the simple truth that when the eighty-six billion neurons stop firing and death occurs, then the consciousness disappears. However, this thinking was then challenged by my reading, of all things, quantum physics. As I understood it, the theory is explained through something called quantum entanglement: When a particle comes into existence, it seems to have a double, and they interact or share spatial proximity. They do this in such a way that the quantum state of each particle cannot be defined as independent, and even when the particles are separated by a large distance, they act as one. Einstein called it 'spooky action at a distance' because he dismissed the idea of quantum entanglement but couldn't deny the connection between the two distant particles.

The above ruminations were important because my mind, at the time, was wildly contemplating the nature of existence. I would never say I'd found some holy grail. I only offer my thinking at the time. As I lay there, endlessly waiting for my body to fail, I couldn't stop thinking that given the questions science was throwing up, consciousness itself could be something special in the universe, which carried meaning and purpose, while being part of its physical laws. As I was exploring different realities through thought, my strong belief that consciousness was an artefact of the brain created by evolution was starting to be challenged. I still clung to the idea that religious theosophy was an exaggerated superstition by human misperception, though.

I started to think or hope that consciousness was special. This conflicting questioning of consciousness left me confused and unable to hang my hat on any idea of existence or nonexistence after death. Strange as it might seem, this confusion gave me comfort. Ever since turning my back on the dogma, superstition, and misperception of religion, I had to admit to a feeling of emptiness, a deep-hearted concept of loneliness. Now, by looking at things scientifically as well as spiritually, I started to wonder, even hope, that we all had a larger role to play in the universe than our existence on earth.

CHAPTER 10

THE VISITORS

As the days went by, I felt weaker and weaker. One day, Paul visited and joked (inappropriately) that I looked like a concentration camp victim. Later that day, I saw myself in the lift mirror and realised that he was right. I was skinny, half my head was shaved, and I looked exhausted. As the days and nights went by, I started to believe I was slowly dying. I contemplated it for a few days and then decided there was nothing I could do about it; therefore, I was going to ignore it.

I was again in a room by myself.

A nurse came in and said, 'You have a visitor, but we are only letting one person in at a time.'

'Who is it?' I asked.

'Your brother I think.' Then she left.

The whole world was still upside down, and I couldn't see straight. People were split into three and floating upside down, faces smudged and unrecognisable.

The visitor came in, and he was like everyone else, all smudged up and split into three. I thought it was Geoff at first, but the visitor stood at the end of my bed and stared at me. Geoff would have sat next to me. *Why is he standing there?* I realised the visitor's smudge was different from Geoff's. The visitor never announced himself. And when I asked him who he was, he just said, 'What's wrong with you? You have seen the truth of things. You know there's no "I". There is only the one. Surely this gives you comfort?'

I looked at him and said, 'It's because of the one that I feel at peace at last and feel I can move on.'

He seemed to look hard into my soul.

I wasn't afraid. In fact, I felt some kind of connection with him, almost like the love of my family.

He said, 'You have to fight through the bad days to make it to the best days of your life. When you realise nothing is lacking, your world belongs to you. This isn't your time to die. Just giving up isn't enough. You're not at peace. The giant inside of you still rages, and it's time for him to die, not you.' He continued talking in a soft tone, which made me feel at ease. 'You have become no more than a fool who believes he has reached his destination. You need to see there is no destination. There is only the journey itself, and your journey has not finished. You're still afraid of death. I can feel it like the wind on my face. Look deeper, son. What you are suppressing is deep down, and you know nothing. You are yet to see what you stand for and your purpose. You can't continue on the journey until you discover your true state of being.'

Who are you? Is this the 'him' that Doctor Dark was talking about? I thought. I was quite happy to just slip away now. This man demanded something new from me. I was conflicted: On one hand, I was ready to move. On the other hand, I was being pulled back to life by an unknown force. The man's eyes bore into me so much so that I could feel my whole soul stiffen up. Even though he was a blur, I could tell he was looking at me with a determined look that burnt through my confused and blurred view. He said simply, 'You're no fool. Kill him. You needed him once, but now he's making you feel that being paralysed makes you worthless. You are neither worthless nor a fool. You know what it is that pulls you back? The three of them need you.'

'I'm dying. What can I do?'

'Why did you want to survive before?' he asked.

'Because of my family, but I can't hold on for much longer.'

'Nonsense! You can fight this for them. They still need you, but to win, you can't let him live. He has to die for you to even see them.'

'What do I do now?' I asked.

'Death is not to be feared by those who have lived wisely. But you haven't lived wisely. You have lived for yourself. Kill him and live. There's no place for a giant anymore. The truth is and has always been that you are the strength, the drive. You have always been larger than the giant himself.'

'I fear it's too late now. My death seems unavoidable.'

I felt him looking at me. I couldn't see his face properly, but I could feel the strength of his stare. I knew that stare from somewhere, but I just couldn't put my finger on it. He was caring, strong, and reassuring, and I seemed to be hanging on every word he said. Whoever he was remained a mystery to me. He looked at me with an intent stare, and his words hit me like missiles exploding in my soul.

'Sickness and death are unavoidable, but your time hasn't arrived yet to be defeated by illness or paralysis. They are misfortunes, but to allow them to take over without a fight is sickness of the mind. Your human spirt is greater than anything else. All you have to do is grab hold of it but this time without the giant. You don't need him, and you never did.'

I replied, 'I worked hard to see the truth, and I really do feel like I have found it. I'm not scared of death anymore. I'm not scared of the abyss.' I paused for a second and then continued, 'Will I still feel them once I have moved on?'

'No, this is not the movies. You don't take the love with you, but you do experience the oneness. And sometimes they call you from across the dark. You're not ready. You think you have found peace, but you're deluded. You have just told yourself you have. That's not peace, just an intellectual understanding of what it should be. Neither have you allowed your ego to die; nor are you anywhere near ready to let go of those you love. You're just ignoring them because something inside you says they will be better off without you. Was that your experience? No! You carried the hurt for far too long. Don't do the same to them. No sorrow like separation exists, and anything can become the sickness of the heart. Life is your greatest possession as long as you live it wisely. Being free of attachment does not mean you give up on yourself and others, especially when others need you. Find strength, not from within the real self—the self that is not there. Nothing needs protecting, and no facades or personas are needed. Give them up, and that will be the greatest gift.'

He went quiet for a moment and looked out the door. I didn't know what he saw, but he seemed to be in a rush now. He said softly, 'They need you. This is about your attachment being conquered, and that will come.

This is about three people who need you. You have yet a lot to do. You will suffer in the future, but you will fight like you always have and conquer your paralysis before your attachment. I can't be standing next to you, but I will be a part of the one. Hence, I will always be there. It is better to travel well than to arrive. You seek inner freedom, which is not guided by your outer efforts. It comes from seeing what is true. The more you get involved in events, the more you get distracted from seeing the actual cause of your suffering— you still believe in the self, and there is no "I", my son. Doctor Dark's words only make you think of the dark options, so you know the option of life is the real one. Don't be swayed by him. He himself does not believe in what he says.' After a second's pause, he said, 'This is not the end. It is just the beginning.' As he left the room, he said sternly, 'I'm proud of you.'

Those were his words. I couldn't get what he'd said out of my mind. And slowly those words started shifting my dark thinking.

During his visit, Paul had turned up to see me. The nurse told him my other brother was inside with me now, and only one person was allowed inside at a time. When Paul looked through my open door, he just saw the back of a man, who from behind looked like Geoff. When Geoff turned up with Caz, they were all confused about who the visitor was—so much so they chatted about it and then missed him leave. After the visitor left, the nurse said to them that they could visit me now but only one at a time. They all took their turn to visit, and they all asked me who the visitor had been, but all I could tell them was I had no clue.

The next morning, I woke up in a different single-occupancy room. I must have been moved yet again in the night. I lay there thinking of my encounter with the stranger. He was right. I still had my family, and they needed me. I kept thinking about the mysterious visitor. I hadn't lived a wise life, and I still needed time alive to do so. I also knew who he had meant. If I lived or died, neither could be done with the giant. I needed to live, and the giant needed to die. *But how do I do this?*

Later that morning, Rob visited me. He was his usual self, relaxed and aloof. We talked and joked about everything and nothing. Once we started discussing food, I explained to him how bad the vegetarian options were in the hospital and how I was starving to death. He, like me, was a vegetarian, and in the past when either of us had almost faltered, we had been there

117

for each other to keep straight and true as a vegetarian. I explained to him that I had lost five and a half stones. He looked at me and said, 'Mike, if you were locked in a cellar with a pig and there was no food, then the pig would eat you. Mate, eat some bloody meat. You're not going to get any protein otherwise. How fucking weak are you? You have a rare disease attacking your nervous system, and you need all the strength you can get. Also, you're not eating any protein so you're getting weaker and weaker. Just eat the bloody meat!'

That day on, I started to eat meat. At first, I found eating meat difficult. Then I was given the cure to vegetarianism—a bacon sandwich—and there was no going back after that. My strength began to come back, and I started putting on some weight. Rob's interventions were always short and hard-hitting but effective.

Having a room to myself gave me my own space, which made a big difference. Being isolated gave me no choice but to consider all that was going on. As I lay there thinking, I smelled a horrible odour of sweat and bad breath. The odour was intermittent. I knew who it was, but I had learnt to just ignore it. My monkey mind skipped from place to place. I certainly wasn't achieving mindfulness and one-pointedness of the mind. I was getting stronger. Strangely because of Doctor Dark's intervention the other night, I started to fight myself away from death's door, with, of course, great help from all the doctors and nurses. I wondered if he had meant to do that. I was still vomiting up food but not as much as I was eating, which was a good thing.

Questions ran through my head over and over, giving me a headache and driving any calm I had into a spin. I couldn't stop thinking about my family and how much of a burden I would be to them if all my limbs stopped working. I closed my eyes and took in three deep breaths, each one slower than the previous. I tried very hard to just concentrate on the breath going into and out my lungs. As I did, my mind slowly calmed down, and the smell of sweat and bad breath entered the room.

When I opened my eyes, the whole room had disappeared. In its stead, on both sides of me and above, were dark veils moving like waves in the wind. On the floor, I could see a cobbled path that seemed to just disappear into what now was a horizon in the dark distance. I felt cold, yet I was aware I was sweating. The atmosphere was heavy with a sense of foreboding fear. Above the overwhelming smell of burning flesh, the even stronger and unmistakable smell of bad breath and bad body odour wafted over me. My eyes were transfixed on the dark horizon, and there he appeared—Doctor Dark—first in the distance. His arms were down by his side, outwards.

He slowly came closer and closer. As he did, my heart started beating faster, and the atmosphere appeared to get heavier. Eventually, he was at the end of my bed. He stood there in all his dark presence. The horizon from which he had come was now gone, replaced by a dark veil. He stood large as life over my bed, yet he seemed incomplete. All around him, the edges of his body seemed to shimmer and move yet in some way stay connected to the dark. His face was white with cracking white face paint, and his eyes had dark black rings around them. He gave me a stare, which seemed to pierce my very soul. His lips started moving well before any sound was produced. Eventually, I heard his crackling and distorted voice.

'You must know that you have got it utterly wrong.' He paused, almost to rub it in.

As he did, a chill ran through me, and I could feel myself in bed, unable to move, trapped by my body.

He spouted, 'You have a choice, you know. Just walk with me down the path, and I can show you the way out.'

'You mean the way to letting myself die?' I asked.

Before I even finished talking, he growled, 'No, you're duty-bound to kill yourself, but not the complete self, only the self that changes your perception of reality. If you don't do it now, you won't be able to soon. End the fear, the desperation, and the pain. He is making you feel worthless. But if that's how you feel, then make the ultimate sacrifice.'

'No. I will never kill myself. Or at least not now, not yet, not while there's hope, not while they still need me.'

He was clearly taunting me. It was him, in part, who made me fight to carry on. And now he seemed to want me to kill myself. Every time I found peace and was ready to move on, he appeared and shouted at me. Every time I contemplated something, he jumped on me.

Spitting out a sarcastic laugh, he said, 'Don't you feel it? Are you not pinned to the ground by it? Don't you sense it? There's no hope. You're wasting everyone's time. You can't move your legs already. Every day you wake up, your body gets weaker and weaker. This disease is creeping through your central nervous system, limb by limb, and you're losing your grip on life.'

'I'm not giving up,' I replied. 'I can't leave Amanda and the boys.'

'It's inevitable,' he coughed out. 'Your survival will be a complete burden on your whole family. If you love them, then you know this is the right thing to do.'

The idea of killing myself before I became a burden once again became a strong thought. *He's right. I may be about to make Amanda and the boys' life utter hell.* All I could think about was the same question over and over. *Isn't it better to go while I still can?*

The stranger's words came to my mind. 'Doctor Dark's words are only to make you think of the dark options, so you know the option of life is the real one. Don't be swayed by him. He himself does not believe in what he says.'

The smell of sweat and bad breath seemed to intensify.

When I looked up, he was sitting beside me on my bed. His eyes had changed, no longer piercing through my soul, instead showing sympathy. He opened his mouth, and his voice synchronised with his lips this time. 'You know it can be quite painless. Take the pills, enjoy the trip, and let all this go.'

'No, it doesn't matter what you say. I'm not doing it!'

'Then you know what happens next. It's either you or him,' he shouted. 'Think of the burden you have been on your family and friends, not with this illness but with yourself. Now think about how you will double that if the giant still lives, only to make you feel worthless for being disabled. If your burden is to become physical, then for you to live, he must die because he will see your physical disability as worthless and weak and drive you where you are fighting to avoid.'

Then a nurse came into the room and introduced herself as Jenny. After checking my vitals, she put her hand on my shoulder and said, 'Don't be afraid. Don't allow the doubt in. Don't stop fighting. I have been here for some time, and I have seen those who fought and those who just gave in to their injuries. You're a fighter. I can spot that from a mile away. Concentrate on your family. They love you and you them, and that forms the bridge for you to cross, and you will never be a burden.'

Feeling comfortable with her, I told her about the army of doctors, about how one had lied just so that he could leave the room. I also told her about my fears and my family.

She tightened her grip on my shoulder in a comforting way and said, 'You, like many people, have dedicated your life to your family. They are your reason for waking, living, and fighting, day in and day out. They are the centre of every atom in your body, the nucleus of your whole life. If paralysis is your fate, then just remember that life is always moving forward though in many cases not as we planned. The only thing we can rely on is the transience of things. Yet we are never ready for a big change. We think life will always be slow changing and we can cope, but life isn't that fair. You have chosen your reason to live. Now live. If you want to connect where you have either not connected or lost connection, then just show kindness, and you will be able to connect. I'll be honest with you. It's going to be a challenge, but it will define you more than anything in your life has defined you yet.'

Then the crushing ball smashed through the window and hit me straight in the head. All those great achievements and challenging times in my life were worth nothing. All that I held up as that which defined me was only of any use in the past. *I have to start my life anew, and God knows in what state, and find a way to support my family.* I had defined myself once, but my life was changing, and I needed to change with it. I suddenly felt shielded from all the dark thoughts.

As I lay there considering the new possibilities, a nurse came into the room and said, 'I'm here to take your vitals.'

I said to her, 'Oh, don't worry. I just had them.'

'By whom?' she asked. 'The sheet says your last check was three hours ago.'

'The nurse just left a minute back,' I pleaded.

'Well, she hasn't filled in the sheet, and no one has told me your results. If you don't mind, I will just take them again.'

'Fine.' I resigned to my fate.

As she left, the room instantly went dark. The foul smell of burning flesh choked me, and the familiar crackle of Doctor Dark's voice broke through any shield I had just built up. He paused to let as much dread as possible soak in and then said, 'It's time to take action.' In a quiet yet

121

threatening tone, he continued, 'You have to come close to taking your own life to kill the giant, preserve your dignity, prevent your suffering; and it will free your family because, let's face it, you're not going to get any better.' Then he disappeared.

He seemed to have always been there in my life, but the truth was he had appeared only after I'd left the army. *Did I create him?* He was always just a fearful feeling and presence and a faraway thought. Until now, I'd only ever glimpsed him in the dark. But now I saw him completely. Now he was a man, fully formed and as large as life, talking to me. Strangely, I wasn't surprised at his appearance though I had never fully seen him. I had caught enough glimpses of him to paint a mental picture of him, and he looked exactly as I had imagined—a frightening phantom.

His face looked familiar, but all the white cracked paint on his face disguised his real face. I knew his eyes. I had seen them before, but I just couldn't place them. I always dismissed him as a bad dream, but everything seemed very real this time.

Was I asleep? Was he real? Am I going mad? I didn't know anymore. I could have dozed off when I had started breathing slowly or when had I calmed my mind, and I could have let him in. The rest of the day, thoughts ran through my mind. *How bad is this going to be? What am I going to do? How will I cope? How will this affect my family?*

I lay in the hospital bed with these thoughts spinning around my head as the inner monkey went mad. I started vomiting. My paralysis was creeping up on me. My legs were now lifeless, and I had given up all hope of ever walking again. Life seemed bleak, and Doctor Dark's words kept playing in my mind. Now my mind was failing. Slowly but gradually, I was falling into a pit of depression and desperation. My mind was usually strong and resistant, but now it was starting to rationalise suicide again. This was unbearable. One minute I was up, and the next minute, I was down. The darkness fell again, and there he was—Doctor Dark. I tried not to look at him, but not staring at the phantom was hard. His face was still covered with dried cracking white paint, and he was smoking a large cigar. After a moment's pause, he spat out, 'You must feel it—that uncontrollable anguish and despair, that pull to take your life now and save everyone from anguish.'

122

I rolled over in bed and pulled the covers over my head with the little strength I had left, like a six-year-old scared of the dark. 'Leave me alone,' I demanded.

Thwarting my attempt to ignore him, he said in a soft, almost caring voice, 'Michael, you've worked hard all your life. You've tried your best. You've given what you can to your family, yet life has become difficult and pointless. Surely somewhere inside, you're telling yourself it's unfair and time to go.'

I rolled over and saw him sitting at the end of my bed. For the first time, I mustered the courage to engage with him like a confidant and not a haunting phantom. 'I haven't told anyone about this, about thoughts of suicide.'

'Why would you?' he asked. 'How could this be anyone's business but your own? You are the master of your own destiny, and no one and no mysterious force is coming to save you. Taking your own life is your decision; therefore, only you should make that decision. I'm only here to help you see the truth.'

His reasoning started to feel right and even comforting. But something inside me wanted to argue my case for life. I made the best argument I could think of. 'My feelings of suicide were an emotional reaction to my current circumstances; therefore, my outlook was dark and hopeless. The future isn't set, and emotion clouds my decisions. Much is unknown and frightening, but suicide itself is too definitive. I can't get out of my mind that it's a very drastic solution to take, and these feelings may be only temporary. I haven't exhausted all the facts and personal feelings, so I can't commit suicide.'

Doctor Dark looked at me with anger in his eyes. I braced myself for his tirade, but his reaction surprised me. He leant forward and said softly, 'Suicide is a personal choice. You must reject the thought that suicide is irrational and see that it is, instead, a solution to a real problem. Your condition isn't temporary. You're not going to get better. Suicide can be a last resort that you can legitimately take, as your alternative is worse. No being should be made to suffer unnecessarily like you're going to, and your suicide can provide an escape from your suffering.'

I thought for a minute about what he'd said.

Then the voice of my visitor entered my thoughts. 'You" can fight this for them, but to win, you can't let him live. He has to die for you to even see them. Death is not to be feared by those who have lived wisely, but you haven't lived wisely. You have lived for yourself. Kill him and live. There's no place for a giant anymore. The truth is and has always been that you are the strength, the drive, and you have always been larger than the giant himself.'

With a newfound resolve, I spoke to Doctor Dark. 'Suicide makes everyone around you suffer. I might resolve my suffering, but my family and friends will suffer because of me for the rest of their lives. I can't even contemplate passing my suffering over to my wife and boys. What kind of man would I be?'

Irritated and angry, he said, 'That sounds very definite to me, almost like you have made your mind up.'

'For now,' I replied, perhaps realising I had made my mind up at last, and taking my own life was out of the question. But it didn't mean I wouldn't consider it in the future.

He took a deep breath, looked at me, and spat out, 'If you are to live, then he must fall, Mike. Otherwise, your pain will always be felt, not just by you but also by those you love. They will be forced to watch you live in pain and suffering, and you might not be able to rid yourself of the pain, but you can from the suffering.'

With that, he faded away but, surprisingly, with a smile on his face. As he smiled, the white paint around his mouth cracked and fell away. I had never made a decision without hearing all the facts. I always looked for someone to give me what we called in consultancy, 'the black-hat opinion', which was always described as a black top hat, just like the one Doctor Dark wore. In a strange and painful way, Doctor Dark had done exactly that for me. He had prompted me to make my decision to carry on and fight; it was like he'd turned up to argue with me, in order to make me see all the options. I had done so with full confidence after hearing both sides of the argument. Now, I had to turn my mind to murder for me to survive. *The giant must go. But how do I kill such a big part of myself?*

I tried to think of a way to kill the giant. *Do I just tell him to leave? Can I just ignore him? Should I enact some ritual?* As I was thinking through the possible methods of self-murder, I heard a deep, dark laughter as the darkness surrounded me again. It felt like a prickly horse-haired blanket, uncomfortable and itchy. I experienced the oddest of feelings. I felt like I was standing on a wall, and the bricks of the wall were just sliding out of place, forcing it to almost collapse. I saw myself standing in front of me, dressed in a suit and ready for work. It was the giant, and he said, 'You think you could live without me? You won't even leave this hospital without me. I am your strength. It's me people admire. It's me who drives everything forward. You're just a bystander.'

I replied, 'You're me, and I am you. All this time, I have been the one with the strength. I just couldn't bring myself to believe it.'

He retorted, 'When you're scared, it's me who pushes you to act. When your indecisive, it's me who forces you to make a decision.' His twisted and out-of-shape face revealed his anger.

'Life is created in part by thought. Things arise because we perceive them. When thoughts vanish, then either the problem vanishes or at least the problem changes. I need to rest and start to be kind to myself. I have nothing to prove anymore. I'm going to live by letting things happen and see where things take me. Resistance itself to unpleasant situations brings on suffering. I must learn to be comfortable in adversity and to be still and content when bored. I'm going to leap into the boundless and live there with peace of mind, in the knowledge that I have faced the worst and accepted my fate as it reveals itself. I don't need you anymore, and I don't want you anymore.'

A dreadful, violent, and nasty scream filled the room. I could feel the bricks slide from underneath me, and I experienced the feeling of falling uncontrollably. The giant me threw out his arms to try and catch me, but he missed, as I jumped backwards on the collapsing brick. I fell for what felt like a lifetime. As I finally hit the bottom, I was back in the misty forest, lying on the dew-wet grass. All the horror of the past months ran through my mind—the pain, the paramedics, the wheelchair, the endless waiting, the coma, the meningitis, the bladder and bowel troubles, the hallucinations, the sickness, the PICC line, the failing body, the boredom, the operations, the intermittent hospital admissions, and so forth.

My heart was beating so hard that it felt like it was lifting me up and dropping me down. The self-determined giant in me came into focus, and I watched him go about his business as if I was watching him on TV. *He's a wanker. How the hell did I become him?* That was all I could think of. I couldn't believe how much he thought of himself or how his thought only went to his family when he needed comfort. I couldn't stand to watch myself anymore. I lay on the floor, broken. My mind shot to Amanda. I realised that, despite having a lovely, caring, determined and beautiful wife who did so much to care for her family, I had taken her for granted. My boys' faces came into view, and my heart broke. I had missed too much of their lives trying to be the big I, and I wasn't even that. I felt my whole body start to fade, and slowly my heart slowed down.

After watching myself like that, I just knew I had to die in some way for the giant in me to die. I started to allow my own death so that the giant could die. My heart slowed and slowed until it was just a fading tick. Realising his approaching death, he fought back and started to fill my mind with thoughts of cowardice, failure, and worthlessness. He reminded me how I needed him if I was to live. Something inside me just wouldn't give up, and I tried to keep my heart beating by breathing harder and trying to will it to restart. Then I heard Doctor Dark's voice gently say, 'It's time. You have no more use of what is, ultimately, you. Just let go.'

Soon after, I heard the mystery visitor. 'You can fight this for them. To win, you can't let him live. He has to die for you to even see them.'

I stopped trying to keep my heart from stopping, as it wasn't making any difference anyway. Slowly, it ground to a halt, and I heard myself shout, 'You pathetic wanker, stand up and fight!' For a second, my whole body reacted like a soldier having orders shouted at it. My heart started to beat, but I had made my decision: It was better to die now than to live on as I was. My heart stopped dead, and my whole body seemed to smash into small pieces, scattering all over the floor.

Then Doctor Dark whispered, 'Three things cannot be long hidden—the sun, the moon, and the truth. Even death is not to be feared by one who has lived wisely. Every morning, we are born again.'

The giant was dead. I couldn't feel that drive to be a top dog anymore or the feeling of being a worthless cripple. The giant facade had died, leaving behind my previous facade, which clung to me and reminded me of my shame—an angry, violet man, a soldier willing to do as ordered, with a questionable morality at best. I couldn't put my finger on a single point. As soon as I did, I would feel even greater shame about all my actions. All this created a great conflict in me, with one half telling me to move on and the other half asking me how I could move on from such a self-loathing shame. I realised that I didn't have just one facade. I was like an onion. Peel away one layer, and there lay another.

Nodding and stroking his chin, Doctor Dark paused. I thought I had shut him up, but I hadn't. In a slightly louder whisper, he said, 'Your death was spectacular. The fall you took smashed you into pieces, and now you fail to see your chance to grow. You mutter wise words like a fool trying to get out of prison. There is more to come with the fall of the giant facade, which was given so much power to hide your previous facade, the one that carries shame for you. You now need to let him die too. Maybe the only way to destroy him is to take your own life, to fall upon your sword and extinguish everything.'

As he finished talking, I heard a man's voice I knew so well. 'Michael!' He shouted out my name like I was doing something wrong. I knew that voice; it was that of my father. On hearing him, my heart restarted, just as a foul wind started blowing through the forest, picking up all the leaves and carrying them everywhere. The leaves started to circle me with speed. Soon, I was engulfed by the leaves as they created a whirlwind all around me. The whirlwind started to choke me, and panic set in.

Then, I heard Doctor Dark's voice. 'Shame, it drags you back. Let go. Let it be. See through everything and be free, complete; kill the self and be at ease.'

I felt my past get sucked into the storm and start swirling around me as if I was in a glass. Suddenly, with the loudest of cries, I felt the facade of shame hanging on to me like a man trying not to fall from a great height. Doctor Dark's voice penetrated the roar of the storm and leaves around me and said, 'This is not the end. It's just the beginning.'

As his voice faded, I heard a laugh, a horrid, mocking laugh. I knew instantly it was not Doctor Dark's laugh. It was something else, something that made a chill run down my spine. The leaves fell away, and I found myself in bed, clinging tightly to the quilt and sweating from head to toe.

'You have always been stuck in the past, not through action but through your own stupidity.' That was the last thing I heard before my mind collapsed with overexertion. My mind seemed stripped of all its thought, and my brain felt like it had been spinning inside my skull for hours. I didn't feel the giant anymore. It was like a weight had been lifted off. For the first time in my life, I really did feel at peace—no more anger, no more regret. I had faced death by bringing it on myself, killing my facades and false personas. Yet I had underestimated the draw of the past, which would catch up with me later. I hadn't reached nirvana (enlightenment), but I did escape samsara (a living hell, life without some kind of enlightenment).

The transformation started a new conflict of interest. On the one hand, I felt less fear of dying, making the idea of ending my pain no longer a frightening prospect. I certainly didn't believe the universe had a set of written rules of do's and don'ts with 'don't commit suicide' written down somewhere. On the other hand, the thought of having such a possible connection to the universe was a strong reason to live and perhaps experience what came next. Not forgetting my solid connection to my wife and two boys, I felt even closer to them, as this new thinking made me feel as we were all one. They were as much a part of me as I was them, and the right to self-determine my death was now questionable at best. As I lay in bed, I found a way to manage the excruciating boredom and painful wait for death or advanced paralysis. I used the time to meditate on the question of not what was next but what I had been experiencing for the past forty-five years. Right now, any Zen practitioner would assert that Zen was about the here and now and neither the past nor the future. However, I would say tell them to try lying in a bed, slowly dying and losing the use of their limbs as the weeks went by. Then looking back would be inevitable. That said, I would also say, 'Be patient. I did get there in the end.'

The room instantly went black. The smell of the dark made me retch, and lying on my bed was Doctor Dark. He was almost a friend now. He no longer instilled fear, anger, or hatred in me. Without looking at me, he said, 'You're getting close. But are you ready to make the great sacrifice and find out the answers to your questions?'

I thought for a while, and I looked at him. He turned his head, but I held my gaze directed straight at his eyes. I instantly shifted my gaze, as with one look at his eyes, all I could see was fear, despair, and anguish. I took a deep breath, looked him in his anguished eyes, and said, 'Yes, I'm ready to make the sacrifice.' I paused and took another deep breath and said, 'I'm going to deny myself the release from this existence—from this so-called life. I'm going to deal with the physical world, and I'm going to deny myself the experience of facing reality through my consciousness. I'm going to make this work for my family, my wife, and my boys. Whatever happens, happens because I think I have glimpsed somehow the truth of reality. I can see now that, beyond my first three levels of consciousness, furthermore exists. Reality itself exists well beyond my mental formations and perceptions of life. In this reality, I will remain a husband to my wife and a father to my boys. They don't deserve my death, though I don't feel afraid of death anymore. If I see death, then I will shake his hand and walk on by.'

Doctor Dark just lay there listening to me, and without uttering a single word, he got up, turned, and glided into the darkness. As he slowly walked away and faded, I could see a small child. He seemed trapped, like he was handcuffed to a wall. He was shouting something out at me, but I could neither could fully see him nor hear what he was trying to say. The darkness lifted, and he was gone.

Is this finally the end of the long goodbye? Did I defeat Doctor Dark? Who is that boy, and why is he chained to the wall? More to the point, what is he trying to say to me? What does all this mean? What has that boy got to do with me?

CHAPTER 11

THE CASE OF MISTAKEN IDENTITY (SURELY)

My decision that life had more to offer me gave me the strength to fight to stay alive. I chose a goal, which was to get better enough to go back to work. I didn't know why. I was probably trying to make things normal again. *I will be in a wheelchair, but no reason exists for that to stop me*, I thought. I just needed to retain the use of my arms and be able to bang a keyboard to make a report. I told myself that, if I just got back to work, then this whole ordeal would just be a blip in my life. From that day on, everyone with whom I came in contact was told about my goal.

I looked like a survivor of a prisoner of war camp, skinny and gaunt with a shaven head. The condition of my eyes was so messed up that scores of trainee doctors still came to take a look at them. I still didn't know why each student would ask me to look up and then be fascinated. All I knew was, when I did, my eyes started jumping all over the place. I was such a star that I had to ask the nurse to limit them coming in so that I could get some sleep. Otherwise, I quite enjoyed their visits.

Life did seem better because I now possessed a goal and the realisation that the true goal was my family and not work. Telling myself that I would go back to work was just the way I pushed myself beyond the possible.

James, the neurosurgeon, once visited me to see how I was doing. When I told him my new goal about work, he said, 'Of course, that sounds great.'

I detected a sense of doubt in his voice, but it didn't surprise me. I knew I was pretty messed up, and my chances of going back to life as it had been were low, but James was always positive and believed in goals.

Another doctor who visited me regularly was Dr Ellis, the eye doctor in charge of all the students and somebody who would become a major contributor to my progress in the near future. I told him my goal regularly, and whenever he visited with students, I told them the same too. He always smiled and said, 'That's great.' However, I found out later that he didn't think I stood a chance.

Each day, I exercised with the resistance band on my bed, fighting to keep my arms from weakening. I would synchronise each pull with the clock and imagine that each tick and pull was fighting the paralysis back. I had started to believe that everything was truly connected, and I really believed it was all joined as one. I knew one couldn't ever really see atoms, but I liked to imagine I could. I would visualise uncountable plains of existence rippling through space and time and me being enveloped inside a vast movement of atoms and the lover's dance of the particles, whose love held the whole universe together. I liked to picture this image as much as I could, while exercising, lying on my bed staring at the fluorescent lights, meditating, and trying to fall asleep.

I would wait in anticipation for the ward physiotherapist to come, collect me, and take me to the gym, where I put my heart and soul into working as hard as possible. Though I mainly caught a ball and attempted to throw it back or was put on an automatic exercise bike to which my feet were strapped, I would try to make the best of it. Turning a pair of crank arms to keep my arms going made me feel like I was getting something out of the experience. I would discover later that the whole thing maintained the muscle tone in my legs and maintained blood flow. I wasn't looking to maintain myself. I was looking to gain all the strength I had lost and improve.

In my spare time, I started pushing myself in my wheelchair around the ward, which was set out in a large circle, making it a perfect exercise circuit. I would run into other patients who were also doing the same thing. So, I got to know people from different parts of the ward. Each time I saw them, they would want to talk. Even though socialising took my time away from exercising, I now saw human contact as important and realised others craved the same. I was, of course, now too polite to say I was going to get on with exercising and gave them the time they wanted to chat. Listening intently to all their stories, I would imagine particles dancing around in and out of us. Eventually, a porter and nurse would come around, pushing someone in a bed off to surgery, and split up the gathering, as we were in the way. Both parties probably took the intrusion as a sign to move on, or at least I took it as my chance to get on with exercising.

I started feeling better. The surgeries seemed to have stopped. My face was still paralysed, but I was learning to live with it. I couldn't lift my arms over my head, but I could use them below that point. My belief in oneness and the unity of all gave me a new reason to live, and no matter how bad my condition was, I had stopped seeing myself as an individual separate from all that around me and started seeing myself as one with everything and everyone. As broken as I was, I still felt like a collection of atoms that was part of a single existence. There, my physical being never mattered to our connection as one. As with all belief, I had decided on an existence. And to make it real, I imagined a whole picture of it until it started to feel real.

I soon started to pester James about getting me into a rehabilitation centre. He suggested Swindon. But as I told him I was done with Swindon, he tried to get me into the Oxford Centre for Enablement (OCE), which sounded perfect. A week later, the consultant in charge of the OCE came and interviewed me to see if I was an eligible candidate for the centre. He probably just wanted to check whether I wanted to get better and I had the will to do so. When I told him about my goal, he seemed doubtful but impressed. Then and there, he agreed to temporarily admit me to the centre. 'Let's get you transferred ASAP, but there is a waiting list. Therefore, it could be a while.'

Out of an outburst of emotion, I had to fight back tears as I said thank you.

That night, I daydreamed about getting better and just being a management consultant again. I imagined riding my wheelchair into my company's impressive London office like nothing had happened.

Remarkably, the next day, I was told I was being transferred to the OCE. A bed had become free, and I had been allowed to jump the queue due to my condition and determination. At the time, I imagined I was halfway there, and I must paint a strong image of myself in the wheelchair. The aspiration couldn't have been further from the truth, as I looked terrible and had the posture of the Leaning Tower of Pisa even though I thought I was sitting up straight. My drooped paralysed face likely did the trick. I looked like hell on wheels, and I didn't think my strength of character got me bumped up the list. It was more likely because I looked like I needed immediate rehabilitation.

Not long after, an ambulance team arrived, transferred me into a gurney, and strapped me in, ready to go. I said goodbye and thanks to Pedro, and off we went. When the ambulance got stuck in the Oxford traffic, the paramedics told me to get some rest. As I closed my eyes, I felt a great weight on my chest. The whole ambulance went black, and the back doors ripped open to reveal Doctor Dark standing in the doorway. With a smile on his face, he looked like he was very happy to find me again.

'What do you want?' I asked belligerently.

'Just because you think you have decided to fight, you haven't seen the end of me,' he growled. 'You fought from day one, even when you were in a coma. All you have done is see through the dark veil of perceived reality. I wonder how far you will go.'

'I intend to go back,' I grumbled.

Doctor Dark just laughed, looking like a condescending parent, and said, 'The body is only an instrument for the true self. Work on your goal, but do not lose sight of the truth. You will make mistakes, because you are focused on the target and not your actions. Be noble-minded, calm, and steady. Little people are forever fussing and fretting. What are you, noble minded or little?'

I had no answer to provide him, and my lack of response seemed to please him. He inched closer and said, 'Nothing ever goes away until it has taught us what we need to know.'

At first, I thought he was talking about himself. As he said it, he looked out of the back of the ambulance, and he seemed perplexed and unhappy. At first, I tried not to look, but the suspense was too much. I looked at the dark veil that had replaced the back doors of the ambulance. I couldn't see anything at first, but then I saw some kind of phantom lurking deep in the darkness. The phantom was less visual and transmitted more of a dark feeling than any other on my journey. Whatever it was, I felt more afraid of it than I ever did with Doctor Dark. I looked at Doctor Dark and asked, 'Who is it? What do they want?'

He looked at me as if I were a naughty schoolboy and said, 'You know who it is. You have been so afraid of me for so long that you never saw I was just a mirror of your fears. Maybe I have no power over you now, but you have called upon another phantom to help you do what you could never do, which is torture yourself. The reason you can't see him right now is that he is from your past.'

He looked at me with fatherly eyes and said, 'If you are depressed, you are living in the past. If you are anxious, you are living in the future. If you are at peace, you are living in the present'. He looked back at the phantom and said, 'I must go now, but you haven't finished with me yet. Forget the years. Forget distinctions. Leap into the boundless and make it your home. Don't seek, don't search, don't ask, don't knock, and don't demand; you will still achieve your goal if you relax. Remember, when you're relaxed, he can't hurt you.'

With that warning, he was gone. The dark veil lifted, and the ambulance doors had returned. The paramedic kept apologising for how cold the inside of the ambulance was. She told me that the traffic was bad, but we should reach the hospital in fifteen minutes. The wait gave me time to think. *What the hell is going on with Doctor Dark?* It seemed almost like he was trying to help me. *What was that in the darkness that even Doctor Dark himself seemed afraid of?*

When we arrived, we had to park away from the hospital entrance. I was transferred onto an old hospital wheelchair with wheels that only wanted to go left, giving the paramedics a hard time in pushing me into the hospital. I was leaning to the right as always; my face was still drooping, and I couldn't lift my arms up very high. I was very conscious. I must have looked like a hopeless case, but I was about to meet my fellow patients. As the swing doors into the OCE were locked, the paramedics had to ring a bell. That should have been my first omen about what lay ahead, but I was too excited and couldn't wait to get going.

The doors opened to reveal a nurse. She said, 'You must be Michael.'

Though I tried hard to respond in a normal way, 'All mer Mike,' was all I could get out of my paralysed mouth.

As I was pushed into the ward, I saw many tables in a big common room, and on them were different people, from old ladies to young men. They hung out in their wheelchairs, some drooling on the floor, others trying to move their arms to wave hello. *Poor souls*, I thought, not realising that was exactly how I looked.

I was pushed into my room and introduced to Giovanni, a man whose body odour was probably the worst I had ever known, as it penetrated your nose and stayed there. I was horrified to hear he was my assigned nurse. He checked my vitals and hoisted me into a bed with a machine that lifted me with a harness. He made me comfortable, which was terrible because it meant he got up close and personal. The odour choked me. I told myself that he must have had a hard day, and this was a one-off incident; he would smell better tomorrow. I was soon proven wrong, as such was his permanent state. I later learnt he feared getting cancer from the use of deodorant and chose to stink all day rather than risk it. Moving on, I was always surprised that his superiors never said a word. I never worked in health care, but if one of my team members smelt that bad, I would have brought them in and discussed it. I knew he was part of the one, but come on!

He left the room having tucked me into bed. Then, I heard a voice from next door, which I could only crudely explain as not from this realm. A loud growl with different tones, it just sounded like something from a horror film such as *The Exorcist*. Intermittently, the growl would stop for a few minutes and then start again, without words, just grunts and growls. I wasn't scared, rather annoyed that I would have to listen to the cacophony the whole time I was here, as well as deal with Giovanni's choking body odour. My belief of oneness was being tested. Quite frankly, it wasn't some religious belief that was all well and good until reality came crashing in.

The next day, I was put into a wheelchair and pushed to the common room to meet everybody. As we went, I looked into the room next door to vaguely see what seemed like a demon-possessed man. The sight broke my heart—makeshift padded walls with plastic mattresses lined the room. On the bed, a young girl, no more than twenty-five years of age, lay crying. The realisation that the possessed man had been this poor young girl ripped my guts out. When she spoke, only a growl came out of her mouth, and I didn't see a monster anymore. Instead, I saw a young girl crying and struggling to communicate.

The nurse inched my wheelchair forward, put a hand on my shoulder, and said, 'Don't worry. She's moving on soon. Poor girl had a brain injury that affected her speech.'

135

I wasn't pleased or relieved to hear the news like I thought I would be. I just felt incredibly sorry for her and ashamed of myself for my first thoughts. She was moved three days later, and everyone who came and visited me would comment, 'What the hell is that?' But all I heard was a young girl struggling to communicate. At times, I didn't think my heart could take it because I felt miserable. Such empathy seemed new to me— being emotionally involved with someone I hadn't even met. Here we were again with more proof of the random universe. If some godhead had done this to that young girl, then I would have mustered every bit of strength in my body and struck him down. The random universe wasn't cruel, kind, or otherwise; it just was. I still carry the young girl in my head wherever I go. She's not a ghost or a phantom, rather a guest.

I found my whole experience at the OCE daunting and depressing. As I was pushed into the common room each day, I was speechless. Everyone had brain injuries or were stroke victims, all affected in different ways. You could talk to some, as they just had some physical impairment. Some could just grunt at you as they drooled. Overall, seeing those poor people in such a state was distressing. I was also considered like them and had been sent to this place, and I hadn't realised yet that I was one of them.

At dinnertime, we were all given aprons to protect us from spilling food on our clothes. At first, I felt insulted when the nursing assistant put an apron on me, but once I started eating, food spilled everywhere, and I understood the reason. We were like lost souls on the river Styx, the mythical river that took you to death. Stuck between two worlds, I felt like we were just rudderless, floating through oblivion. We would all come out of our cabins to eat together and then return to our own misery.

After a few days of being in the OCE, I started to settle in and realise I looked like everyone else. I made some friends on the ward, mainly from the shared horror of being nursed by Giovanni and the smell that seemed to linger in our rooms minutes after he had left.

Amanda came to visit as always, and the different conditions of the patients and the plight of the poor soul next door affected her. As always, she talked about each one with compassion and never once said anything derogatory about anyone. As she cradled me in her arms, I looked up at her and said in my best voice, 'Am I going to become like these poor people?'

136

'No, you're just here to get better,' she answered with tears in her eyes, well aware I was already one of those poor people.

I felt better even though I knew she was lying. I knew I wasn't going to become like the other patients, as I was already like them—unable to sit up straight or speak or eat properly, my face drooped, my eyes pointing in different directions. Without speaking, we just held hands and cuddled. The silence between us was broken by the growls and grunts of the girl next door. Though I could feel Amanda's eyes on me, I didn't meet her eye and kept my head nestled in her chest. She stayed for the rest of the day, but when she had to leave, both of us were heartbroken.

I was wheeled into the dinner hall. At the dinner hall, like in school, I would look for the people I liked to chat with over dinner. But if the table was full, I had to find somewhere else to sit, which, on this occasion, I did. Those on my new table were very nice, and like me, they struggled to eat without making too much of a mess, trying to preserve whatever dignity they had left.

While I was at the OCE, my brain damage had started affecting my hippocampus, which, in turn, affected my memory. So, from here on, my ability to remember names is patchy at best. While sitting at the dining room table, I met a lovely lady in her sixties or seventies. After introducing herself to me, she told me not to worry, as she had a stroke and the OCE had nursed her back to health. She was still working on regaining the full use of her right arm and hand. Her bright blue eyes penetrated my new facade, and I felt that she was talking to my soul. 'Never give up. If you want something, then fight for it. You're here to get better, and you might not walk out of here, but you will feel as if you have started your journey home.'

'Look at me,' I said. 'Do you really think I can get better?'

'Of course,' she said. 'I was like you, even worse in fact.' She whispered, 'There are some in here who are just not going to get better. Most, however, come in like you and walk out like nothing happened. It's this place. It's a place of miracles.'

She laid her hand on mine for comfort, which made me feel safe. I settled down, and my constant panicking instantly stopped. She was undoubtedly a shining beacon of hope. She seemed quite well, though you could see she had issues with her arm. She talked about the OCE as if it was a miracle place where you come in broken and leave fixed. *This is a little optimistic*, I thought, as the girl in the room next to me wasn't getting any better. But hey, it was good to hear there was hope.

She pointed out to me people in their forties and fifties who had fallen off horses or bicycles and sustained head injuries that had affected their movement. She told me to keep fighting, as she had come in crippled and broken, and now she was on her way to full health. She raised my spirts, and I realised that the OCE wasn't a dumping ground for people with no hope but a place where I could get better. If I believed in myself and never gave up trying to get better, then I would. I sadly cannot remember the elderly lady's name, but I am forever grateful to her because she lit the fire back in me. She totally changed the perception I had of the OCE. If I didn't know better, I would have said she was an angel. But I saw her every day at the OCE, and angels didn't stick around that long. Her name was probably Melody. Sorry. I can't be sure; my memory blocks the truth. I looked up from my angel and scanned the table, and everyone was staring at us as if we were mad. I just ignored them.

Soon after, a physiotherapist walked into my room, pushing a bright red wheelchair that looked like it had been through a war. She introduced herself as Kim. I'm not entirely sure of her now. She told me I needed to get into the wheelchair. She got help to hoist me into the chair and pushed me off to the gym. I was transferred using a transfer board, from my chair to a plinth. There, Kim slowly checked out my whole body, writing the results down as she went.

'OK,' she said, 'you have some good flexibility, but your strength and balance are not very good. You don't have any core muscle anymore, which is why you're very floppy when we move you. Your core will take a long time to improve, if at all, but I can help with your strength and flexibility. I will also teach you techniques for moving from chair to bed and back as well. If it's all right with you, I would like to film you now and a few weeks later to show how you have improved. Is that OK?'

'That's fine with me.' I felt really optimistic for the first time in months.

Each morning, two Polish health care assistants (HCAs) would get me up, wash me, and dress me. We would all have a laugh as we went through the same routine every day. They were good lads who really enjoyed their job and cared about their patients. I couldn't tell you how much of a breath of fresh air that was. When breakfast was served, I would always have Weetabix, and when they put a plastic apron on me, I no longer minded. Then off I would go, in my old tank of a wheelchair, to the gym where Kim would help me learn, not to walk again, but to move my body using the limbs and muscles that worked. After a few weeks, she showed me on the computer the comparison of my state when I had started and now, and I was amazed at the progress I had made in movement and flexibility. I was very grateful to Kim. Before her, everyone had been fighting to save my life, but she helped me to start my recovery and restart my life. I couldn't emphasise enough how this made me feel and how much life was getting better.

One morning, I was wheeling back from a gym session feeling a bit flat because my movement wasn't very good. I struggled for some reason that day to do most things at the gym. At the common room, I saw Melody and wheeled over to her. She was always happy to see me. She smiled, and the whole room lit up. She was working on a puzzle on the lid of a puzzle box. I couldn't see what the puzzle was, and I never did until the day I left. Every time I came across her, she would be alone, doing her puzzle, quite happy in her own thoughts.

'What's up?' she asked as if she already knew the answer.

'Oh, I just had a bad session at the gym. It's like I have started going backwards,' I whinged.

'Don't be hard on yourself. We all have bad days, weeks, even months, but you just have to keep trying. Never give up. Look at me. I just kept going, failing, picking myself up, and fighting on.' She sounded like me, as that was the sort of thing I would say to people.

I had never heard it said back to me before. It sounded good, and something inside of me started to awaken and pull me out of my bad mood.

Kim walked past, and she reminded me that I had to go back to my room to get some rest. I bid goodbye to Melody and let Kim wheel me back to the room.

'What made you stop there?' Kim asked.

'Oh, I was talking to Melody,' I replied.

'I don't think I have met Melody,' she said.

Before long, I was being lifted by a hoist under the watchful eye of Kim and an HCA who Kim had recruited to help her. I was lowered on to my bed where I fell asleep and stayed until Paul's ex-wife Sarah and his daughter Jasmine came to visit. They had become regular visitors. Though Sarah and I didn't always get along in the past, she visited me every Monday, and we soon became good friends. Jasmine was my godchild, and I loved her very much. She was as sweet as apple pie, and I was always pleased to see her.

One exhausted afternoon, I was woken from sleep by two nurses kissing me gently on my cheek. They then sat on the windowsill at the end of my bed and quietly chatted away. The kisses, though gentle, had woken me up, and I was a bit confused. I kept my eyes closed and pretended to be asleep. As I thought I had been woken up by nurses, I wondered, *Why did a nurse kiss me? And why are they chatting at the end of my bed?*

I decided to ask the nurses to leave, as I was trying to get some sleep. I turned, and that was when I saw Sarah and Jasmine. They had turned up for their visit, and instead of waking me up, they'd just given me a kiss. I was pleased to see them and secretly glad to have been woken up. In my dream, I had been running from the new phantom, who was even more hateful and fearful than Doctor Dark. Unlike Dark, the new phantom had no form, just a presence of fear and anger and the intention of forcing me to take my own life for the sake of everyone else. It was a terrible feeling; and unlike with Dark, I couldn't argue with the new phantom, as he just wasn't there, just his dark presence. I truly felt that, if the phantom caught me, then I wouldn't have the willpower to stop him. Given the pain, the disability, and the uncertainty of a bleak future, I wouldn't need much of a push. Sarah and Jasmine were more than a distraction; they were welcome visitors.

That night's meal was all right, much better than what had been served in the JRH. The food here was edible and even tasty sometimes. As the meal ended, the nurses started handing out the meds. A nurse came around and handed out meds to everyone at my table except me. As I didn't get mine, I asked the nurse for mine. She told me another nurse was looking after me. I was later wheeled off to bed without being given my meds, regardless of my protests. The situation made me panic and anxious because one of those pills was an antibiotic, which, James had said, was keeping me alive by fighting off further infection and I must always have it.

That night as I lay in bed, all I could think about was not having taken my meds. I complained to the nurse about the necessity of my meds. She told me she would look into it, but somehow, I didn't believe her. I was right, as I didn't see the meds or the nurse again that evening. By quarter to nine at night, the night staff was on duty, and my nurse was Giovanni. When I told him I hadn't been given my meds and why my meds were important, he said he would check the chart. Five minutes later, he returned after checking the chart. He said it was noted that I had refused my medication. I told him that was a blatant lie and clearly someone was just covering their tracks. I told him I didn't care who had done what, but I needed my meds. He just turned his back on me and said that was the problem of the last shift's staff and had nothing to do with him. That got my blood pumping, and I conjured up images of the old giant. Just for a moment, the old Mike emerged, encouraged by Melody's words, 'You have to fight.' As Giovanni turned his back on me and started to walk away, I growled, 'Giovanni, I'm not taking this shit. Get me your supervisor now, or all you will hear all night is my call bell.'

'All right, whatever,' he grumbled back at me in his Italian accent and with a wave of his hand. I waited for ten minutes and then rang the bell.

Giovanni came in. 'What is it?' he asked in his Italian accent.

'You know very well what it is.' I wasn't taking prisoners. 'Get me your supervisor, Giovanni. I mean it.'

He turned and said, 'We will see.'

About half an hour later, a young nurse dressed in dark blue entered the room and said, 'Hello, Mr Fisher. How can I help you?' Her dark blue uniform indicated she was a senior nurse, but it irritated me that she didn't introduce herself. Dark blue dress or not, introducing oneself was common courtesy.

I replied, 'Are you the senior nurse of the night shift?'

'Yes,' she answered, almost frustrated that I didn't know her designation even though I had never met her before.

In the mood for a fight, I replied, 'Have you been informed of my issue?'

'Yes, and I have checked the chart. It says you refused your pills.'

'OK,' I said, 'but here's the thing. *I don't care what the chart says*. At best, it's an error. At worst, it's a lie. Either one of your nurses made a genuine mistake, or they lied to cover up an even bigger mistake. Besides, I don't care what it was or how you deal with it. Please I'm begging you to find my file, and you will see it says I must have the antibiotics. And if, for whatever reason I do not, then my neurosurgeon James must be contacted and told why.'

She tried to stare me down, but I wasn't having any of it. She just turned and said, 'I will have a look.'

I didn't see her again, but Giovanni came in an hour later with my meds. I checked them, partly to make sure the antibiotic was there, partly to piss Giovanni off, which it did. He left the room without uttering a word, and I finally took the meds.

The next morning, the head nurse came into my room and started to prepare me for my shower, which wasn't the norm. I told her about the incident the night before, though I left out names.

Under her breath, the nurse asked quietly, 'Do you mean Giovanni?'

At that point, I got the feeling from the tone of her voice that Giovanni's attitude was well known to them.

'Yes,' I replied.

At my response, she tutted and lifted her head in annoyance. Nothing more was ever said to me, but from that day on, Giovanni worked in a different ward. The next day, the two Polish HCAs were back, and they took the best care of me and were willing to even confront the head nurse about my care. Again, I don't remember their names. We always had a three-way conversation, and they made everything light, even me having a toilet accident in the shower room. They made me feel like a human being again, and they were good company. Things were starting to look up.

The following Monday, I was visited by Sarah and Jasmine. We chatted for hours, which was unusual for me. I enjoyed their visits, which never stopped all the while I was in the hospital.

When they left, and the door was shut behind them, the room became instantly dark. I saw Doctor Dark standing at the door. He walked towards me, stopped, and looked behind him. He didn't have to utter a word, as it was evident the dark phantom was not far away. I could feel him, and so could Doctor Dark.

Doctor Dark sat at the end of my bed and asked, 'Well, how you getting on?

'OK,' I answered.

'You never were a good liar. You're uncertain and fearful of something, so you summoned me up,' he said mockingly.

Trying to hide my fear, I replied, 'I never ever summoned you. You just turned up.'

'Your fear summoned me,' he snorted.

'Fuck, you piss me off!' I growled.

Bursting into laughter, he threw his head back. He then looked me straight in the eye and said, 'Of course, I do. How do you think you conquered your fear? All that we are is a result of what we have thought. We grow fearless by walking into our fears. Well, you grew fearless by facing your fears through me. Then becoming angry with what I showed you was possible in the dark of life. You got angry and walked straight into your fears almost to spite me.'

He was right. I had dealt with my fear and desperation by proving to him that I wasn't going to take his road. He had been with me since I was in the army. One day, I'd been desperate and scared, and he'd showed up, mocking me. That had made me get up and face the fear head-on. *Can this be true? Has Doctor Dark actually been a help in my life and not a weight, as I have always believed?*

Doctor Dark turned his head around quickly, his eyes fixed on the door. I could feel it too, the phantom, his presence getting closer. Doctor Dark turned his head, and as he did, the paint on his face cracked and slowly peeled away.

'There is a darkness greater than me here. I have always been the fear of your present, whereas he is the fear of your past and future. He's ten times stronger than me, and he has no form to argue with. Keep away from him, for he will be the end of us both. Remember, it is during our darkest moments that we must focus on the light. If being in this place makes you scared, then focus on the light. That flame will keep him at bay. Find what it was that created me in the first place and destroy it, because he has it now, and it's feeding his anger.' Doctor Dark seemed scared.

I had never seen him like that, and it freaked me out. As I shouted for the nurse, the room returned to normal. When the nurse came running in, I just looked at her blankly, as I didn't know what to say. She helped me get into a comfortable position and made the bed around me. As she did, I looked out the now open door and saw Melody wheeling past. As she smiled at me, the whole room seemed to light up. Then she winked at me, and my head fell back on the pillow, and I fell asleep not long after.

I started concentrating on the light as Doctor Dark had told me. This time, I didn't concentrate on the light of my family, but on the light of my disability or what wasn't disabled, and the light in me did grow. My spinal injury was severe, rendering me a quadriplegic, yet thankfully I had my arms. Though I couldn't lift them above my head, and my hands hardly worked, at first sight, I presented as a paraplegic, which seemed to be a positive to me. Every emotion including fear was a choice. Every belief was a choice. I could either let this battle beat me or choose to be the one in control. I shifted all my energy to being positive and no longer being afraid, but I had to find what it was that had created Doctor Dark in the first place. And that would be a dark road for sure. Each battle had to be dealt with one at a time. Today's battle was dinner.

Meals were a battle. I struggled to get food on the fork and then the fork to my mouth without the food falling off. Once it got there, my face was so paralysed that the food would fall out again. I was glad about the plastic apron. I no longer thought I was becoming like the other patients, as I was already one of those poor people; and I had been from the day I'd been wheeled in. That was a dark moment. I looked up and stared into the distance with no thoughts, just a feeling of despair. As I did, positivity lost the battle that day. I caught the eye of Melody, who was having her tea at another table and listening to people's conversation. She smiled at me, and she broke my stare. Now, all I could do was smile back.

The OCE offered many different therapies. I took various sessions with various therapists, from speech therapy to learning how to eat again. I even got to have a session with an ophthalmologist called Caroline who worked for Dr Ellis. She introduced me to different strategies to help me live with double vision. She told me I could see normally again with patches and such. From that day on, I wore an eye patch, and all the doubling I saw focused into one image. Though I looked like a pirate, the patch helped me to see the world straight again. The kaleidoscope vision that made up my whole world was not back to normal. Wearing the eyepatch was difficult at first. I had to keep trying to keep it straight, the constant feeling of a strap around my head was irritating, and an odd glance in a mirror or a reflection in a window would make me realise how silly I looked. I kept telling myself that perception was everything. If I stopped perceiving it to be bad, then it wouldn't be. However, in the future, I would scare small children, who thought I was some robotic pirate on wheels, and they would burst into tears. So, I changed to a pair of frosted glasses.

Two old friends, with whom I used to work, visited me at the OCE. They did their best to maintain a neutral exterior, but I could see in their eyes that they were thinking, *This isn't the Fish I knew.* Fish had been my nickname during my consultant days. They were right. The high and mighty management consultant was gone, and the hard-faced man they knew now could barely even smile. They stayed long enough to come across as polite and then left. The visit would have normally made the darkness come, but all I could think was, *They made an effort to come and see me, which was good of them, and I appreciate it.*

All I tried to focus on was the light. Every time I felt the dark coming, I would talk to Melody, and she would always look away from her puzzle and cheer me up. She seemed to always be in the common room, sitting in the same place, happy with her endeavours, which was always solving the jigsaw. She seemed like she was in no rush to finish it. When I told her about my phantom, her reaction was strange. She seemed to know him. She tapped me on the hand and said, 'Don't you worry about him. He's just filled with hate and his own self-importance. Keeping focusing on the positive, and you will be fine.'

Then, she said something that seemed to answer the confusion in my soul. 'In my experience, hate has never dispelled hate. Only love dispels hate. This is the way it is, ancient and inexhaustible; peace comes from within. No one has a secret box of peace hidden away, so don't seek it. Let go of the hot coal of anger and hate. Whatever happened in the past is the past. Your physical state now is just something that happened. The person who holds on to the hot coal only gets hurt. Don't worry about your phantom's hatred, anger, and fear. We all have them. You're lucky you can see them. It means you can confront them, whereas most people are just reacting to the phantoms inside of them and not the external world.' With that, she wheeled off down the corridor.

Her words were very familiar. I know I had come across them before, perhaps heard them in a different context or read them in a book. It didn't matter. What she said was like a song. After that encounter, I still enjoyed her company, but I couldn't shake a feeling of suspicion or not help question my reality.

Letting go of my anger was difficult, as all I could think was my failing body was all someone else's fault. Dropping the burning coal wasn't as easy as Melody had put it. I knew I had some work to do. Keeping calm while at the OCE wasn't an easy task, as many patients were angry about their situation and liked to take out their frustration on others, all very passive aggressive, of course, nothing overt or obvious.

For instance, a lady would deliberately park herself and her wheelchair right in the middle of the corridor so that you would have to ask her to move out of the way. When asked to move, she would give you a dirty look; whisper something under her breath, something to this day I couldn't make out; and then shout, 'Oh, you want me to move, do you? I'll just get out your way, shall I?'. Then, she would move very slowly, only to take up her blocking position again for the next victim.

She wasn't the only such character there. Another lady used to stream music on the computer so loudly you couldn't hear what the people next to you were saying. Another chap would go around and around in his electric wheelchair and then suddenly stop, pick someone, and stare at them for the rest of the night. Another guy who had no inhibitions due to brain damage would shout and swear for no apparent reason. When asked the time, he would say, 'It's 3 fucking p.m. The thing I found most annoying was that he would spontaneously shout, 'Arsenal, Arsenal, fucking Arsenal.'

Then there was this bloke who couldn't sit up in his wheelchair and speak properly. He would give everyone a look as if to say, *Don't talk to me. Just leave me alone.* If you tried to talk to him, he would hardly respond because he couldn't. He would spend days in his room just facing the wall in his wheelchair, happy with his own company, which, of course, was me.

One day, when Paul came to visit, he found me in my room quietly facing a blank wall, all by myself. He probably thought I was just spending my days staring at a wall without talking to anyone. The truth was I was meditating. In Zen practice, you face a wall to help you not get distracted by the outside world. Paul didn't know that then. But in the future, he would take up meditation and understand. At that moment, he probably thought I was off my rocker. He quickly moved me, even though I didn't want to move, and we had a cup of coffee together in the common room. When he left, he called Amanda all worried and told her I needed to get out of my room more.

For a short time, the Arsenal supporter from the neuro ward was in the bed opposite me. At the time, we all thought he was a goner; here he was. As much as he irritated me, I was glad he had made it this far. As soon as he arrived, I recognised him, but it took my damaged brain some time to work out who he actually was. However, by the time I had worked it out, I decided not to make the effort to engage with him due to the swearing and the not-so-occasional shouts about Arsenal. He would resort to his rants and shouts mainly when everyone sat together eating, though it was generally whenever the mood took him. He became universally disliked by everyone, and he only made my burning coal hotter.

I started to get used to the passive-aggressive behaviour and just kept to myself. I broke my hermit existence only to talk to Melody, who would always fill me with hope. I confided in her once and told her what I saw when I looked in the mirror. I would never forget her response. 'What you think, you become. It's you who's putting all that ugliness into your image. It's only you looking in the mirror. What you feel, you attract. And others will see you how you do. What you imagine, you create, Mike.'

When I told her I was scared of what people would think of me, she just smiled, put her hand on mine, and said, 'Not everyone will understand your journey. That's OK. You're here to live your life, not to make everyone understand.'

She then pulled herself closer, which normally would have made me feel uncomfortable. However, with Melody, I was quite at ease, maybe because of her advancing years or the fact she only ever wanted to pass on messages of hope. She'd once told me, 'Miracles start when you give as much energy to your dreams as you do to your fears.'

She never told me not to worry; rather, she just pointed out it was up to me to create and believe in my own future. She was a ray of sunshine in a very dark place.

Whenever Amanda visited me, I would beg her to get me out of the OCE. I just wanted to be with those with spinal injury and not brain damage. Amanda was supportive as always. She never said a word to me, as she never wanted to get my hopes up. But behind the scenes, she was ringing up nurses to help, getting pissed off when they didn't, and calling up spinal rehabilitation hospitals until she found me a place. I didn't know she had succeeded, as she kept it from me, just in case it fell through. She was tired on her feet, still managing everything and juggling everyone's needs. Somehow, she kept a positive outlook and never accepted no for an answer.

The boys had become used to their visits to the hospital to see me. Now that I was no longer dying, they started to get bored and restless and even not want to come. They can't be blamed, as they were just kids. As they were secure in the belief that their father was going to live, they had better things to do. Amanda wasn't having any of it. The boys had to come to see their father, regardless of whether they liked it. She would then deal with the fallout from them later. But that was later, and right now, she was getting me moved.

The OCE was a fabulous rehabilitation centre with some very committed staff and doctors. I will always be indebted to Kim for helping me move again. The same was the case with the various speech and eating therapists who helped me talk again and, of course, the two Polish lads who helped me feel like a man again. However, the centre just wasn't for me because I was insecure and didn't want to see myself in the poor patients.

My last night at the centre was a hectic one. Though I didn't know it was my last night, I certainly prayed for it. A new patient had arrived, a middle-aged man with brain damage. He was another shouter. For some reason, the young Arsenal fan took a disliking towards him, likely because he shouted at him to be quiet. It was something we all wanted to do but never did. Perhaps we never had the courage to do so. The corridor blocker also took a disliking towards him. And at one point, she and the Arsenal fan both turned on the poor chap. The exchange got a bit heated, and they were all told to go to bed like naughty children. A nurse appeared, and each one was pushed off in his or her wheelchair back to his or her room. But that wasn't the end of it. Owing to some great ward management, all three ended up in bedrooms next to each other and opposite me. The Arsenal fan started shouting at the new guy, who shouted back in response. The corridor blocker then shouted at them both to shut up, and they both turned on her. The Arsenal fan started back on the new guy for shouting at the corridor blocker, and it went on.

At this point, I was in bed, and I was in complete disbelief of what was happening. All I could do was say to myself, *Get me out of here.* The shouting went on for hours, with staff coming in now and again to tell them all to shut up, which they would do. But ten minutes later, they would start again. Sleep seemed an impossibility, as even the loudest of music couldn't drown out their voices. I was close to tears, thinking I'd have to put up with the cacophony for the rest of my life. Like in *One Flew Over the Cuckoo's Nest*, I felt I needed a big Native American to suffocate me and then escape through a window. I banged my head against the pillow in despair as the shouting got louder and louder. A nurse would turn up, and they would all shut up. As soon as the nurse was gone, they would start again. I found myself starting to laugh, which eventually turned into a hysterical laughter. Instead of wallowing in despair, I started to create my own reality; and from that moment, it just all felt laughable. I laughed myself to sleep, giggling all the way.

The next morning, I woke up to the two Polish guys coming into my room. They announced, 'Right, Michael, it's time to get up. It's a very sad day today. You're leaving us and going to another hospital.'

'Which one?' I asked.

The head guy looked at his file and said, 'Stoke Mandeville. It's a good place. That's where all the UK Paralympic teams train.'

Though I said nothing back, all I could think was, *Thank god! I'm getting out of here.*

The lads got me ready for the last time and bid their goodbyes. Before my transport arrived, I had the time to go and say goodbye to all those I had gotten to know, after of course asking the corridor blocker if I could pass, which had become a game by then.

The last person to say goodbye to me was Melody. I found her sitting at her regular table. She looked like an angel, with her long white hair and her slender slightly age-bent figure and, of course, her jigsaw. As I approached her slowly in my chair, she turned her head, and her face lit up with a smile that would make anyone's day. She took my hand and said, 'I hear you're leaving us.'

'Yes, I'm off to Stoke Mandeville.'

'Oh, I hear that's a great hospital. You're very lucky.'

'Yes, I am,' I replied, thinking, *Yeah, how come I'm this lucky? What has changed to make them send me elsewhere?* I looked her in the eyes and said, 'Thank you. You really helped me at a difficult time. I'm going to miss you.'

She just smiled even more and said, 'Mike, don't dwell on the past, and don't have too many expectations of the future. Concentrate on yourself from here and now. You will have many battles to fight, and I know you will face them all down. But remember to conquer yourself because that will be your greatest victory.' She inched closer to me and squeezed my hand harder. 'Peace comes from inside. No matter how broken your body is, don't seek it without. No matter how many failures you face, the only real failure in life is not to be true to oneself. We are what we think. All that we are arises with our thoughts. With our thoughts, we make the world. What we think, we become.'

I gave her a gentle kiss on her cheek. As I moved away, I looked down and saw her jigsaw, which was nearly finished. 'Wow! You only have one piece left, and you're finished,' I said.

She handed me the last piece and said, 'Here, you finish it for me.'

I took the piece but argued, 'No, it's the last piece of your jigsaw.'

She replied, 'This isn't my jigsaw. I don't have any compulsion to be the person who finishes it.'

So, I placed the piece into the jigsaw for her. I waited for a feeling of satisfaction to wash over me, but it never came.

She looked at me and said, 'It only matters when the jigsaw you complete is yours.'

I told her I was honoured to have met her and that she'd made a big difference in my life.

At that point, two ambulance personnel arrived and asked, 'Where's Mike Fisher?'

'Here,' I called out.

Next minute, I was being transferred into the ambulance chair. A nurse came running with my meds and all my belongings in several plastic bags and said, 'I'm coming with you.'

Quite unceremoniously, we all then left. Once the ambulance started moving, my phone rang, and it was Amanda. I told her all about my transfer, and I was on my way. She didn't sound surprised at all. So, I asked her, 'Why do I feel you have had a hand in this?'

She laughed and said, 'Of course, I have. How do you think it all happened? I didn't want to say anything until I knew for sure.

'I thought as much. What's this place like?'

'It's a proper spinal rehabilitation unit. I had a choice of either Stoke Mandeville or Salisbury. I choose Stoke Mandeville because it was closer to Oxford and the neuro unit.'

'Thank you, darling. I can't express how happy I am that I'm leaving that house of poor souls.' I then told her all about my last night at the OCE and the three shouting three stoogess. I enhanced the story, as I always did, to make it funnier than it really was.

She laughed and said, 'Thank God you're out of there.'

CHAPTER 12

THE ISLAND IN THE STORM

I arrived at Stoke Mandeville and was taken to the triage room. The paramedics left me in the care of a nurse, who checked my vitals and swabbed me for MRSA. She said she was waiting for a bed on the ward where all new patients went, and she would be back soon. A few hours later, another nurse entered the room. She was dressed in a dark blue nurse uniform and wore an old-fashioned nurse hat. At the time, I found her appearance odd, but her overall look was like that of one of those old matrons of yesteryears, which strangely put me at ease.

'Oh, I'm sorry,' she said. 'I didn't know someone was in here. I have just come for some supplies. Do you mind if I look around? I won't be long.'

'No, not at all,' I replied. 'Please take as long as you need.'

'Thank you,' she said. She pottered about, looking through different drawers and cupboards. Her face was stern and determined. She was a middle-aged woman in her early fifties. Her face was weathered with crow's feet on each eye. She was slim, but middle age was starting to spread about her. I wouldn't have called her either attractive or unattractive. Perhaps, the best way to describe her was as mumsy. Her lip was curled up on one side as she was clearly concentrating. 'Oh, here it is!' she said, looking all chuffed with herself. Now more relaxed, she approached me and asked, 'Now what's your name?'

'Mike.'

'I'm Sally. What's your story?'

I told her about the entire ordeal, from the abscess, sepsis, meningitis, coma, arachnoiditis, and paralysis to the OCE. She listened intently with a sympathetic but determined look on her face.

Talking about my ordeal to someone new was liberating, and I felt like I had gotten a load off my chest.

She had a motherly air about her. She picked up my left hand and held it very gently yet hard enough not to drop it. She looked me in the eyes and said, 'Well, this is where people come to get better and go home, but you have to want to get better, and you will have to fight all the way.'

When I told her about my goal to get back to work, she replied, 'Never stop fighting until you reach your goal, and even then, keep fighting. Even when you're home, your life from now on will be a fight, and what you need to do is tell yourself that you're up for it.' Her thumb gently rubbed my hand as she said, 'Life is always about how much you can take. For us all, we all keep fighting in our own way. I like to think a person defines themselves by how much they can suffer and yet keep moving forward'. She smiled at me and added, 'I have to go now, but I will be around. Come and have a chat with me anytime you want, and remember this place is all about going home.' She put my hand down gently and left the room.

As soon as the door closed behind her, the room turned black, and the smell of burning flesh overpowered everything. *Oh, here we go.* I expected Doctor Dark this time, but it was the new phantom. It had no form, just a large patch of darkness that was darker than the dark it came from. As it approached my right side, my heart filled with fear. I felt like I was falling as depression and hopelessness washed over me. I wanted to cry out for Amanda, but I felt what seemed a cold hand covering my mouth. The despair was so bad that I wanted to beg for my own death. Suddenly, I could smell the distinctive smell of Doctor Dark's bad breath.

'Get a load of Sally strong nickers?' he growled while sitting on a stool to the left.

I quickly diverted my gaze from the phantom and looked around to my left. There he was, Doctor Dark, in the same crumbled-up mix and match of clothing and his face still covered in white cracking paint.

'What?' I asked in a shaking voice.

'Old Miss Fighting Pants! I mean "we all keep fighting in our own way". What a load of drivel!'

'I thought she was inspirational, and she made me feel expectant of the future, which is something I haven't felt in a long while,' I replied to him, almost angry that he was criticising her.

'That's because you don't listen,' he growled back at me. 'Fighting is just suffering, and suffering is just the reality that no one can escape from. But you know that; I've told you already.'

'What do you want me to do?' I shouted back.

'Remember,' he growled, 'we create a world of suffering for ourselves and others, simply by believing there is an eternal self. You still think you're eternal. To escape your suffering, you must let go of attachment and realise nothing is permanent, and even you will turn to dust.'

'So, what are you saying? Don't fight?' I asked, almost sarcastically.

'Of course you have to fight. You are still part of this universe. But if you want to stop suffering, then you must reach a level where you feel no loss and no attachment, as nothing is permanent, and everything turns to dust. Fear comes from the inability to see the universe in the right way. That's why that's still here,' he said, gesturing with his head over to my right side and the phantom.

Doctor Dark made me so angry that I had totally forgotten about the new phantom. I looked around quickly and saw the deep darkness. I heard a loud scream, but no words were spoken. However, I was sure I heard or felt someone say, 'You never let go.' With that, the darkness in the room lifted. I looked to my left, and Doctor Dark was gone as quickly as he had appeared.

At this point, Amanda arrived. She never missed an operation or a move. She was always there, keeping me strong.

A doctor finally came in and checked me and read the ops chart. I was told I was going to St David Ward, but first I must spend some time in the high-dependency ward; that way, they could keep an eye on me. By that time, a nurse and a porter had arrived, and I was moved into a ward of people of different ages and different severities of spinal cord injury. I was wheeled straight up to a window bay, which was a blessing and a curse. The summer was hot, giving me a great summer view. No one was on my left, and I didn't feel boxed in. In the summer sunshine, I felt just a little normal for once. However, I was sweating buckets because of the heat. As I looked around, I noticed everyone in the ward was suffering, but they all had fans, which seemed to give them relief. When a nurse came to check my vitals, I asked her if I could have one. She said she would try and find me one and went off to look. It was such a lovely day. I didn't want to moan, especially in England, as a hot summer's day was rare. Though the heat gave a great summer vista out of the window, in my view, it was so intense that it was dangerous. *Typical*, I thought. It was the first great summer in years, and I was stuck in the hospital.

The old man opposite me had two fans, and he looked quite comfortable. Shamefully, I thought about asking Amanda to go and get me one, but I didn't. She wouldn't do that to a soul anyway, though she would go and have a sharp word with the nurse about getting me one, which of course she did. Suddenly, I had two fans, one brand new and still in the box, which stayed in the box and followed me around from ward to ward for the rest of my stay in the hospital. I couldn't tell you how many times we offered it up to people, and they turned us down. No one probably wanted to take it out the box and set it up. That was certainly how we felt, especially because they provided another fan that was old but still did the job and cooled me down. So, we never bothered with the one in the box either.

The next day, a nurse came up to me with a valve and asked if I could open and close it with my paralysed hands. I opened and closed it but very slowly and shakily.

'Keep practising,' he said. 'You will need that for your catheter.'

At that point, I didn't quite know what he meant, but I kept practising.

Two days later, I was given a wheelchair and told to make my way to St David Ward. Paul was with me, and after being given instructions, the two of us set off. I pushed the wheelchair forward as Kim had shown me, but Paul helped on the slopes.

We took the outside route and came across some young lads in wheelchairs smoking cigarettes next to a six-foot sign saying, 'This is a nonsmoking area.' The sun was shining, and they looked quite happy. If I smoked, I would have joined them. Having seen me sitting in my wheelchair and staring at a wall while I was at the OCE, Paul had probably decided I needed to make friends. Bless him, he introduced me to those around like a parent helping a child to meet their classmates on the first day of school. The encounter was awkward because they were teenagers, and

I was a forty-five-year-old man. They offered their greetings as teenagers did. One of the teenagers was on my new ward. He was probably called Mark. He had broken his back messing about while riding a motorbike. I came across quite a few young people there with a similar story.

We moved on and went through the entrance of the spinal unit. The building was under refurbishment, making the entrance literally a construction site. Six months later when I left the facility, they had just finished the work, and the lobby finally looked crisp and fresh. The sight did not give Paul much confidence, and he complained bitterly. When we reached the ward, things were looking up, as it looked and felt like a hospital should.

After being given a bed and bay number, I was sent to settle in. We found the bed in a bay of six people. Unhappy about having gotten the middle bed, I turned to Paul and said, 'No more rooms to myself.'

Paul replied, 'That's a good thing, as you can get to know people now and stop sitting in a room, staring at a wall'. He still didn't realise what I had been doing was meditating. He just saw his little brother on his own, facing a wall.

He was right, of course. I made some good friends on that ward. And for the next few months, we all had a good laugh, which made us feel human again.

In the bed opposite mine, a man of similar age was unpacking. His girlfriend and kids were there, helping. Paul introduced himself first and then explained I was his brother, and my name was Mike. The chap's name was Colin, and he was in the Army Signals and attached to the Paras. He had jumped from a plane at a thousand feet while on a mass exercise drop. His parachute didn't open, and he fell straight to the ground. I didn't know how he survived. With leg bones sticking out of him, they rushed him off to hospital, and here he was. He was only here for a short stay, as he was waiting for a place at the army's rehabilitation centre Headley Court. During his time at Stoke Mandeville, he and I became good friends. My brief stint in the army probably helped us form a connection. We both thought in the same way and both had a can-do attitude and a dark sense of humour, as all soldiers did.

That night, the ward bay started to fill up. Next to me and next to the window was Steve, a nice chap. He struggled a bit with Colin and my army sense of humour, but he was up for it and made a good bay buddy. He had fallen off a ladder while welding on a farm and broken his back. Next to Colin and opposite Steve, near the window, was a young man of about twenty called Tristen. He had dived into a garden pop-up swimming pool and broken his neck. He had already been in the hospital for a year, nearly two, and now he was back because of pressure sores. At first, Tristen had little to do with us oldies, but he came around and turned out to be a funny guy. To Colin's right was Mark, the young man I had met earlier that day. He was always off with his teenage mates from other wards and made little effort with his bay mates. On my left was a chap in his sixties. He was a good laugh and had a sarcastic sense of humour. He could take the piss-taking and give back as good as he got. He was always grumbling about things, which allowed Colin and I to take the piss, and we would all have a good laugh. We forged a friendship like soldiers in a war. We would be there for each other; we would laugh at adversity together, and we would bond like war buddies.

Early one morning, I took myself off to the gym for some scheduled physiotherapy. I had to join a queue of two people, one of whom was Mark from my ward bay. He and the other chap were talking and laughing about shitting themselves and the situation they found themselves in. I was never one to find toilet humour funny, even in the army, so I never joined in. I just sat there quietly smiling, not really listening.

Mark turned to me and said, 'In the end, we all talk about shitting ourselves no matter who we are.'

He was right. Toilet conversation became a pastime for everyone. Being paralyzed meant everything under the paralysed line didn't work— bladder, lungs, bowel, and cock, which came as a bit of a shock to me. When paralysed, your bowel would run your life. Some days, it would work, some days it would all get stuck inside you, and some days you wouldn't be able to move without shitting. If I had a good bowel day, then I would have a good day. If I had a bad bowel day, then I would be miserable all day. All dignity would be lost, and my deep desire to be treated as someone of value would be wrenched from me. No matter well or not, I was treated by the nursing staff the same no matter what.. I had to give up my own self-value and want for respect. At six every morning, we were all woken up and made to lie on our sides while two gel suppositories were unceremoniously inserted into our backsides. We were all left for thirty minutes, during which all sort of noises came from behind our drawn curtains as we all struggled with our bowel movements. If you hadn't gone in thirty minutes, a nurse would appear, stick their finger up your bum, and waggle it about until you defecated.

In the future, whenever Paul came to visit and eyed up a female nurse, I would simply say, 'She's had her finger up my arse.' My comment would stop Paul in his tracks. He would stop eyeing them, laugh, and move on— enough said. Of course, I could only hope for a female nurse at that point, as they had smaller fingers and a lighter touch than the male nurses. That daily routine was, in itself, a trauma. Though medically necessary, it was a horror. If you didn't defecate in the morning, you couldn't be sure of an accident-free day, and, more importantly, you couldn't go to hydrotherapy, for fear of an accident in the pool. Hydrotherapy was the best release we all had because they would float us and help us swim like we weren't paralysed. On bad bowel days, it was a pleasure ruined, as, for the whole hour, all I could think about was having an accident in the pool.

Life in Stoke Mandeville became routine. The days were full of therapy—hands, arms, legs, speech, eating, you name it. My consultant was Dr Lock, who was a nice old chap. But all he ever did was prescribe me stronger dosages of hard drugs for the pain. I couldn't blame him, as everyone had different levels of broken backs, which they treated for the individual level of injury. I had arachnoiditis, a rare disease of the central nervous system that slowly and surely was crushing my spine. No one knew how to treat it and didn't want to mess with it because of its progressive nature.

I had a physiotherapist called Lyndsey, a Scottish lady with a caring nature. She helped me a great deal and showed me how to move on a bed past what Kim had had time to show me during my short stint at the OCE. She taught me how to transfer and how to stretch so that I could start moving with less help from others. Every day, we would spend an hour in the gym. My session was always after lunch. We would all line up like schoolchildren in wheelchairs waiting for the physiotherapists to return from their break and open the door. Everyone wheeled to the bit of equipment they wanted to use and then wait to be helped on to it. I would just seek out Lyndsey and trust myself to her treatment plan. That was not to say I didn't try different equipment. I enjoyed the functional electric stimulation (FES) bike that sent electric shocks through my legs and made the muscles move the peddles of a bike around.

I also enjoyed standing. We would wheel up to a wooden frame, grab on, and pull ourselves up with the assistant physiotherapist tightening a belt behind us. This allowed us to stand on our legs as if we were able. By doing this, we would strengthen our bones and increase blood circulation in our legs.

Around the five stands all lined up together, we would stand, having a chat and a laugh. I would meet people I wouldn't normally meet because they were on other wards. I learnt a great deal by listening to people's stories. Despite different backgrounds and upbringings, everyone had similar hopes and fears. I learnt about Islam from a Muslim inmate and Hinduism from an Indian woman. I always left time for me to stand. Sometimes, I would spend the whole session standing and chatting. I hadn't for a long time just chatted with people outside of a work environment. My conversations in the past always followed a structure, and people's answers needed to fit into one of my predetermined boxes, as I would be thinking all the time about my preconceived ideas of living structure. Now as I was learning about people and listening to them, thought became the conversation itself, with two people of completely different backgrounds but with a shared disability and pain exploring a topic together.

Every day, I saw in my mind's eye the oneness of us all. On the one hand, I would feel euphoric; on the other hand, I would feel angry, as I thought of all the people in this world creating division from nothing but misplaced, misguided, and ignorant words. I would consider the deaths, the human suffering, and the money poured into killing people who were just different, especially when children were starving. It made me ashamed of having joined the war machine and played my small part. Before, I would tell stories of my time in the army. After the experience, I stopped and saw no need to do so.

However, do not take this as a criticism of our armed forces in anyway. I have simplified conflict here. Would you have let Hitler just have his way? Could you allow Bosnia to happen again? How do you stop the blood diamond wars and child soldiers in Sierra Leone? It's not the soldiers who make the decisions of war, and without those brave men and women willing to make the ultimate sacrifice, this country and others would be undefended. My problem was with myself, not the brave.

For the first two months, I really came along and got stronger and stronger, yet something was missing in me. I was driven, but I didn't have the energy to fight. My energy levels dropped, and I started accepting things as the norm and no longer something to fight for. The giant in me had gone and, with him, the sense of fight. I tried to remember his anger and energy when faced with a hurdle in life and simulate it now so that I could put more into my recovery, but my fight seemed to have gone.

This came to a head on one dreary afternoon when I was wasting the session, pretending to pull ropes to strengthen my arms. I heard a voice next to me. 'For fuck's sake, mate, why don't you just go back to bed and suck on your thumb?'

At first, I ignored it and thought two people were having an argument next to me, but I could feel someone to my side staring straight at me. He had black shorts on, along with black socks, black trainers, and a maroon T-shirt. He was in his late forties or early fifties and had a rough exterior. He looked like he had been around the block a few times. He was strenuously lifting a medicine ball and doing lunges.

I looked right at him and said, 'I'm sorry. Are you talking to me, pal?'

'Who the fuck else would I be talking to?'

At the time, several different people were around us, all of whom seemed to be just going through the motions like I was. I didn't know why he had singled me out. I later suspected he was ex-army and spotted me to be of his kind as well. When I left the army, I was told, 'Once a soldier, always a soldier.' Strangely enough, even now whenever I came in contact with ex-soldiers, we would both recognise each other and instantly hit it off.

'You've lost it, mate. You need some fire in that belly.'

'I'm a tetraplegic, mate. Nothing is how it seems,' I replied with a snigger.

'Your arms look all right to me.'

'That's because I have been pulling the resistance bands tied to my bed. It has kept my arms going,' I retorted.

He just looked at me and asked, 'What happened to that determination then?'

Becoming weary of him, I just answered, 'Fuck off, mate!'

He looked away in disgust and carried on with his exercises, which were quite impressive. He then stopped and picked up his towel and walked out. As he did, his injury became apparent. He walked with a pronounced limp. Clearly, he had done some major damage, and I assumed he had fought his way back to health. At that moment, I instantly regretted what I had said to him. I had thought he had some minor injury and was trying to tell me I didn't have enough fight in me, someone who was a tetraplegic.

The next day, when I entered the gym, there he was lifting a medicine ball and doing lunges. I rolled up to him and apologised for my rudeness the day before. He instantly stuck his hand out and said, 'I'm Pete.'

I took his hand and replied, 'Mike.'

He looked me in the eye with a stare I could feel in my stomach and said, 'I was tough on you yesterday because, when you first entered this gym, you put your heart and soul into every exercise you did. But now you seem to have given up.'

I was about to go into my long and boring story of slowly dying, paralysis, nerve pain, and heavy drugs, but I could see in his eyes he wasn't interested in my excuses. 'You know you're right. I seem to have lost my fight.'

'Then find it. Your fight isn't out here somewhere. It's inside you, and only you can tap into it. Mike, all animals have at the core of their psyche a fight or flight response. You know, inside there.' He pushed my head with his finger. 'Is there enough fight to win this battle in there?'

I've tried to put away my angry side and be softer in my approach to others. It makes no difference at all. I'm just talking about swapping one facade with another. There's still fight in me, and it may be something I don't want anymore, but it's still there, and it's useful in circumstances like these.

I wheeled myself up to a weights machine, especially made for wheelchair users, and started pumping iron as if, somehow, I were fighting against something. Pete carried on with his lunges and medicine ball lifting and gave me a wry smile. From that day, on I took on every excise like I was fighting a personal war. I would see Pete from time to time. We never really spoke again, but we always acknowledged each other and got on with our fitness training. Strangely, whenever I saw Pete, I was encouraged from inside to work harder. I would freely use the gym in my own way and do as much as possible with the equipment, mainly because Lyndsey would have three patients at a time, each hour of the day, and she had to split her time between us all. She did a great job, and though she found it stressful, she would never show it. She explained my condition to me and really helped me to get home, encouraging me to use as much equipment as possible in our sessions.

In the later days, I found myself in a standing frame, stretching on a plinth, biking with FES, or mainly just free working the weights. I used to watch Lyndsey help the other patients while I was in these various positions and machines. I took Lyndsey's lack of attention towards me a little personally at first and thought I had upset her because I seemed to be left standing or exercising, never learning to walk again. But when I looked back on it with wiser eyes, I realised she would never act in such a way. She only had an hour with three patients, and she probably concentrated on those she could help walk again. We both knew I wasn't going to walk, and there was little need for words between us. I asked her once if I would walk again. She did a muscle test and shook her head, and that was it. Besides, I had gotten to know many people in the hospital. When people she could help started to tentatively walk, I would be happy for them, as I now considered them either friends or people I really wanted to see get better.

Not long after this epiphany, I met a person who brightened my life in the Spinal Injury Unit and made me laugh—something I hadn't done in a long time. Her name was Marine, a lady approaching or in her fifties, with bleached blonde hair and an infectious laugh. The day I met her she was pushing her wheelchair into the gym. At first, she wasn't that happy, but she managed a smile as I said hello and introduced myself. This was all done in passing, as I was leaving the gym and she was entering it for the first time. Marine and I soon became solid friends, and we were always having a laugh together about one thing or another.

The spinal unit had a kitchen in the exit ward, where we would gather in teams to cook so that we could all feel like we could do normal things. Once a day, four different people would come together in a cooking team and make something relatively easy, like fajitas. Marine and I were in the same cooking team, and we would always have a blast. The two of us decided to start a weekly takeaway night, where we would order in Chinese food and have it delivered. Though alcohol was banned from the hospital,

Marine and I would sneak off to the local ASDA across the road, buy some wine, and hide it under the table so that the nurses didn't see it. It started off with just four of us and then ended up with over fifteen people each time. We would ask the nurses to put tables together in the dining area and sit there having a banquet, wine hidden away under the table.

Things were brightening up, and Marine always brought a real funny side to it all. Everything being fleeting, including happiness, I would find every reason to be laughing. Marine made friends all over the place, and even though she had been there less time than me, she knew almost everyone and all types of people. I would enjoy talking to them, and if I didn't like them or if they didn't like me, I would just say goodbye and simply wheel off at an appropriate moment.

One miserable rainy day, I was with Lyndsey. The cold was spreading down my legs, and my backside felt like lead. When I told Lyndsey about how I was feeling, she told me not to worry but to inform the doctor anyway. The doctor didn't say anything, as he wasn't sure as usual. The feeling turned out to be the start of constant nerve pain, which was unbearable at the best of times. It would drive me close to suicide. Each day, I would wake up with my legs in a tangle, my feet feeling like they were being crushed by freezing blocks of ice. My legs felt like they were burning from inside. I would try to move, but my whole body would put the handbrake on, and everything stayed in place no matter how much I tried. Spasms ran up my body, from my feet to my chest. My only release was medication. They tried different drugs and different cocktails of medications on me. Some had no effect whatsoever, while some made me so drowsy I couldn't talk or get out of bed. During one visit to the gym, I started crying uncontrollably, an effect of the drugs, and was sent back to bed. The drugs they had me on just pushed me to the edge. I had them changed immediately and started to refuse meds that I knew took the fight out of me.

Matters were dark and desperate, and I felt like giving up. In an occupational-therapy session on exercising paralysed hands, I was approached by an occupational therapist called Ruth. She asked me if I were willing to try a new FES therapy to help my face find its position again. The therapy had never been tried in Stoke Mandeville, and only the Salisbury Spinal Unit had tested it, so no promises could be made, and significant risks were involved. I almost bit her hand off. She told me I had to be patient because she needed to get all the papers on it from Salisbury, write a case for it, get my consultant to sign it off, and then get the chief spinal consultant to sign it off. I thanked her about a hundred times and went on my way, excited about this future treatment. I would have to wait a long time, so my excitement turned into anxiety, as I kept giving my mind to the future and not the here and now.

At first, I didn't see Doctor Dark or the phantom, not even the dark of the other world. I just felt low and desperate. The feeling of loneliness forced me to withdraw into myself. No matter how many visitors Geoff organised, I would shake with the fear of being alone. I felt like a prisoner of war waiting to be tortured over and over. I had come a long way physically and emotionally, only to be crushed against the rocks of reality and left to waste away in a stormy bay of pain. My consultant didn't really know how to treat arachnoiditis, as it was too rare a disease for most doctors. Being the nice man he was, he didn't want to see me in pain. So, he kept increasing my dosage of gabapentin and baclofen. On their own, they were strong drugs and could space me out; in combination, they sent me to another universe. The drugs didn't really relieve the pain, but I was completely spaced out and just didn't think about it. When I reported this to the consultant, he switched baclofen with dantrolene, another muscle relaxant. This new combination of drugs just left me completely off in the head and drooling. I was terribly depressed. I might have looked the part, but I thought and spoke negatively.

I finally managed to get out of bed and join people in the common room. One evening after waiting for everyone to go to bed, Marine said to me, 'Mike, you must promise me that you will never give up; just keep working through it all. You have to promise.' She was very emotional.

I took her hand and said, 'I promise, but now you have to promise too.'

She did. We had just made a pact to stay alive and keep fighting. Once we had both agreed to keep going, she rolled off to bed, leaving me alone in the common room.

At that moment, Sally, the nurse who I'd met on my first day, came in and said, 'I thought that was you. How're things?'

'All right,' I replied.

She gave me a little smile and said, 'You don't sound all right. Do you want to talk about it?'

Suddenly, it all poured out—being left to stretch because I had no hope of walking, the drugs and their effect, and now my constant nerve pain. Opening up to her was like someone pulling the plug from an old crumbling dam, and suddenly the whole weight of water just gushed out. I talked for what seemed like hours. And during all that time, Sally never once looked bored or anxious to get away. As I talked, I felt like the desperate and depressing darkness that had me in its clasp was slowly letting me go. When I finished, I looked up from a bowed position and expected to see Sally wanting to get away; instead, she just sat there and quietly listened to me.

Once I was finished, she took my hand and said, 'I told you it was going to be hard. You're not ready to give up, are you?'

I replied, 'My fate is decided for me. I'm to suffer in constant pain until I find the courage to die.'

'I don't believe in fate. No one's life is planned out or pans out as they imagine.' In a motherly manner, she said, 'Anything can happen in this life at any time. Do you have faith?'

'No, I have no religion. I believe it's all superstition,' I answered.

'I didn't say religion. I said faith. What do you believe in or what do you think happens when we die?' she asked.

'I don't know. I always just believed we are over as soon as our bodies stop working. Who we are is consciousness created from the mechanical organ, the brain.'

'And now?' she asked softly.

'That's it. I don't know. I'm more comforted now. I have an open mind and don't believe that it's just over. We perceive this world, we perceive the solar system, and we perceive the unperceivable, the universe. Past that, beyond the universe, there's nothing but the unknown, and even scientists don't know. So given how vast all this is and how unthinkable it is, I have started to see that as part of the universe, which is vast and mainly unexplainable. No one knows for sure what it is or how it really works. Some people call upon an unknown God, and they all have different names for it and superstitions of how it works. But I just see the unknown and take comfort that there may be more than we know.'

'And do you think that somehow someone or something has a plan for you?' she enquired.

'No, I don't. I think everything is random. We live an unpredictable life. We're just organisms clinging to the third rock from the sun, waiting to see what's the next thing,' I replied, fully aware of the trap that had just been laid for me.

She then delivered her masterpiece, not with a triumphant blow, but with a motherly pride. 'So, if that's the case, how is it you think your fate is in any way set?'

'I guess I don't really,' I replied.

'So why are you telling me there is?' she asked, still not finished with her masterpiece.

'Because that's how I feel right now,' I replied.

Her response came quickly. 'Be careful of how you feel about the future when all these random things seem to conspire against you. They're just random. Who knows what's next? You, naturally, have a negative perception of life right now, which is expected. But be careful as that perception can form into a mental belief, and you can start to see all life as negative. You will even start to do things and think things that will reinforce your negative view. By that time, it may be too late to change such a belief, and you may see that the only way out is to end your life, whereas if you recognise it now as just a fleeting perception, then you can avoid the negative and start to see what you really want to see. You alter the universe by thought, by thinking something and then taking action, conscious and unconscious. Thereby, you can make your own world. It won't be perfect, and it won't ever fully meet your expectations, mainly because of the random effect of the universe, but you will live inside a world of your own perceptions and mental beliefs.'

'I can't change the fact that I have arachnoiditis, which leaves me in constant pain,' was all I could say.

She looked at me sympathetically and said, 'No, but you can change the meaning of it.'

'You have given me a lot to think about,' I replied.

She squeezed my hand and said, 'You have given yourself something to think about, Mike.' With that, she stood up and quietly left the room, leaving me to ponder what she'd said.

That day on, I kept what Sally had said in my mind, and every time I felt negative, I would work on the positive, and things started to get better again.

On 30 September 2015 was Amanda and my twentieth wedding anniversary, which, luckily, fell on a weekend. In Stoke Mandeville, we could go home at weekends, as long as the doctor in charge gave permission and the local district nurses were informed. From the day I entered the ward, I had told all the staff I was going home on my anniversary weekend no matter what. I didn't care what paperwork was needed. I was going home that weekend. The head nurse, Sue, and I had become good friends, and Sue instructed my allocated nurse to get all the paperwork done. Come the Thursday of that week, I had everything—my permission, my pills. All I was waiting for was for my nurse to write to the district nurse in Swindon and inform them about me being in their care that weekend. The nurse had forgotten to do, it even though I had told him a hundred times. He'd then taken the Friday off, and I was left out in the cold.

I went to Sue and told her, 'I don't care if you haven't done your paperwork. I am going home no matter what.'

She marched off, got my nurse in on his day off, and made him write the letter so that I could go home. Come the weekend, I thanked Sue for her help, gave her a hug, and wheeled off to meet Paul, who was waiting to take me home.

It was a great weekend but a difficult one as well. Amanda had managed to get hold of a bariatric electric profile bed, which I found a little insulting because those were for people who were obese. In the end, I had to bow to her wisdom. As she had noticed me struggling to turn in the hospital beds, she'd had the local occupational therapist source her a bariatric bed. It was wide and allowed me to turn with ease. She had set it up in the living room, which became our bedroom once I returned home. We had no shower or shower/commode chair downstairs, and no way could I get to the bathroom downstairs or the one upstairs. That was when we realised we were woefully unprepared and that life was going to change for us all. The next morning, she helped me go to the toilet while I was still in bed, which she cleaned up without a word. She then washed her hands and cooked us both a breakfast. I handed her the anniversary card and present, which my mother had purchased for me, and she handed me mine. Given what she had already done for me and what she was about to go through, whatever I gave her was inadequate and almost pathetic.

That evening, before we went out, she gave me a thorough bed wash and then dressed me. We struggled to get out of the door and over the stone doorstep, and then with my effort, she got me safely to the front of the car. Applying Lyndsey's training on how to get into a car, I finally got myself in. By this time, I just broke down and sobbed. From the driving seat, Amanda leant across and gave me a long, lingering cuddle.

I didn't have to say anything, as she knew what was wrong, but I did anyway. 'I can't go through all that again, sweetheart. I can't shit in my bed every day, and you can't keep clearing up after me, bed bathing me, and dressing me.'

She whispered in my ear, like there was someone else in the car who could overhear us, 'I don't mind. I still have my Mikey, and I would do anything for you.'

Whispering back, I said, 'No, we have to make some changes to the house. We could turn the downstairs bathroom into a wet room. Then I could do everything there.'

Gently, with no fuss, she said, 'Leave it to me. I will take care of it. Let's go and enjoy our anniversary night out.' Saying no more, she started the car, and we drove off.

About a hundred yards from the house, Amanda sharply applied the brakes. 'Shit,' she shouted, and I quickly looked out. I saw our dog just a few centimetres away from the car running down the road.

As Amanda was about to park up and get straight to checking whether the dog was all right, I reached over, grabbed her arm, and said, 'Do you know what merry hell I have gone through to get here tonight over all that we have just been through? I care about that dog, but it has run away. I love you more than a damn dog. Just drive on like nothing has happened because we're going out for our anniversary by hook or crook.'

Amanda put the car into gear and drove off as if we were fleeing a bank robbery.

'What about Charlie? I love that dog,' she said.

'Don't worry. She will just run to the house with the greyhound, and the dog's owners will bring her back as usual.'

'It's not fair to them. We should get her,' she protested.

'Not on your life,' I replied. 'Phone Myles and ask him to go over and collect her.'

She dialled Myles up immediately.

'Yes, Mum.' said Myles.

'Myles, you need to go and get Charlie.'

'Don't worry, Mum. I'm on my way around now.'

'Do you know where to go?' she asked caringly.

'Yes, Mum. I have been there before.' Myles seemed slightly annoyed.

'Thanks, son. You got this,' I said, hoping we could just move on.

'OK, call me when you're home.' With that, she ended the call.

Just as we were going into the restaurant, Amanda got a call from Myles telling her that he had gotten Charlie and was home.

'He's got her,' she said with a sigh of relief.

'Good lad! Now let's eat,' I said expectantly.

She finally looked a bit relaxed, as both Myles and Charlie were safe. We had a very enjoyable night, though she seemed on edge. I could tell she was still worried about the dog. So, I put the discussion on having a wet room on hold and said, 'Shall we finish up and go home?'

'Yes, please.' She sounded relieved.

So, we finished off dinner and went home to check on the family. They were, of course, just fine. My mother was there, babysitting them for us, which Myles was unaware of. He thought she was just visiting, as he was old enough now to babysit Max, and he would have been insulted if he knew we had asked her to come over and sit them.

That night, Amanda slept on the bed behind the sofa while I slept on my big bariatric bed on the other side of the room. The whole night had been quite low-key for a twentieth wedding anniversary. I didn't mind that, as I just wanted to be with Amanda that night.

When Sunday evening arrived, Amanda took me back to Stoke Mandeville. We brought along the boys, who weren't impressed but went along with it anyway. Once I was tucked up in bed in the ward, she and the boys kissed me goodbye and left me to sleep. The ward had changed around a bit.

Steve, one of my bay buddies from when I'd arrived, had gone to St Joseph Ward, which was the exit ward everyone went to before leaving. I was now in Steve's old bed space by the window. Tristen had gone home to his new specially adapted flat. An elderly chap called Keith had taken his place instead. He was over sixty and had just broken his back. He was a good laugh. We used to challenge each other to physical tasks, such as how many times we could push our wheelchairs up the hill path outside our window. Keith really earned my respect, as he matched me point for point. Colin had moved on to the army rehab centre, and his old bed space had been filled by a young chap in his thirties called Mark. His back had just popped one day as he was bending over, blowing two discs and a vertebra. To his right was an old chap called Michael. He had gone in for routine fusion of the spine, which went wrong, and he woke up in Stoke Mandeville, paralysed. He complained so much that the other patients asked him to shut up, as all of us were in pain. I guess everyone had their stories of how they ended up in Stoke Mandeville. Everyone got a hearing but then you shut up and just got on with it. Finally, next to me was Kevin, who had broken his back in a motorbike crash. When they first brought him down from upstairs, he was out of it, and they had him in traction. I was convinced he wouldn't make it, but I didn't know him then. He was a fighter and had a young family, which clearly gave him something to fight for. Over the coming weeks, he got stronger and stronger and soon joined the takeaway club.

The only constant in life was change, and almost everything had changed overnight. I neither let the past hold on to me nor allowed the future to drag me along. I tried very hard just to stay in the moment, here and now. Though I missed my earlier friends in the ward, my new bay buddies were just as enjoyable this time around. *What really changed then?* My usual way of meeting and making new friends involved showing off so that they would like me. Sad, right? Now I recognised people always judged me in the end, regardless of what I said or did, and there was no point trying to impress people anymore. I was who I was, and they were who they were. That sentiment would be tested in the near future, and I doubted I passed muster.

We were also joined by an East European HCA called Gretta. She was a good laugh and built like a brick house. One didn't mess with Gretta, as she didn't take any shit and wanted things done at the earliest. She liked to take the mickey out of us, and I enjoyed doing the same in return. I used to call her 'the Commandant', as she reminded me of a Russian

Gulag commander. The whole ward enjoyed Gretta's sense of humour, and everyone got as good as they gave.

One day, I probably took it a bit too far, mainly by accident, but afterwards we never saw her in our ward again. I kept a sponge on a stick next to my bed. When I went to the toilet, I would clean my arse with it in the shower, as I couldn't bend down that far to do it myself. The day in question, as I came out of the shower, I saw Gretta rubbing it on her face, saying, 'Look at me! I'm Michael with my girly sponge.'

I coolly pushed myself out of the shower room and simply said, 'I clean my arse with that!'

Screaming, she threw the brush in the air and ran off. The whole ward roared with laughter, and even Michael, the miserable chap, cracked a smile. I honestly didn't think much of it. I found her exit hilarious, not in a cruel way but in a comic way. *Well played, Gretta*, I thought. However, she was genuinely upset because we never saw her in our ward again. I really didn't mean that to happen, and I was telling her the truth.

Stoke Mandeville wasn't having an easy ride of things either. First, five Spanish nurses left all at once over the matter of bed washes. In Spain, the patient's family came in every day and gave the patient a bed bath, and nurses didn't do the bed wash duty. They protested that they shouldn't do it even when they worked for the NHS. The ward management was having none of it and told them they had to do it, as it was part of NHS nurses' role. The trouble was that they were unable to recruit any replacements, so the centre faced severe staff capacity crunch.

The patients complained about the inadequacies in nursing care, so the senior nurses called for a meeting with all the patients. The meeting turned out to be a dogfight, with people tearing off strips of them with little suggestion of how they could do better. I tried my hardest to keep quiet. But as matters got worse, I took over and led the meeting, only allowing people to raise a grievance if they had a suggested solution. At the end of the meeting, I was invited to a meeting with the senior nurses, who had realised I was someone with organisational knowledge. They asked me how to improve things. I told them to be seen and approachable to patients and staff; to allow showers in the morning and evening, as people had different habits; and to create a rota board for patients to show who was doing what activity in a day. The next day, we were provided bits of paper with the head nurses' names and numbers if we wanted a chat with them. They then spent one day working the morning shift. And instead of bringing extra hands to see what it was like, they took over and pissed off all the nurses. I decided I wasn't going to open my mouth again.

A few nights later, a Spanish nurse came up to my bed and asked, 'When did you eat last?'

'Five in the evening,' I replied.

She then hung a sign saying, 'nil by mouth'.

'What the hell?' I asked.

In a very dismissive manner, she said, 'You're having an operation tomorrow to insert a suprapubic catheter.'

'I didn't know about that,' I protested.

'Your consultant should have talked to you about it,' she grunted at me.

'He hasn't said a word about it,' I retorted.

'Well, talk to your consultant. That's all I know.' With that, she turned and walked out as quickly as she could without making her escape obvious.

The next day came, and I was visited by an anaesthetist and a surgeon. I complained to them both about knowing nothing about the operation.

The surgeon said, 'Your consultant should have discussed the matter with you.'

'Well, he didn't,' I retorted.

To make things simpler, he explained, 'A suprapubic catheter is a type of catheter that is left in place. Rather than being inserted through your urethra, the catheter is inserted through a hole in your abdomen and then directly into your bladder. A urinary catheter valve is fitted, which is like a small tap or switch fitted directly to your urinary catheter instead of a drainage bag. You just release the valve every four hours in your case. Any questions?'

'No, I guess that explains it,' I said.

'Right then, just sign the consent form, and we will see you soon.'

I signed it, and he was gone. Later that day, I woke up in bed, feeling light-headed and confused. In my stomach, I felt a pipe with a valve, as promised.

Seeing my distress, Keith, the patient on the opposite bed, said, 'Don't worry, Mike. I have one of those. It's just like going to the toilet normally. I use a piece of cut-off catheter pipe, attach it, and then just pull it up by the side of a loo point, and Bob's your uncle.'

As I reached down to feel the new catheter, I felt something very familiar. It was the valve I had been told to practise opening and closing. Suddenly, the point of the exercise became evident. The valve was an important part of the suprapubic catheter. From day one, they had known I would need one, and it was just a matter of time.

I became aware of my whole body and started to feel all its faults and strengths. I tried my hardest to channel the here and now. My head swam from the anaesthetic, and my mind was pulled away from the concentration of my body. The whole room swayed back and forth like a boat on rough seas. I had just had my twenty-third anaesthetic since I'd first entered hospital, and now it was getting harder to recover from them. It was starting to leave a taste in my mouth and a smell in my nose. My body felt like a testbed for doctors, which wasn't true, as they were only trying to make my life better. I smiled and lay back while considering not the benefit of the suprapubic catheter but the level of my growing predicament.

As I lay in the bed trying to shake off the effects of the anaesthetic, I started to ponder the events of last year and all that had happened to me and my family. I also thought hard about my encounters with Doctor Dark and the people I'd met on the way who talked sense to me, such as Melody, Marine, Pete, and Sally. It then occurred to me that they had not said anything new but only reminded me of what I had learnt before, when studying Eastern philosophy more than ten years ago. Though they'd told me nothing new, they'd certainly awakened something inside me, made me focus on the here and now, and reminded me to take each day as it came. Every time a part of my body failed, I saw it just as the next thing in an existence of random occurrences happening in a nonpermanent state.

My mind still reeling from the effects of the anaesthetic, I focused between Keith and Mark's beds. I saw a black figure there, which I couldn't make out. From the wall, it approached me, waving and shuddering like it was a black cape flapping in a storm. A deafening angry raw came from the dark menace, and my whole body was gripped by fear. In that moment, I glimpsed the little boy again. With one hand pinned to the wall, he tied hard to stretch his whole body out. As he did, his mouth opened as to shout, but I couldn't hear him over the roar of the dark menace, which was creeping ever closer to me. My whole being was pinned to the bed, my fists gripping the sheets as tight as they could. However, my paralysis prevented any real tight grip. I could hear my own blood rushing through my ears as the fear grabbed my heart and started crushing it. There was no human shape like Doctor Dark, just a dark presence creeping up on me as I lay unable to move in so many ways.

CHAPTER 13

REALISATION OF THE DARK

I soon withdrew from the early mindset of being here and now and lost my fight with the dark, as it engulfed my consciousness. The change was an indication of how close I was to the edge of darkness and how easily I could be knocked back into it. The whole room was now covered in darkness. Everyone in the room had faded to being just transparent objects in the night.

'Just ignore him,' ordered a crackling voice.

The smell of cigarettes and bad breath filled the air and sitting next to me was Doctor Dark.

'Why is he here?' I asked.

'Wherever the darkness is, there he is. As I live in the dark, he kind of follows me about, though lately it feels more like I'm following him,' grunted Doctor Dark.

'OK, that's why he's here. Why are you here?'

'Don't ask me, boy! You're the one who calls me from across the dark.'

'I call you? I have never called you. You just haunt me.'

'Is that what you think?' he asked, almost holding back laughter.

'What do you want?' I asked angrily.

'Nothing,' he said indignantly. 'How's your new cock?' he asked, signalling to my suprapubic catheter.

'Fine,' I said. 'I guess it's just the next thing.'

'Bloody hell,' exclaimed Doctor Dark. 'You're finally getting it.'

'Getting what?' I asked.

'This existence is random. Random things just happen to random people in random ways,' he stated with a patronising glee in his voice.

'I know. I have known that for a long time now.' My voice was calm, my argumentative tone gone, realising I had finally started to connect with what he had been telling me.

He crackled with laughter and said, 'At last you see! We create meaning to the point we believe everything should have meaning, and it doesn't. Why do children get cancer? Why is there war? Why do people abuse others? It's all random, but if you look in the right place, you may just be able to glimpse some meaning.'

I found myself joining the conversation with Dark. 'The meaning is simply how we deal with this existence and the random things that happen. Even then, the meaning is seen through the individual's own perception of meaning.'

He gave me the look of an old teacher finally getting through to a difficult student. He paused, took a deep breath and said, 'If you empty your mind of desire, including that of being able-bodied again, you will lose all fear. Work out your own salvation. Do not look to others. No one can save us but ourselves.' As he talked, his face slowly changed into Melody's; his voice became her soft calming tone full of hope. He/she laid her hand on mine and said, 'No one can, and no one may. We ourselves must walk the path. The demon that follows you is of your own making, and in the end, only you can defeat him.'

I looked around and saw the phantom darkness had moved to the end of my bed. I still couldn't see anything but darkness, other than the odd glimpse of the boy, which made me even more afraid.

Doctor Dark clicked his fingers, and I instantly turned back to him. He was back to himself. 'All that we are is the result of what we have thought. All that we fear is a creation of our own making. Even death is not to be feared by one who has lived wisely and seen the universe and our existence for what it is, which is nothing more than the result of atoms crashing into each other.'

'Yet there seems to be more,' I replied.

'Yes, but it can't be comprehended. We make our own meaning or share that of others, which is where religions come into existence,' he responded.

'I'm not religious. I find the practice of following others' perception of meaning to be that of fear.'

He looked at me with an eye of suspicion and said, 'You're closer to the truth than you know.' Then, he suddenly turned into Pete, from the gym, and said, 'There's nothing to be afraid of, except fear itself. But to fight is natural to humans, just like any other beast. You just need to focus yourself at fear itself, and once you conquer it, you may find some peace.'

From Pete, he transformed into Sally. Looking at me softly like a mother reassuring her child, she said, 'Silence the angry phantom with love. Silence the ill-natured phantom with kindness. Silence his lies with truth and show him your generosity. Don't show him your fear. Show him the best of yourself; then the fear will lose its strength. Only you can defeat the phantom.'

From Sally, he turned into Jenny the nurse and then back to himself again. 'I have no power here, but you have all that is needed.'

The realisation brought about by Doctor Dark slapped me in the face hard, as I felt almost stupid for not seeing it. Melody, Sally, Jenny, and Pete were all there for me when I needed someone the most. All along, it had been Doctor Dark helping me across the bridge of pain. He had been there each time I'd felt like giving up.

He suddenly turned into Jenny and simply said, 'This is not the end. It's still just the beginning.'

I thought, *How can this still be the beginning? I have been through so much, yet I'm just starting out.* Little did I know that the real challenge ahead of me was to keep living, and only death was the end.

He looked at me as if he knew what I was thinking and said, 'The real meaning of death is the meaning we attribute to life. Look around. There are others better off than you and others worse off. You are who you are, and it may not seem so, but you're pretty well off. Bring some real meaning to your life, get off autopilot, and see the world for what it is.'

I wondered, *Why did he try so hard for me to kill myself when I was dying?*

I looked hard at him and said, 'What happened to all the talk about killing myself? You seemed to have changed your tune.'

He sniffed and said, 'You did kill yourself. It's you who has changed his tune, and there's no going back now. The Mike Fisher you were when you entered the hospital is dead and gone, and you killed him by bringing

177

yourself to death's doors. Now, all that's left is the true you, and all you have to do is open your eyes and allow your body to take its course without fear. It has less importance than the truth of your reality. Your own mind is the prize.'

I thought for a moment. I felt like Doctor Dark had punched me through my head and placed a jewel in my mind, lighting up the path. Yet all I could see was that the path only led right back to me, here and now. Like a burst of knowledge, it occurred to me that he was right. The old me was dead. I had taken my own life by choosing to be a different man. I thought of all the time I'd spent in the hospital, being cared for by people willing to do any job, no matter how degrading. I thought of people who were a thousand times worse than myself, like the young girl who had been hurt in such a way that she seemed so far gone. When she talked, all she could manage was to sound possessed by some demonic creature. Yes, the shouters who clearly couldn't communicate in any other way. I had been humbled by them all.

I realised the progress of the arachnoiditis in the body and its effects were being made worse by my fear of losing my limbs and no longer being able to be the man I once had been. The fear of loss only manifested by clinging to what is naturally an impermanent world. The giant's suicide wasn't quick. It wasn't some great act of valour or something simple like taking the painkillers to kill myself. It was slow. Each day allowed him to get by unchallenged, uncelebrated, unmissed, and unseen, as he wasn't quite dead yet. I still clung on to him, mainly because I thought he had a lot to do with me still being alive. But this time, I controlled him. For the first time, I engaged in a discussion with Doctor Dark as an equal.

With a smile on my face, I stuttered out, 'You're not my nemesis, are you? Have I misjudged you?'

Doctor Dark looked uncomfortable and quietly spoke as if he had a lump in his throat. 'No one can save us but ourselves. No one can, and no one may. We ourselves must walk the path that leads only to us. All that we are is the result of what we have thought. You created me because you needed to punish yourself over your perceived bad deeds. You fed me with your fear, and I became fear itself. By conquering me, you conquered yourself. You were so focused on me that you missed the real danger.' He gestured to the new phantom. 'I always shielded you from him, but he has always been there. I am your perceived fears, whereas he is fear itself. You conquered me. Now, you must conquer him. When you do, you will have reached nirvana, a state of calm and pure life. Until that day, he will always be there. Don't fear him, as that feeds him. Don't engage with him, as he will trick you. Don't ignore him, or he will sneak up on you. Just be aware of him and remember he is as much you as I was.'

Before I could question him on what he had just said, he stood up and took a deep breath. As he did, all the paint on his face cracked and fell off. I was astonished, as I looked up and saw the real Doctor Dark: He was me! Just an older version. He/I was standing there, in those black trousers, the big black coat and the grey hoody with the hood up, holding the top hat in his/my hand. When he looked at me, his face turned into Melody's again and then Pete's and then Sally's and then Jenny's. He transformed into me, put on his top hat, and said, 'You don't need me anymore.' With that, he walked straight into the middle of the new phantom's darkness and disappeared into it, almost like he was sacrificing himself to help save me from the dark phantom.

I could swear I heard his voice from the darkness say, 'Stop, stop. Do not speak. The ultimate truth is not even to think.'

The phantom reacted violently to Doctor Dark entering it. The waving sheets turned into a tornado, the darkness twisting and turning as if it were fighting something. The whole mass seemed to shrink, and its grip of fear on me loosened. Doctor Dark had diminished its power somehow. Or had it been me? I had created Doctor Dark, who was a version of me. I finally realised it wasn't Doctor Dark I was afraid of. I was afraid of the menace of fear behind him, which he'd shielded me from. I had misjudged him and seen him as the dark in my soul, when, all along, he was always trying to help me to see the truth. Even when I believed he was trying to persuade me to kill myself, he was just showing me my own resolve while trying to get me to let go of the old me. He made me face my fears and regrets, and by making me angry, he made me fight against the dark.

The darkness lifted, and I could see the ward again. Dressed, Keith lay on his bed reading the paper, which he had folded into quarters. Kevin lay on his bed next to me, talking to his family. Mark was in his wheelchair and looked like he was getting ready to go out for the day. The old man Michael was slumped in his wheelchair as usual, looking beaten.

I pondered what had just happened in the other world. *What did it mean? How did I misunderstand Dark all this time? Could it be that all this time I was just afraid of myself? Is Dark just a manifestation of all my fears? What did it mean when Dark walked into the new phantom?* I had plenty of time to consider those questions, as I still had to spend another three months in the hospital before I could finally go home for good. Those three months were much the same and uneventful, which I was grateful for in a way, as it meant I had finally stabilised, physically at least. For some reason, my early life kept troubling me.

I'd left state education with a big fat zero, so I'd wrapped a blanket of failure around myself for strange comfort. I'd started working in a local department store in Exeter for £27.50 a week under the government Youth Training Scheme (YTS). Working the job was better than being unemployed and slowly wasting away at home. To me, not having a job was like having my soul sucked out through my nostrils, an unpleasant experience that lay waste to my identity.

I finally left home at seventeen, scared, excited, and anticipating the future. I first worked as a warehouseman while living with Paul and his first wife, Denise. I slept on a sofa bed in their living room and lived out of a luggage bag. It was a cold and damp one-bedroom basement flat in Cheltenham. Still wrapped in my blanket of failure, I had given up on any real hope of a life that included a family, career, house, and car. The building we lived in had a drug dealer of its own, and he lived in the flat next door. When the world was concealed in darkness, his flat attracted strange stick figures, who hovered like zombies outside our window. In reality, they were trying to gather the courage to go and ask for drugs. Some lost souls arrived at our door by mistake. We always answered as if we had no idea what they wanted, being as friendly as we could, but the encounter was always short.

Some thanked us and apologised for bothering us, while others just gave us a dirty look and walked away. One night, the police raided the flat, all dressed in their riot gear and looking to smash a few heads. Thankfully, they kicked down the right door, and everyone came peacefully, a bit of an anticlimax, but it did give us something to watch that night, and no one got hurt.

Rob, our cousin, also went to college and lived in Cheltenham. He rented a bedsit that he shared with his two pet albino rats. At the time, Rob and I became good friends, and we did the most insane things to pass the time. He had a unique outlook on life, and he was one of the kindest and most giving of people I had the honour to call a friend. Rob and I would talk for hours about life, the world, the human condition, and so much more, conversations that still go on today in our fifties. Rob helped me on my journey, always keeping things real for me, and I would like to think I did the same for him.

Paul, Rob, and I would spend our free hours drinking until we ran out of money and stash of grass and then head home to the basement flat. It had fewer redeeming features, other than a large open fireplace in the living room, which served both as a heat source and an occasional distraction. With nothing to do, Paul, Rob and I would put the fire out with plant sprayers set to jet, something that allowed the invisible dimension of time to pass unseen and unfelt. There's a whole backstory about those days, but I won't delve into that now. You would be forgiven for thinking they were pitiful times, but when I look back, they were full of freedom and fun.

Later, Paul and his wife chose to stay in Cheltenham; Rob moved back home to Swindon; and I moved to Torquay, working as a trainee deputy manager of a men's fashion shop. Torquay had its own fruits to offer—great weekends on the beach; exciting night life; and well, that was it really. At first, I shared a flat with two herberts I met at work. They were from Wolverhampton and seemed to be running away from something, but I never knew what. They were obsessed with sex and tried every day and night to find some poor lost soul, devoid of self-respect, who would agree to come home with them. They would search the Torquay pubs and clubs until they got lucky. It wasn't an ideal way to exist for me, apart from witnessing their obsession, and they didn't know what it meant to live in a habitable state. Though we lived as three so-called mates, I always felt like the third wheel. They had a strange relationship, like two brothers with a dark secret.

I eventually became tired of their bullshit and found a little haven of my own. My new flat shared a large balcony over a garage with one other flat, where a middle-aged lady lived with her thirty-year-old girlfriend. The three of us instantly became friends, and I attended the odd party.

Big butch women would, by proximity, pin me to the wall and interrogate me as to the legitimacy of my heterosexuality. They meant no harm, and all interrogations ended in hysterics for everyone. Since then, I have always been comfortable with my sexuality, simply because I was so thoroughly interrogated that I was 99 percent certain of not being gay, not 100 percent, as I have never tried it, so I'll never know. One thing was for sure—it did not matter to me if one was lesbian, gay, bisexual, or transgender. During my time at the flat, I met many people of many persuasions, all great company and no different to anyone else, perhaps a bit more colourful, sweet, caring, and fun. It was a time when I was never judged, never belittled, and never tolerated, just accepted. How I miss those days!

When I was eighteen, I was promoted to a store manager and was transferred to Exmouth. Not bad, I thought, for a guy who had left school with nothing. I dare not dream any higher than that as I snuggled into my blanket of failure. I was bored stiff; I felt that retail really wasn't for me; and I was living with my parents again, just outside Exeter, which felt like I was going backwards in life, not forwards. So, in the vain hope of creating some form of meaning, I joined the army for a complete change in life. I had no idea what I was doing, and it just seemed the only way out. The army was very challenging and gave me a fantastic life and a place of good friends. The training staff and others tried to break me down and build me in their image. But unconsciously, I seemed to fight their attempts, which made me not exactly the most disciplined of soldiers, though they proved successful in casting away my blanket of failure for good and replacing it with a straight back, a never-say-never attitude, and a uniform. I might have been a bit of a wild card, but in a fight, I was always there for my friends and unit. It was also a dark place where one minute I was filled with terror and the next full of laughter. When I look back on those days, I see them through a kaleidoscope with such a mixture of experiences and feelings—making good friends; learning to parachute, abseil, and drive a heavy-goods vehicle; serving overseas postings; undertaking NATO exercises; performing countless inspections; being put in army jail; walking the streets of Belfast in the twilight of the troubles; and, of course, drinking.

When I joined the army, I had sworn I would never go back to retail. But when I did leave, after a failed attempt at being a lorry driver, I ended back in retail, selling shampoo and suntan lotion in a drugstore. After my life in the army and all I had done, it was a personally humiliating experience. However, I pacified myself that a job was a job and that it was better than having my soul sucked out through my nostrils.

I was back in Cheltenham and living again with Paul, now with his second wife, Sarah. The three of us lived in a little three-bed semi-detached house with a lodger friend called Lee. Paul and I had bought the house together with the inheritance our father left us. It was a modern house situated in a cul-de-sac called Huxley Way. For some reason, which I forgot now, we called it Huxley Pig.

Through Lee, I met Amanda on 9 September 1994. We were living together by October 1994, engaged in November 1994, and married on 30 September 1995—dates that are fixed in my mind. It would be fair to say ours was a lightning romance. We've been together now for over twenty-four years, and though we drive each other nuts, our love for each other only gets stronger and stronger.

After getting married, Amanda and I moved around a bit, chasing my different jobs. With my blanket of failure ripped from me in the army, I now grabbed every possibility. I gained a business qualification and started on a new route up the career cliff. From an in-house recruitment manager, I rose quickly to managing director of a small human resources consulting agency to an independent consultant to a managing consultant working for a large outsourcing business.

We ended up living in Swindon in a three-bed 1930s semi with our two boys, Myles and Max. It was like watching myself in two angled mirrors. They were both completely different, but at the same time, they were like me in many ways. I often felt like a ghost watching myself as a child, realising for the first time why I had struggled so much in life. Wishing them a different existence than mine, I tried to guide them to avoid the same painful pitfalls I'd made. But like me, they had their own minds and grew up in their ways. As I reached forty-four, I'd finally managed to carve a life that gave me meaning. The life wasn't one of work and ambition; instead, meaning for me was my family. I had ascended to a suitable plateau on the career cliff, but by then, I hardly cared. I had become a reasonably successful management consultant, yet it held little real meaning to me, other than a means to support my family.

I do regret my father not being alive long enough to witness my success. He left us behind on this plane of perceived existence randomly, far too early, and I still miss him today. My mother has been and is a kind soul who has always showered us all with love and affection. When my father died, she clucked over us, almost putting aside her own grief to ensure we were all right.

One of my oldest memories, if it can be trusted, is from when my father was still at base camp on the career cliff, and resultantly he was out selling insurance every night. So, my mother would light the fire; pull the sofa close; and Paul, she, and I would watch TV. She got up early every day and lit the fire to make sure the room was warm when we got up for school. To me, her only fault was that she was so utterly convinced of God that she couldn't help sharing her loves and, mainly, fears with us. The situation got worse when Geoff and then Paul left home, leaving me to blunt the oncoming storm of her fear of the apocalypse on my own. I just shrugged it off and kept playing, but I did start my life convinced of a God, with a hint of distress at the thought of a possible apocalypse.

It's not a bad story of someone's life, but the bit I left out was that my best friend, Paul, and I drifted into different lives. I guess we both just grew up. However, when we do get together, we still laugh loads. I was too busy at work to carry on like we used to and unfortunately too busy to make new friends. Though I only have a few friends—and I can count them on my hands, including Paul and Rob—they are good friends indeed. Back in our thirties, Paul, Rob, and I used to go to Glastonbury Festival, where I met some of Rob's mates with whom I became lifelong friends. Unfortunately, they all lived around different parts of the country, so we all used to get together in the Beehive Pub in Swindon once every Christmas, to see each other and catch up. We might have been distant, but when we did meet up, it meant a lot.

It's hard to spot where the hinges came off. I might have been the big thing at work, or at least I thought I was, but somewhere along the way, my mind derailed; I suddenly found myself trapped under a tonne of different personas and a giant facade, of which I had lost control. On the outside, I kept things together. But on the inside, the dark forces were getting out of control and wreaking havoc through the recesses of my mind. Dark phantoms appeared, and my dark thoughts started to feel real. It's at this point I decided to add to the madness and start looking for the real me in all this confusion. A journey that ends with a tentative truth about the self.

The starting point of this journey was breaking the shackles of oppression forced upon me in the form of religion. In my early years, I considered death a judgement on life. I believed in an invisible God, guarding angels, and an imagined idea that all my actions were being monitored and judged. It was like a self-imposed fascist state. Thankfully, I found the strength to break away and bring all that to an end; and the so-called wisdom of an ancient book filled with dogma and stories written by superstitious men have no hold on me anymore. However, ironically, I felt lost and a little alone with no belief system or God to pray to. This led to me becoming spiritually lost. I missed the comfort of blaming someone or some being for letting life happen to me and then wanting to beg that being for life. So, I concentrated my mind and became fascinated by how modern psychology and thousands of years of Middle Eastern thinking, not religious thinking, Zen thinking, were starting to merge.

The new freedom of thought allowed me to explore everything, including different belief systems that cannot be ignored. If a considerable number of people hold such a perception, by that thought alone a god or gods are created, and they become wrapped in dogma for protection. I didn't always think like this. As I discarded the shackles of religion, I became dismissive of the belief of a god, a single consciousness controlling everything. People of religion just seemed deluded to me. Such thinking changed, and when it did, it was like getting hit in the head by a baseball bat.

The hard part of the journey for me was exploring the dark side of life. I witnessed darkness close up, and not always in the army. It confounded me how someone could torture or beat another half to death, freely kill innocent people, rape, hide weapons under babies' mattresses, and be devoid of a sense of conscience while causing endless misery. My only reasoning was not an encouraging one. I believe that all of us have both good and bad in us, and we define our lives by choosing to be good or bad consciously or unconsciously. Ironically, both sides can use religion to justify their actions. Some blow themselves and others up, while many wage war to impose their belief on others, which is all such a lack of enlightenment.

185

As I have said, I am no saint. I have always lived my life believing that everyone I meet and every circumstance I face have something to teach me. I don't believe in mistakes. I believe every situation, good or bad, is an opportunity for people to learn. I think that people who make repeated mistakes are either those refusing to learn or listen or lacking basic intelligence. I'm quick to judge and don't suffer fools gladly. To me, if you yield results, you're worthy; and if you bring me problems without even a starting solution, then you're wasting my time. Such an attitude didn't mean I was cruel to people, just fearless when it came to separating the wheat from the chaff. I worked in the field of project management, where results were the currency of our existence. Now you start to see who I am and judge me as you will. As you read on, you will learn more. Who I am, who I was, who I might be is a changing feast full of bitter food and spoilt wine.

CHAPTER 14

THE WAY HOME

Ruth came back to me and told me I had been approved for the new FES therapy to help my face find its position again. She reminded me it had never been done in Stoke Mandeville before and only the Salisbury Spinal Unit had tested it, so no promises could be made, and significant risks were involved. I was still keen, so we got started at the earliest. The treatment took about a year, and I had to carry on with the treatment while I was at home, but eventually it worked. Now you would never know my faced had once drooped. Ruth was my occupational therapist heroine.

Another notable event in those last three months of hospital stay was facing the first challenge to my calming mind. The challenge came across in the form of a new patient. As I can't recall his name, I'm going to call him Wayne. The first I saw of him was in the gym. He entered in his wheelchair and circled the whole place a few times, almost trying to make people take notice of his arrival. He had tattoos all over his arms, and he clearly liked showing them off, as he always wore a vest revealing his arms. I liked tattoos and had two of them myself, but one of Wayne's tattoos was that of a naked woman with large breasts. I couldn't help thinking that, in this supposedly enlightened era, objectifying women in a tattoo was really an unenlightened thing to do. He appeared to be in his early thirties, which ruled out the possibility of him having been too young and had the tattoo done in a bygone era when objectifying women had been considered normal. He also always wore a flat cap inside, obviously to make a statement, all right.

That day, after I finished my session at the gym, I was helped back into my wheelchair, and I headed back to the ward. That was when Wayne and I crossed paths for the first time. Neither I nor he made any attempts to say hello. However, he looked annoyed that I just ignored him. Pretty much every encounter between Wayne and I went that way.

I never really knew how much I got to him until we had a takeaway night, to which, as with everyone, he was invited. As I was laughing and joking with some friends, Wayne from across the room asked, 'Mike, when are you leaving?'

His tone was so passive aggressive that the whole room just went quiet while everyone waited for my response. He wanted it to be known that he didn't like me.

I answered in a jovial voice, 'Oh, I wish I knew, mate. I have been here almost a year now, and they don't seem any closer to sending me home; hopefully some time at the end of this year.'

He gave absolutely no response, another passive-aggressive sign. However, I knew straight away he was trying to rile me up, and I just wasn't going to join in. I carried on talking and joking with the rest of the people next to me.

Later, a bunch of people came and found me and said, 'What was his problem?'

'Don't know, don't care.'

The next encounter I had with him was when I volunteered to collect the takeaway menu. I wanted to rise above any pettiness, so I went to find him to ask him what he wanted for food. He was at his bed space, and I opened the conversation: 'Er ... Wayne, there you are!' I made sure my tone was upbeat and friendly.

His response was passive aggressive again. This time, with no others to see, he was more upfront and showed genuine annoyance that I had the audacity to seek him out.

'What?' he growled back at me.

I ignored his tone and jovially asked, 'Are you joining us tonight? If so, what do want to eat? We are all having a chicken takeaway tonight. Are you in?'

'Yes,' he growled again through gritted teeth.

'OK, then we need your order and money please,' I calmly replied.

He snatched the menu from me and said, 'I'll have the chicken burger.'

'Fine,' I replied. 'We will need your money now please'.

My response seemed to have angered him, and he thrust the menu back at me, saying, 'I will give it to you later.'

'That's fine,' I said, trying my hardest not to lose it.

Amid the hostile exchange, I forgot, consciously or subconsciously, to inform him that we had changed the venue to the café, as the common room had been booked for something else. That night, he arrived in the café after what seemed like a long search for us. He handed over his money to me with no words, no thank you, just childish silence. When the order arrived, we realised his burger had been left out. I really didn't do it deliberately; in fact, I had used Marine's help to order the food, as my speech still wasn't good enough to make a long order. It was a genuine mistake. As much as I didn't like him, I did now feel responsible, so I phoned the restaurant and got his order sent over. When it arrived, he just took it, sat on a table on his own, and ate it. Earlier that day, I had noticed that he had found a small group of Wayne worshipers, none of whom were there that night. Rather than mix and make new friends, as we all did, he chose to sit and eat alone. I was hoping to build a bridge with him that night, but instead, I just made things worse by accident. I decided to leave him bend kept out of his way for the remainder of my time there.

I did have one more encounter with him. As I rolled through the hospital's circle junction, which always had stalls around it, I saw him chatting with a girl on one of the stands. I ignored the encounter and rolled by, well aware he was giving me the hairy eyeball as I passed. When I passed him, I heard him say, 'Wanker,' under his breath.

The old me—the six-foot fully able ex-squaddie—would have turned around, gone back, and repeatedly punched him to the ground. At that moment and even now, I couldn't punch my way out of a wet paper bag. Yet I hope that wasn't the reason I ignored his comment, and I hope that now my mind is calmer, and peace is my approach to all situations.

It was a shame really because this one person made what was a great vibe into an uneasy atmosphere, at least for a small few. It could have been a shared misperception of the situation. But then that was life, and there was always someone who spoiled a good day. I could feel the darkness behind me almost egging me on to react negatively to him. Holding on to anything like that where anger prevailed, I just burned myself. When I ignored him, the darkness almost crackled with anger in my mind. It never spoke to me. I never knew what it wanted, but it knew when to keep its distance and when to get up close in my face. I was starting to reach some level of peace, but I was still dogged by the darkness. Adding this part of the story in the book is probably me still holding on to some burning embers of the hot coal, or maybe it's me free of it. I don't mind discussing it, and you decide for yourself. Maybe we all have our phantoms bear. If we do, then we certainly have created our own nemeses. I always knew that the phantom was just the other side of me that I no longer wanted or gave any credence to.

Yet there was something else; something kept my mind partly in the other world. When Doctor Dark had walked into the darkness and my new phantom with him, I caught another glimpse of that small boy being held back, as he tried to free himself and shout something to me across the dark. As I passed Wayne, I focused my eyes straight ahead. As I did, I saw the boy again in front of me, still trying to shout out to me. I tried to ignore the vision, but his presence felt overwhelming. Little did I know that he carried the most important message of all. So the story continues.

I was finally moved to St Joseph Ward, as my carers or Stoke Mandeville's staff were starting to think about my release. I was in a two-man bay, and I only had to deal with one person's noises. Wayne had left weeks ago, so the pleasant equilibrium of patients looking out for each other returned. I forget yet again the name of my bay buddy, so I will call him Andy. He was a nice chap, a big fella, both length and width ways, and he had been in a wheelchair for over sixteen years. He was in the hospital to recover from his hurting leg. People with spinal injury needed to maintain all aspects of their health, as the smallest ailment could turn into a giant problem and even kill us.

Andy used to give me advice on being disabled—availing benefits, using wheelchair, and circumventing accessibility issues. The wheelchair I'd been lent by the hospital turned out to be the wheelchair he'd had when he was in sixteen years ago. When he'd had it, it had been brand new, which just showed that the hospital was making do with old equipment. Andy and I got on well, and I enjoyed his wisdom and advice.

Marine had bagged herself a private room on the same ward, and we had a good laugh when we saw each other. Strangely, being on the same ward but in two completely different parts seemed more of a barrier than being in two completely different wards. It never mattered, as there was plenty of fun to be had with Andy and others also waiting to go home.

At that time, I was becoming more and more forgetful of names. One night, as I was talking to Andy, I totally forgot where I was, who Andy was, and what we were discussing. The curtain between us was drawn, so he never saw me, but I lay there, confused and bewildered. He finally said goodnight. As soon as he turned the light off, I remembered who he was and where we were. I wished him goodnight and then lay in bed, wondering what had happened. I feared the arachnoiditis was affecting my brain or all the brain surgery I had was taking a negative effect or the shunts were failing.

I checked this out with Dr Lock the next day. He told me not to worry; it was very unlikely I had any of those problems. This, of course, turned out to be untrue.

Just when I started recovering normal speech, or at least I thought I was, I found myself grappling with another problem. I kept forgetting words, and instead of taking the conversation forward, I stopped and thought, *What the hell is that word?*' People just switched off and moved on to another conversation, which just confused me and made me forget entirely what it was I had been thinking that hard about.

I ignored it all and decided I wasn't rocking the boat, as I was going home soon. As I lay in bed, the memory of who I was and where I was became lost in a thick cloud that would have images of reality flash past as if strong winds were blowing them away. All I could envision was right there and right then; the past had become a giant black hole. As I lay there, trying desperately to remember, I saw the small boy in the corner of the room. The room was small, and that was as close as I had ever been to him. Yet every time I focused on him, he slipped into the distance of the other world. I closed my eyes and I heard something being shouted at me, but all I could understand was 'this is' and nothing else. My mind then grasped who I was again and where I was. By this time, I was worn out, and my eyes closed by themselves as I faded off to sleep.

A couple of days later, I was approached by my case manager. As I don't remember her name, I will call her Dawn. She was a lovely lady, very helpful and always willing to chat. She had a mumsy quality about her like Sally, which made me wonder whether she was real. My doubts were quenched when I learnt others had her as a case manager as well, and they all spoke very highly of her. So, I could trust she was real. She asked me to join her in her office, and we spoke candidly. She asked me if I had any carers lined up for when I left. I told her I couldn't afford it and the council wouldn't help me, as I had over £28,000 in the bank (a lifetime of saving). She asked me if I had applied for Community Health Care (CHC) funding from the NHS. She said it wasn't means tested, but the application was very rigorous and long, which meant not many people got it. She said to me that I was very disabled, and given all my new challenges, I may qualify for CHC funding for having care at home. She saw in my eyes that I was not keen, so she reminded me that I wasn't a paraplegic but a tetraplegic, which meant not only would I struggle at home but my family would also. It was a harsh message but true.

Together, over a period of meetings, we completed the application form. She asked me the questions, which were mainly about my ability to do tasks, like brush my teeth, eat food, and other such things. Dawn then completed the form for me with the answers I should give, given my condition. She also recruited Amanda. And when I went home at weekends, we continued our quest to finish the application, which was a small book rather than an easy-to-complete form. Once it was completed, I had to have a panel interview with Dawn; Lyndsey, my physiotherapist; and my psychologist, Mark. Amanda was allowed in to give me support. We all crammed into a small meeting room. I was in the middle and surrounded by the panel, and Amanda sat behind me. Being crammed into the small room was intimidating, but it was just the only room available for us. We went through the form one question at a time. I had to discuss each question in terms of my disability, and I was scored against each activity on a scale ranging from low dependency to high dependency. The interview went well, and I was as honest as I could be, as I saw no other way. Now and again, I said I was capable of doing things, but then Amanda quizzed me on it, and my attempt to be more positive about my ability collapsed, and I had to rethink my answer.

Finally nearing the end of the interview, we got on to the last set of questions—psychology. I wanted to be honest, so I told them the truth about my depression, about the dark phantom that I imagined stalking me, and how often I considered suicide. I told them of my many plans to kill myself and how the love of my family always stopped me. By the time, I had finished, I could hear Amanda weeping behind me. Both Dawn and Lyndsey had red eyes and were fighting back tears. As Amanda and I were about to leave, Dawn held my arm and said, 'If you need to talk, then you know where I am.'

Amanda spent half an hour holding me and making me promise that I wouldn't kill myself. I promised and told her I'd had no intention of ever telling her, but I had to be honest with them. Amanda and I packed my bags to go home for the weekend and then made our way to her car.

Then, Lyndsey came running out and said, 'This is a great time to practise your car transfers, Mike. Can we try?'

I looked at Amanda and asked, 'Shall we?'

'Yes, of course,' she said excitedly.

We then spent about an hour getting me in and out of Amanda's car. Lyndsey showed Amanda as much as she coached me what to do and when I needed help. When we had finally finished, I was exhausted. As I sat in the car recovering, Lyndsey and Amanda chatted on. Lyndsey's face revealed that she was keen to get away, probably because she was busy.

I called out, 'Amanda, I'm really tired now. We need to go. Plus, I'm sure Lyndsey has things to take care of.'

'I do actually,' Lyndsey replied in an apologetic tone.

Amanda immediately broke off the conversation and apologised for keeping her. She got in the driving seat and started the engine while Lyndsey closed my door for me.

Amanda and I held hands all the way home, the only words spoken were a brief exchange initiated by me.

'You're the greatest. Thank you.'

'No, I'm not. You are,' she said.

And that was it.

That was all that was needed. We knew how much we meant to each other. After all, she and the boys were my reason for staying alive, and she knew that now and understood my anguish.

193

The following week was much the same as most. I had now managed to bag the private room next to Marine, and the only downside to it was that Marine was a big George Michael and Wham fan. I had nothing against either, but she played their songs constantly, almost on a loop. One morning, she had set her morning alarm to 'Wake Me Up Before You Go-Go'. It woke me up, and I lay there as it played on a loop over and over again until I couldn't take it anymore. In the end, I had to call a nurse and ask her to check on Marine and just mention that I was going a little mad next door. When the nurse went in, she was still asleep. She then woke up and turned it off. We had a good laugh about it later, no hard feelings.

Opposite us, in another private room was a bodybuilder called Ed. He had fallen asleep on a balcony while on holiday and rolled off, breaking his back. He was a massive guy, full of muscles, but he also had a very quiet and unassuming personality. The three of us would have a good laugh together, making my remaining days in hospital more bearable.

Later that week, Dawn came and found me to say I had scored enough points on my CHC application to be taken forward to the next step. She told me, however, not to hold my breath, as I had scored just enough points, and usually the application took weeks to come back. So, I didn't give it much thought. As the week went by, I routinely went to different therapy sessions.

Come Wednesday of the following week, Dawn came to my bedside. She was ecstatic and in a hurry to talk to me. I hadn't even gotten up. She popped her head around the curtain and said, 'Mike, you're not going to believe this! You've been accepted for CHC funding. I have never known it to go through that quickly. Your file must have really moved them, and your complex condition swayed them. I can't believe things came through that quickly.'

Trying to reciprocate the enthusiasm, I said, 'That's great news! What's next then?'

'Oh, that might be some time, but I will try and move it along.'

Dawn's head disappeared from around the curtain, and off she went.

I immediately phoned Amanda and told her the good news.

She said, 'Right. I will get on to the social worker and start the process.'

'OK,' I said, not really believing anything would happen.

Of course, I was wrong. On Friday, Amanda picked me up early for a meeting with my new social worker. By that afternoon, we all sat around the small table that Amanda had managed to get in the utility room.

The social worker was very upbeat and told us that she had read my file and had spoken to CHC. They had asked her to proceed. She then said, 'I know the perfect agency for you. They are my favourite and very good.'

Amanda and I were so happy to be getting help that we just went along and didn't bother to check what we were told. It turned out her favourite agency was about to win a bid process and take over care in the area. This wouldn't matter, but they ran old people's homes and provided basic care. We thought they would know how to deal with spinal injury patients, but it wasn't the case.

The following weekend, we met the agency representative with the social worker and the CHC representative. We all squeezed around the little table and had our meeting. Amanda and I were very naive, and when they offered 24/7 care, we refused. Amanda told them she could do the evening shift. So we agreed for care to be provided between 8:30 a.m. and 6 p.m. Looking back with wiser eyes, it was a massive mistake, which we will cover later. We then agreed that the carers would come to Stoke Mandeville and spend a day being trained on me personally. The arrangement sounded great, and I returned to Stoke Mandeville on Monday feeling relieved.

The care training day wasn't scheduled for a few weeks, so I just got on with my routine. Over the weeks to come, I watched other patients on St Joseph Ward having their care training days. Smart-looking people, always roughly the same age as their patients, would come in and train with their patients. I listened to the carers as they were quizzed on their qualifications to care for tetraplegics, and they all made a very good impression on me. I was looking forward to meeting my new carers.

The agency called to say they couldn't send carers the weekend we had agreed and gave a new date, which was one day after I was due to leave. As my bed was to be filled in St Joseph Ward on my due to leave date, I had to be moved back to the main St David Ward for my care training day. I didn't care, as it was only for one night. The day after was my care training; then I was going home for good.

195

The next day came, and I couldn't wait to meet my carers. I really hoped I would be as impressed by them as I had been with other patients' carers. Amanda arrived too, all excited because, whatever happened today, I was going home for good. Eventually, my new carers turned up—two ladies, both over sixty, one was wearing a well-worn tunic (who I will call Diana) while the other looked like she had just been dragged through a bush (who I will call Sandra). Their agency boss had also turned up, squeezed into a dress two sizes too small for her stature.

When I asked their qualifications to care for tetraplegics, they seemed shocked by the question. The agency boss tried to answer for them, saying they had both been in care for over twenty years. When I probed, it turned out that they had both been working in elderly home care and neither had any experience with tetraplegics. I just thought, *Well, that's Swindon for you.* The age mattered because the carer was supposed to be matched demographically so that they could converse with their patient and create a good working relationship. I doubted such was going to be the case with these two. Diana hadn't made her mind up about whether she wanted to be my carer yet, so she was a bit standoffish, whereas the other had a thick Swindon accent, which immediately rubbed me the wrong way even though she was trying. My state of mind demonstrated I hadn't reached a state of full calm and still associated my own meaning to things.

The day went on. Sue came and showed them how to handle me in bed. We went to the gym, where Lyndsey showed them how to transfer me and the stretches they had to do with me every day. Dawn came, met them, and talked them through skin care. She told them that, when I had injured my spine, my skin integrity had softened and that I could tear my skin very easily, which could turn into an ulcer and land me back in the hospital for months, if not years. Diana told Dawn they had worked in care for twenty years and knew all about pressure sores.

Dawn looked incensed and stated very firmly, 'Yes, pressure sores are possible, and you need to look out for them, but I'm talking about skin tears, which are prevalent among spinal patients. You must treat any marks he has immediately.'

The two carers nodded and moved on. As we were returning to the bed, Amanda stopped in the corridor to talk to Sue, halting the whole entourage.

Sandra then said to me, 'You don't want us to wear our uniforms, do you?'

Unsure, as I hadn't given it any thought, I just said, 'I'm not sure. Likely not.'

I later found out they had reported back that I had specifically asked them not to wear uniforms. The truth was I didn't care either way. But if one of my work stream leads had manipulated a client like that, I would have had them removed from the project immediately. Trust, loyalty, and honesty were the kingpins for anyone working for me. The day ended, and we dispersed, having agreed to meet the next day at home.

Amanda got me into the car. I was leaving for the last time after a year in hospital, having come close to death and then survived a deceased nervous system by some miracle. It was like every other Friday. I didn't know what I had expected, perhaps a marching band or something similar. But it was just get in the car, slam the door shut, and off we went at last. I told Amanda I didn't think either of the carers were good enough to deal with a tetraplegic. She just told me not to worry, as she would be there keeping an eye, which was enough for me to relax about things.

Even at home, I was unable to shake the phantom off. He had followed me thus far in my life, and he wasn't giving up, always threatening, always menacing, always carrying my unknown fear and holding the threat of just ending it all. Unlike Dark, the phantom didn't have an alternative motive, just my death. I could feel his hunger for it and his breath over my shoulder. It wouldn't take much to give up and let him have his prize. Yet, with the right thought, I could avoid him and live beyond my fear of him. I knew he too was me, a combination of my existing fears. I had a higher cause now. I finally saw my family and how they needed me as much as I needed them. I would endure any pain for them and accept discomfort as the price of life and a second chance to be with my family.

I had pushed hard to get rid of Doctor Dark and the fear I believed he represented. I had pushed all my true unknown fear together into another phantom, which was hiding behind the truth. Or he always probably there, meaning fear was a part of us from the start. Although I had managed to escape my known fear and see the impermanency and randomness of life, I carried my phantom wherever I went, as he was the potent unknown. I avoided him by reminding myself that no fear existed for one whose mind was not filled with desires. I tried hard not to become attached to things or the way life was, which also meant my relationship with others. The only attachment I could never shed was that to Amanda and the two boys, but then I never really tried. My love for them was absolute and likely the only thing that could still hurt me. As time went by, I left the world of permanency behind. I still carry my love for my family like a silk purse constantly hanging from my hand.

When I looked back, I finally realised all that Doctor Dark had spoken to me was from the learning of my life that had touched my soul over time. He was created from my unconsciousness to remind me of Dharma. He pushed me through my fears, perceptions, and mental formations to find the truth of myself—life was a manifestation of my thoughts. He and all the ghosts he manifested were me, my mental formation, and my way of talking to myself and encouraging me to pick myself up and to take advantage of the places I found myself in. He himself was a manifestation of all that I was afraid of. I used him to push myself away from the dark in the only way I knew how—a fight between two minds, two perspectives of the same reality. I wondered how I would cope without him.

The answer to that was, of course, by looking at the world with renewed perception and realising I was the one creating all the meaning. I wasn't strong enough to change my mind's reality, and I still clung to the idea of 'self'. However, I was strong enough to recognise the truth of it all. Looking back, at that moment after my operation, I had escaped my bonds and calmed my mind. No longer was I dogged by the effect of my own fear. As long as I didn't look back at the phantom, I could stay strong. Even death was not to be feared by one who had lived wisely.

I now believe I'm privileged to see that much around us is a fragile reality, constituted by misleading mental formations and brought on by wrong perception. This makes many people afraid of the unknown concept called life and death, though they probably wouldn't admit it. For many, death is a dark fear, while others view life as darkness and see death as a release. I now see both as the unknown. Strangely, I often find that many people live their lives based on their beliefs about death and not necessarily life. Many views and beliefs are out there, such as those pertaining to judgement at death and reward. Such views and beliefs can make one either afraid of life or afraid of death, creating a certain approach to living. When trying to understand each approach, action, event, thought, and perception of life, mental formations are formed, which are validated against whatever belief people have. All these mental formations form how people see the world and themselves within it, making reality a very personal concept, difficult to grasp as a real thing. At the time I first fell ill, my personal and un-unique belief was that death was just a light going out and it all just ending. At the time, I didn't believe in judgement or reward, just the end. The view made my approach to life 'simple', and I wanted to die knowing I had led a good life.

Now death seems a different reality. I'm concentrating on my journey as it is now in the here and now. I have shed as much of the past as I can. I'm working hard not to let my past affect me today. The future has been easier to let go of—no more driving ambition and no more worries of the future. I take each day as it comes. As each day brings a different challenge, I don't see a point in looking to the future. I and all the people I love are alive today, so here is where my mind is.

This mental attitude doesn't mean I believe life will be serene from here on. Life is full of challenges, some big, some small, some in your control, some out of your control. Nothing is how it seems. Life is guided by the mental formation created by our perceptions, and perceptions can be deceiving.

My so-called care agency turned out to possess the contract to act as a broker of care in the whole of Swindon. Ideally, they should have noted my needs and found a specialist spinal agency to provide qualified and relevant care. Such an arrangement would have provided the agency only a small cut. However, if they employed their own people from the care homes, they would make a bigger margin. So, they provided me carers with three years of experience at best and sometimes those who just walked into their offices for work with no experience at all. I tried to stay as calm as I could, even when their care was so bad that my safety was regularly put at risk.

CHAPTER 15

JUST WHEN YOU THINK IT'S ALL OVER

Diana turned out to be a good carer. She and I learnt as we went along. She worked like a Trojan around the house and helped Amanda and I with the ironing and housekeeping. She was a sweet lady though we never really had much to talk about. The age gap was too large for us to have any meaningful dialogue. However, she did seem to think she was invited to join every single conversation I had and would even jump in and answer for me, cutting me out the conversation and replacing me. I probably should have been angry about it, but I found it amusing each time. Every time I would complain about my pain or condition, she would top me with a story of her own suffering. In the end, her anecdotes turned out to be useful. She was an epileptic who hadn't had an episode for some time. She was on some pretty strong medication. She used to complain the dosages of her medications were being increased and that made her groggy, which would be vital information for me in the future. We didn't really care about her complaining, as we liked her. However, when you looked at the matter with safeguarding lenses, having someone with epilepsy caring for someone like me wasn't ideal. She did lose concentration a few times, and I ended up out of the chair or back down like a turtle. Over my time with the agency, I was sent another two carers who were epileptics. One had said she hadn't had an episode for a few years. However, when she was asked to drive me, which was part of their duties, she admitted not having a driving license, as it was taken off her because of her epilepsy. The admittance indicated the doctor still saw her as being at risk.

The other was a very polite young man. His accountancy career had come to an end because of his epilepsy, and now he hoped to work in care, as it would be less stressful. When we first met him, I had just had brain surgery after one of my shunts failed, something he wasn't even told about. I was his second ever patient, he hadn't had any training at all, and he was working alone and out of his depth. The poor fellow didn't know if he was coming or going. One thing I could tell just by looking people in their eyes as they transferred me was whether they were experienced in transferring. If they were, then they stayed calm as I moved from surface to surface. If they didn't have any real experience or weren't sure of themselves, then I saw panic in their eyes, and I knew they weren't suitable carers for me. The poor chap who had been sent to me was one such person. He had no experience and no training to help anyone, let alone me. He was removed and replaced with a young girl. She didn't have epilepsy, but she had pure panic in her eyes and almost dropped me on a number of occasions. After that, I called the agency and told them I didn't blame the carers they were sending. Rather, I blamed them, and if anything happened to me, then I would engage my solicitor to go after them, not the poor carer.

Let me not get ahead of myself. The poor lady with the thick Swindon accent (Sandra) was assigned to care for me more than anyone else at first. Working with her, I first saw panic in her eyes. The way I see it, transferring is about technique, not brute force. Get the technique right, and the transfer will always work. Get it wrong, and the patient will end up on the floor. An experienced or trained carer will know these techniques and have techniques of their own for diverting disaster, which meant calm eyes. But without that knowledge, panic is inevitable. Then, there are those who have transferred only old people, and they think they know what they're doing with a tetraplegic, but it's a whole different kettle of fish. Most people with tetraplegia have no core strength, which means they can fall forward without warning or sometimes because they are tilted too much on the transfer.

Often, I didn't have the strength in my arms to fully lift myself during a transfer. I would lift, but sometimes halfway through, I would lose strength and drop. When transferring, tetraplegics would be very weak and unstable. Sometimes, I needed help and support; sometimes, I needed to be left alone when moving, as an unexpected hand of support could knock me off course on to the floor. I still had horizontal and vertical double vision; one part of my technique was to look where I was going before moving. That place for me was a very confused place. I just used to go for it with best judgment. The complexity of my case only induced panic in a carer with no experience or training.

I never got on well with the agency. Once they sent me a carer who had been told I was an easy case, and she could probably take a book and sit in the kitchen and read. Of course, when she arrived and saw how much there was to do and how complex my case was, she was shocked, and we never saw her again.

I had a conversation with the agency boss and aired my grievances. She promised to look into them and get back to me by that Friday with a new care plan. That was three years ago, and I'm still waiting for my call. I've tried calling her, but she had always been too busy to talk.

Over those first three years, the agency and the carers were one problem. The other was I had no aftercare for the first two years. I visited Stoke Mandeville Hospital every three months to have Botox injected into my legs to stop spasticity. Though the outpatient nurses were great for advice, whenever we were referred to a specialist, we never heard a word back, mainly because of the high retirement rates and lack of new people to recruit. Being referred was one thing; there being someone to be referred to was another. I saw Dr Long once a year, and he offered no help at all. In one appointment, he showed me an X-ray image of mine and said he was worried about the two lines on each side of my body. I had to tell him those were my shunt drainage pipes. He was clearly ready for retirement himself.

Amanda became busy raising money from charities for things like a recliner chair, a power wheel, and outside decking, making it possible for me to go outside. Anything to do with disability came shamelessly with an extortionately high cost. The exorbitant prices of necessities made matters difficult for us, as we were living hand to mouth on the remainder of my critical illness insurance, which was running low. Amanda worked hard around the house, being a mother to the boys and acting as a night carer to me. She was also going out to work, so we had some money coming in. She was slowly running herself into the ground. Opting to not have a night carer and believing Amanda could do it were critical mistakes. All the work was making her more and more stressed, and her back was getting affected with all the lifting of me.

Though Amanda had sacrificed everything for me and the boys, there seemed to be no way of helping her. As I had a rare condition that affected my spinal cord, I didn't show up on anyone's radar. Basically, if you broke your back in an accident and couldn't walk, you went on one list, and if you had a stroke or head injury and lost the use of your limbs, you went on another list. Arachnoiditis was not on anyone's radar, so I just fell through the cracks. My only recourse was my GP. Unfortunately, he had no idea about arachnoiditis and never bothered to find out. He never helped me manage my drugs, and when I visited him, he just looked at me and said, 'What do you want me to do about it? There's nothing that can be done.'

So, over a period of two years, I took charge of my own drugs and trialled different dosages with different times, trying to always hold the pain at bay. For the most part, my experiments worked, but I still had a constant freezing feeling, and my feet felt like they were being crushed by ice. Some days were so bad all I could do was take a high dose of diazepam and fall unconscious.

The hospital had given me a wooden standing frame, which I would pull myself into and pull myself up and stand for about an hour. Standing was an important exercise to do when paralysed, as it strengthened bones and helped with blood flow and bowel care. The agency never bothered to train the carer on the standing machine, so we had a tetraplegic who had weak arms that could give out any time, a carer who was normally an old-people's home carer with absolutely no knowledge of or training on working with spinal injuries, and a standing machine really made for paraplegics. To be fair, when I was under strength training every day at the hospital, I could use them. However, now that I was at home and getting no physical care at all, my arms grew weak very quickly. So, one day, I pulled myself up into the frame, but the carer hadn't tightened the leather strap that went under my bum to support the stand. As I leant back into the standing strap, it all gave way, including my arms. My legs bent, and I landed on my knees, which fractured them both. The poor carer tried to catch me, thinking I could also catch myself, but I had used all my strength getting into the frame, so I just went down like a sack of spuds.

Being paralysed, I never felt the fractures in my knees, and I had no idea of the break. We would never have known if we hadn't shortly after that found a private spinal injury physiotherapist called Clare, who was exceptional. She immediately spotted the crunching in my knees and advised me to get an X-ray. By that time, it was too late to do anything about it, and even if they could, all they could do was immobilise my legs, which was already the case with the paralysis.

After being in bed for such a long time, I had given up on my body as a whole. But Amanda, as always, found the solution and arranged for Clare, the private physiotherapist. Clare gave me a new strength and showed me a new way to strengthen and use my body. In short, she gave me something to live for and instilled in me the hope of getting stronger.

When I first got out of hospital, all my friends and family had organised a fun run to raise money for me, with the objective of helping me buy a trike wheel for my wheelchair. They did a great job, and I thanked them all. One of Amanda's friends bought me a standing machine more suited for tetraplegics. It wasn't cheap (we are talking thousands); their generosity was overwhelming.

Before we found Clare the physiotherapist, I had withdrawn into myself and found getting out of bed difficult. I felt trapped in darkness all day long, and when I fell asleep, all I saw was the phantom. He still had no form, but I could hear him screaming insults at me all night long. Every now and again, I glimpsed the small boy in the corner of the dark, and he seemed desperate to get to me, shouting something across the dark, but I couldn't hear it.

While I was in hospital, Amanda had kept her promise and somehow found a plumber/builder to turn the downstairs bathroom into a wet room where I could manoeuvre my shower chair around and deal with my bowel. Every morning, I would have to pump water into my colon to empty everything out of me. The toilet was unfortunately too close to the wall. I could get the shower chair over the toilet, but I was so squeezed up against the wall that I couldn't go to the toilet. When I talked to the nurse about it, I was advised just to go in the shower area and wash it down the drain, and that became my morning routine. Every morning, I would go to the wet room and spend two hours in there. In all that time, I only spent fifteen minutes actually having a shower, and the rest of the time I would be cleaning up the mess I had just made. I would chase faeces around the floor to the drain with the showerhead. Sometimes, the drain would block, and shitty water would go everywhere. If I didn't get all the shit out of me in the morning, I would spend the day desperate for the toilet and then have an accident. I couldn't just go when I wanted because my bowel was paralysed, so it needed a water enema, which you could only do once a day. How it then found its way out when I wasn't expecting it, I would never know. Movement certainly helped me go. In the end, I was able to take control of it. But as time went by, whatever intervention I had would stop working and I would have to find another solution.

When I first got home, I couldn't get out of bed. I was so completely out of it that I couldn't focus on anything. The arachnoiditis pain ran through my body even as I lay in the bed. At that point, I hadn't mastered my drug dosages, resulting in the pain coming and going in waves. My carers seemed to like it that way, as they didn't have to do much. By the time I started seeing Clare, I was convinced my life was confined to a bed with the odd morning trip to the wet room. I was home, but I just couldn't feel anything. The boys still didn't have their dad back, and Amanda was still waiting to see if her Mikey had survived.

My release finally came about six months after I first got home. By pure chance, I heard my carer, who was an epileptic, complaining about a drug she was on that made her confused. The drug was Keppra, which was used to treat seizures. I remembered seeing Keppra on my drug chart, as I'd had a seizure when coming out my coma. Due to the lack of review, my need for it was never reconsidered. We called James to check whether I could be taken off it. He gave his blessing but warned us to stay vigilant of any sign of me slipping into trouble. I immediately stopped taking the drug. And as if like magic, the next day I felt like I had just woken up out of a long nightmare. I probably wasn't affected much by it while I was at the hospital because I was engaged and busy with activities. I started to see that Amanda needed help with the boys, who had been growing up over the last year and a half without a father. I felt like I was back at last. The boys needed some discipline, though whenever I tried, they went upstairs to their room where I couldn't follow.

I started spending a considerable amount of time sitting in the kitchen, as it was the only place I could go in the house, other than bed. Myles and

205

I had long talks, and I tried to pass on some of my knowledge. I didn't know whether he took any of my advice or just learnt life like I did, the hard way. Max started coming down and just sitting with me wherever I was and then playing me up for laughs. I didn't mind, as it was nice to have him around, and he always made me laugh. The boys were great when they weren't having a teenage fit. When they did, like all teenagers, they were hard work. I loved them both, and I treasured the different relationship I had with each of them.

My eyes were still bad, and my vision was all over the place. I was advised to wear an eyepatch when I was at the hospital, which helped me see the world without much confusion. I had three operations on my eyes to try and fix the double vision. Each time, I woke hoping to see significantly better but only found slight improvements. I had my first eye surgery under the NHS. The waiting list was terribly long, and the eye consultant I was seeing worked in two different hospitals, making having a long-term plan with him difficult.

Amanda found Dr Ellis who had treated my eyes while I was at the hospital. He had retired but was in private practice now. I started to see him, and a long-term plan was set. As my eyes got better and I started to feel stronger overall, I went back to work part-time, three days a week, five hours a day. Being able to work again brought more money coming in. With my salary package, I could afford private medical care again, for me and my family. Dr Ellen was always amazed that I had managed to get back to work. He admitted to me that, when I had told him I wanted to go back to work back in the JRH, he'd thought I never stood a chance, given how ill I was. He always treated me with respect, and he did a great job on my eyes. Though my eyes were not perfect, they were a lot better, and I could almost see straight again. Unfortunately, owing to all the operations, the scar tissue on my eyes prevented any more surgery. So, I swapped the eye patch with frozen lenses, which kept only one eye doing all the work, helping me see with a single perspective.

I was also plagued with bladder problems, and I had to seek out another private doctor called Dr Bens. The NHS nurses came over every four weeks to change the suprapubic catheter in my stomach to avoid infection. The trouble was, once the old one was pulled out, the new one had to be put in within thirty minutes. For some reason, most nurses struggled to complete the task within the thirty-minute window, and then, there I was in the back of an ambulance, racing to a hospital that just did not have a clue. As always, whenever I was in the care of paramedics, I felt perfectly safe. However, the moment they left me in the Swindon casualty, I ended up in a worse state than when I'd gone in.

Eventually, Dr Bens widened the hole in my stomach from 14 mil to 18 mil so that the tube could be inserted more easily. However, the trouble was that inserting the tube became too easy. Once, a nurse pushed the catheter into my stomach and then into my urethra pipe. The situation ultimately became worse when she pumped up the stabilising bag inside my penis. I went to sleep that night and then woke up in the middle of the night. My bed was soaking wet, with blood pouring out of my penis. Amanda called the paramedics, and they very calmly got me cleaned up and in the ambulance. At that point, no one knew why I was bleeding. I told the paramedics I didn't want to go to Swindon casualty. If I was going to die, I wanted to do so at home, surrounded by my family. And I meant it.

The paramedics then told me something I never knew: They were obligated to take me to any hospital I wanted as long as I wasn't in any danger of dying. So, I elected to go to the JRH in Oxford. It was the best decision I could make. The JRH casualty was the best in the country, as Oxford was full of teaching hospitals, making everything first class. They, of course, identified the problem and resolved it quickly.

The nurses still came and changed my suprapubic catheter at home. With the introduction of paramedic nurses—paramedics who had been roped into helping out the community nurses—the competency of service providers significantly improved. They never even blinked while changing my suprapubic catheter and were adept at managing unknown and difficult situations, owing to years of experience.

After all that, I started developing bladder stones, which were in danger of blocking my renal system. Each time, I would have another procedure in surgery to have them removed—three times in all. Preventing the stones seemed impossible, until we were given some advice on bladder washes. And to date, no more stones have developed.

I stayed at work for a year and a half. The company didn't trust me with project management again. And when clients saw me, they were put off by the wheelchair and funny speech. They were paying £2,000 per day for a management consultant, and I doubted I gave them the confidence they wanted. So, at first, I worked in the Reading office doing very little and being bullied by a passive-aggressive woman who had just been promoted to a senior management consultant, like myself, and saw me as a threat, for some reason. She was constantly on my back about everything. One day, as I had nothing to do, I packed up a few minutes early to go home. When I looked around, she was sitting in the chair beside me.

She said, 'Half three you finish, isn't it?'

The old giant in me would have cut her a new one, but I just ignored her and went home.

Come New Year, I had myself transferred to the Bristol office, which was a little better. No bullies were around, just an office full of kids in their twenties and early thirties. They were mainly accountants, and we had no common ground to have any discussions. I became very isolated. I was told a human resources management consultant team was in the building, but I never found them. In the end, I just sat at my desk writing manuals on organisational design, well aware no one would ever read them. At least I could say I kept myself busy if anyone ever asked, but no one did.

In 2018, I was told by numerous medical experts that being at work was leaving me with no time to rehabilitate, and I had fallen below my fitness level at Stoke Mandeville. They were right. While I was working, I would get up in the morning and go through a toilet procedure, which took almost two hours. Then, I would be dressed and bundled into a taxi by my carer and driven one hour to Bristol. At the office, I would work, or at least pretend to work, for five hours. Then, I would get back in the taxi and be driven back home. Back home, my carers would make me do some stretches and hurry me into bed before their shift got over at six in the evening. I had no family life, and I was becoming exhausted for no real reason.

Having toilet accidents at work was one of my biggest fears. I used my anal irrigation system every day to clear my bowel. The whole process was a defecation nightmare, but it wasn't the only worry. One day at work, in the disabled toilet, I accidently pulled the catheter pipe out, leaving the valve in my pants. Urine sprayed all over me and the toilet. It was a real mess, and I was soaked head to toe in urine. The experience was like all my nightmares had clubbed together and come true.

Luckily, owing to some quick thinking, I phoned my carer, who was sitting by my desk. She quickly came and helped me clean up, but there wasn't much we could do. We phoned the taxi driver who had parked up locally, waiting for us to return. The then carer called the elevator, and when it arrived, I shot out of the toilet into it, which we took to the basement and into the waiting car, with me half-dressed and smelling of piss. It was not my proudest moment. The next day, I went to the building manager and explained what had happened and apologised about the mess. He was a good sport and told me not to worry about it, but I did.

After that, I took the medical advice (from ten different doctors) and applied for a year's career break so that I could get rehabilitated. The NHS Trust responsible for not giving me the antibiotics when they should have and taking over a day before administering an MRI scan had admitted liability. The turn of events ensured I had a source of income, and I could take a career break more easily. However, at this stage, the income was still limited, as we hadn't settled on a final figure. I had thought long and hard about suing the NHS. They might have caused my plight, but they had also worked hard to save my life and rehabilitate me.

I never held anything against even the people who had messed up and hadn't given me the antibiotics. Working in a setup that was understaffed and under-resourced, they were overworked and exhausted. However, I would say try being a disabled person in today's Britain. The government prefers to recover the national debt by cutting the benefits of those in most need, rather than from the bankers whos fault the country's debt was . Private companies have been brought in to review disabled people's needs, and they are targeted to reduce the overall cost. Thereby, good and honest unfortunate people are being taken advantage of and made out to be the enemy instead of the banks. The weak-minded in society are starting to believe the government spin, as hate crimes against disabled people has risen by 41 percent. I too have been abused by a carload of yobs, who circled the block to find me and spit on me while shouting and swearing. The government says they are trying to cut down on benefit fraud by making the application even harder. The fraudsters are good at filing the applications in, so the new system isn't a deterrent for them. But it becomes a massive barrier for a disabled person. Even if you're lucky enough to secure benefits, it's nowhere close to what a small family needs to live on in this day and age.

As I had saved money up for our old age, I wasn't entitled to any help in adapting our house to meet the needs of a disabled person. I had to use our entire savings to create an environment for a disabled person, which still wasn't enough. We were left with no savings, so Amanda and I had to go to work. My health suffered, and she reached a breaking point. Work almost drove us into early graves, and the boys suffered the effects of a stress-filled home. My strength deteriorated to the point that all my medical advisors told me I couldn't carry on this way.

Though I wanted to leave the past behind, Amanda was still angry and knew, if we didn't do something, we would fall apart as a family. So, she employed a solicitor. He went through our case and reminded us an MRI scan on the first day in the hospital could have detected the abscess in my spine. The abscess could have been easily prevented from turning into sepsis and then infecting my meninges, which, in turn, brought about the meningitis, arachnoiditis, and paralysis with constant pain. If I had been given antibiotics on day one, instead of waiting for three days, the entire tragedy could have been prevented. It wasn't my fault. I hadn't do anything stupid or dangerous, just going out every day and earning for my family. I didn't deserve this, and the fault did lie with the NHS. Now that I was back in the real world, I realised I couldn't take care of my family. Therefore, I decided with a heavy heart to sue the NHS so that my family could live a normal life, and I could get the treatment I needed and a house I could live in.

I found a case manager to help me with my care, which was a requirement of any case. She promised me that, when I went on career break, I would be so busy I wouldn't touch the ground. This didn't happen. When my career break started, most of the time, I was stuck in bed because there was nothing else I could do. To add to that, the house in which I lived was far too small to do anything in, and I had nowhere else to go.

Clare, the physiotherapist, had taken a permanent job in a hospital, so I lost my only release. The case manager found me another private neuro-physiotherapist called Emma, and she was totally different from Clare. Emma concentrated on my weaknesses and worked out fitness solutions.

She was also a great listener, and as a neuro-physiotherapist, she knew a great deal about my condition. Though I only saw her for two hours every Monday and Wednesday, she was a godsend. And even when we were hard up for money, which was quite often, we made sure we could afford Emma.

Out in the real world, I found everything a massive struggle. Coming out of my front door itself was a risk. Terry, our good friend and maintenance man, had built me a ramp that landed me on the only flat surface on the driveway. After that, it was a hair-raising ride down a steep path into the busy road. Many a time, I had considered pushing myself down the driveway into the heavy traffic. However, the consideration of three possibilities stopped me: One, such an act would ruin the driver's life. Two, I would have a horrible death with Amanda, Myles, and Max in the house. Three, the final blame for my demise could end up on the carer, which would be an injustice. Another plan was to just wheel into the woods opposite to the house and take a stash of painkillers. That way, someone other than my family would find me. Yet again, my conscience stopped me, considering how that would affect someone, especially if it was a child who found me.

Every move I made as a wheelchair-bound person seemed doomed to fail. The pavements outside my house were broken, with tree roots sticking out of them. To self-propel was nearly impossible for someone like myself, who had failing arm strength. All nonmodern pavements tilted towards the road for drainage. When I was able bodied, I didn't even notice it. Yet for wheelchair users, it was a nightmare, as I found myself constantly fighting the wheels from slipping down the slope into the road. Most the shops and pubs in Old Town Swindon were old buildings with steps leading to the entrance. That made entry, if any, through the rear entrance where the bins were.

Going to restaurants with friends became a massive undertaking, as access and toilet facilities had to be checked beforehand. Only a few people ever went to the effort of checking—Amanda, Geoff, Paul, Rob, and Jon, who was one of my oldest friends and another good soul. Slowly and gradually, we had lost our other friends, as we weren't an easy choice. Even if they did go through the effort of checking accessibility, there was no guarantee I would turn up; nine times out of ten I kept having a toilet accident just before we were due to go out. I couldn't blame people for backing away, but I did find out who my friends really were. Two people who always stuck by us and couldn't be thanked enough are friends Clare and Terry.

Finding toilets designed to accommodate the needs of people with disability was the hardest. In most regular toilets, the flush was generally on the far side of the toilet, and foot-peddle operated bins were common. Getting around was not easy. One good thing about being disabled was that, wherever I went, I always had somewhere to sit. However, every two hours, I had to do what was called pressure relief, which was leaning all the way forward so that my bum lifted off the chair to allow blood flow to my bum, helping to prevent pressures sores. The trouble was that, as soon as I did it in public, people assumed either I had become ill somehow, or I was sleepy. Sometimes the action was accompanied with a great fart, as pressure in my bowel was released. This happened once at work as I was bending over, my carer standing behind me to shield me. I let out a fart that just seemed to go on and on. I apologised quickly, not realising the discomfort and embarrassment the situation would have caused the carer. Basically, to a third person, it looked like the carer had farted, and it didn't help when the poor woman went red-faced. I couldn't help having a little giggle at her expense. Being disabled was an isolated experience and existence. My only real company was my family, who were, thankfully, always there for me. My pain and troubled bowel kept me from doing anything meaningful.

My existence was miserable at best. Though I had committed to staying alive, killing myself still seemed an attractive idea. I made many plans on how I would do it but always fell short when I thought of my family and the poor person who would find me. Added to all that, at night I wrestled with the phantom. He never spoke and always kept his distance, but his presence alone would make me toss and turn. I would occasionally dream about the little boy holding on to the corner of the wall and trying to shout out to me. I couldn't hear what he was saying, but he seemed desperate to tell me something.

When I had a bad day, I would become so emotionally fragile that I would consider ending things. I would always see the boy desperately trying to call across the dark and tell me something important. Life outside of hospital was harder than I thought. My penis was paralysed, which meant Amanda and I had no sex life. I learnt about this problem when I went to a presentation by a nurse while I was at Stoke Mandeville. As the presentation went on, I slowly started to realise I faced the issue under discussion, and I couldn't believe it was as dead as a doornail for all intents and purposes. It never affected our relationship. In fact, it only made it stronger because we were two people who just wanted to be together, and the pressure of sex was never an issue.

I started to read a lot, pulling out books from my old collection on Zen, psychology, and physics. Going through these books, I came across many of the messages Doctor Dark and the others were trying to give me. I started to realise more and more that it was me who had created all those phantoms and ghosts while trying to get me to cross the bridge from intellectual knowledge of things to one of true belief, enabling me to understand the one. I wouldn't say I fully crossed the bridge, as my own scepticism held me back from following any one belief. Rightly or wrongly, I stopped my mind from being closed to any possibility; the universe was mostly unknown, so who could really say?

CHAPTER 16

BATTLE IN THE DARK

Three months into my career break, Amanda recognised I was starting to get really confused and my speech was getting almost unintelligible. Concerned, she rushed me to GWH Swindon. Guess what they did? You got it! They did nothing and sent me home. Two days later, my condition was so bad that Amanda called the paramedics. The paramedics took me to the casualty, where I had a CT scan. Amanda, of course, demanded to take me to the JRH neuro team, who instructed Swindon to blue light me to Oxford as soon as possible. I woke up again in the JRH with pipes sticking out of my head.

As I came out of the confusion, I saw Paul sitting by my bed. I said to him, 'Don't worry, mate. This time I have decided to go with it and see where it takes me.'

We giggled, and then I must have fallen back into the confusion and the dark, which, yet again, engulfed me. I saw the small boy stretching out one arm; either he was being held back by the other, or he was holding on to something. He seemed not only a long way away but also trapped in the darkness, which obscured everything. The boy, as usual, was shouting at me from across the dark, but I still couldn't hear him.

I called back to him. 'I can't hear you. What are you saying?'

The boy became agitated and started pulling hard at whatever he was holding. He shouted across the dark, but all I could hear were the odd words 'this, the, is'.

'I can't hear you,' I shouted again.

He stretched his hand out even further to me.

I tried to get closer, but the dark rushed in on me and held me back.

214

Once more, I heard the same odd words, and I shouted one more time, 'I can't hear you.'

The dark fell all over us. The boy disappeared. And in my mind, I fell to the ground exhausted, waking up back in a hospital bed.

Lying in bed, once again looking up at the fluorescent lights on the ceiling, I had time a plenty to consider things. The small boy seemed frantic to tell me something, but I couldn't work out what it was. For some reason, I knew he had something important to tell me, but I could never hear him. I pondered why I couldn't hear him and what I could do to resolve this. I tried hard to meditate, but the boy kept appearing in my mind. The thought of him would take over my mind, and my inner monkey would then go mad.

After a few days in the hospital, James, the senior consultant who had treated me previously, came in to see me. He apologised and said the shunt had stopped working, and he was not sure why. They considered the possibility that as I had been in bed for such a long time, gas must have built up inside me and literally blown the CSF fluid back up the pipe through the shunt and back into the brain, but they were never sure.

I was in the hospital for just a week, but during that time, I had a nightmare. My anal irrigation system couldn't work, as I had to stay lying down for the EVD. Therefore, every day I was given a phosphate enema and left on the bed to empty my bowel onto inco pads.

I wasn't in a coma, but my dreams were disturbed and graphic. The coming of the darkness seemed inevitable, as the new phantom was there hidden in the dark. Doctor Dark seemed to be gone, as I hadn't seen him since my time at Stoke Mandeville. I could, however, still see the little boy hanging on to something that stopped him from coming to me. As usual, he was shouting something. I could almost hear his voice, but I still couldn't make out what he was saying. I stared at the darkest patch of darkness, assuming that was the phantom, and I called to him and said, 'Life is uncertain; death is certain. I'm not afraid of death because I know who I am.'

A deep and thunderous voice shouted back, 'You know nothing of your true self. You may have seen off one facade, but you cling to your past like a small boy clinging to its favourite toy. You will never know peace because you will never let go of the shame.'

215

As he spoke, the dark from where he came rippled as if the dark itself was angry.

I shouted, 'I have no shame to let go of.'

My words were followed by a white flash that engulfed everything. As the light faded, I found myself on a street corner in army uniform, including a flak jacket. Looking down, I saw my hands were covered in blood, which was dripping onto the floor. Angry and looking for trouble, the young me just ran tactically up the road. The light flashed again, and now I found myself being punched in the chest by an infantry corporal. As he walked away from me, he counted the money he had just demanded. I should have refused, but I was too stupid at that time. The light flashed again. This time, I was in civilian clothing, chasing someone who had just knocked his girlfriend out down the street. As I caught up to him, I knocked him down and smashed my foot into his mouth. The sound of his jaw cracking penetrated the night air. The light flashed again, and I found myself lying on a pavement outside a kebab shop late at night, fighting someone on the ground. We hung on to each other like schoolchildren, but I rendered the final blow by kneeing him in the face repeatedly until he got up and ran away with blood pouring out his nose. Again, the light flashed, and I was walking out of a girl's bedroom early in the morning, and I didn't even know her name. The flash again, and I was walking out of a police station early in the morning after spending a night in the cells.

This went on and on, speeding up to a frightening pace. Finally, I was standing on the pavement in my army uniform. All around me, people were fighting in the streets and bursting out of the pubs with fists flying. Girls were chasing men down the street and crying for them to come back. And the local police were arresting people and packing them up in police vans. The whole scene was chaos. The sky was blood red with thick black smoke drifting across it from dozens of burning buildings. The smell of burning flesh consumed the air, and I could hear weapons fire in the distance.

The noisy street fell silent, and riot police flooded the streets. They walked straight past the fighting people into a defensive line just in front of me. A menacing crowd of protesters marched down the street from the opposite direction. They were well prepared with gas masks and metal shields made from old car body parts. The police fired tear gas at the approaching crowd. Those who could just flung the gas canisters back and started running towards the police line. As the two forces clashed, they made an almighty noise, and then each side was fighting for their lives.

One of the protesters was wearing a long dark coat, a grey hoody with the hood pulled up, and an old top hat. Unmistakably, it was Doctor Dark. A lit cigarette hung from his mouth. He picked up a recently fired tear gas canister and threw it back at the police. As the canister left his hand, he spotted me and walked over to me calmly and deliberately, as if nothing else was going on. Over the noise, I could hear Doctor Dark singing 'Paint It Black' by the Rolling Stones:

> I see a red door and I want it painted black
> No colours anymore, I want them to turn black
> I see the girls walk by dressed in their summer clothes
> I have to turn my head until my darkness goes

He stopped three feet in front of me. With his halt, the singing came to an end too. As he did, a strong wind rushed from behind me and hit him with a great force. His hat and hood were knocked off, and his coat washed up behind him. I could see all the syringes swinging under his coat like laundry on a line. The white paint on his face cracked and pulled off by the wind. As it broke away, I could see him. His face was familiar. It was familiar because it was mine—a little older, a little worn out and frail, but unmistakably mine. The wind started to break him up, and he was slowly blown away into small pieces. As he broke apart, I heard him call out, 'It's not easy facing up when your whole world is black.'

I stood there staring at the riot. A female protester walked over to me calmly as if everything was normal. She was old and had long grey hair. I recognised her immediately, as it was Melody. She was wearing an old green army Jacket and carrying a banner that said, 'Rise of the Outcast'. She walked up to me and handed me a jigsaw piece while singing 'Jigsaw Puzzle' by the Rolling Stones:

> There's a tramp sitting on my doorstep
> Trying to waste his time
> With his methylated sandwich
> He's a walking clothesline

And here comes the bishop's daughter
On the other side
She looks a trifle jealous
She's been an outcast all her life
Me, I'm waiting so patiently
Lying on the floor
I'm just trying to do my jigsaw puzzle
Before it rains anymore

The wind blew hard again. As it hit Melody, her face changed to mine. Then, she started to break into pieces just like the others. All I wanted to do was finish that jigsaw puzzle. I wondered, *How long until I do?*

The wind carried Doctor Dark's voice: 'I'm just trying to do my jigsaw puzzle.'

Standing behind Melody was Sally in her nurse's uniform. The smoke from the tear gas rose around her, but that made no difference to her stare. She smiled sweetly and sang 'Going Home' by the Rolling Stones:

Spendin' too much time away
I can't stand another day
Maybe you think I've seen the world
But I'd rather see my girl
I'm goin' home, I'm goin' home
I'm goin' home, I'm goin' home

The wind blew a gust once again, and as it hit Sally, her face changed to mine, just like all the others. Then she started to break into pieces, just like the others, and just blew away.

I looked toward the police lines and saw a riot cop run up to me, baton raised high in one hand and a shield in the other. The cop stopped, lowered his baton arm, and removed his helmet to reveal Pete. As he removed the helmet, he was singing 'Street Fighting Man' by the Rolling Stones:

Everywhere I hear the sound
Of marching charging feet, boy
Cause summer's here and the time is right

For fighting in the street, boy
Well now, what can a poor boy do
Except to sing for a rock n' roll band?
Cause in sleepy London town
There's just no place for a street fighting man, no

Until now, Pete had given me courage and, perhaps, the drive to keep on fighting at one of my darkest hours. What I had seen at that point made me want to curl up into a little ball and forget the angry street fighting man I once was. Pete smiled at me, and his face turned into mine. The strong wind hit him, and he blew away as Doctor Dark's voice blew back in the wind: 'There's just no place for a street fighting man, no.'

The riot suddenly stopped as if by a single command. Everyone looked at me, and everyone was me. All of this, every vision, everything was me. The Brethren walked by with their faces uncovered, and yes, they were me too. A voice from behind me reverently said, 'They're the Brethren. They protect us from the darkness.'

As I looked around, there was nobody there. As I looked back, I tried to make sense of what had happened, but I didn't know what any of it meant. The Rolling Stones were my favourite band, but I needed time to pick through the meaning of each song in my context. Everybody disappeared, and I found myself standing on the street by myself. The buildings were all still burning, and at the end of the street, I could feel a dark presence. I felt a deep sense of shame for my role in the army, for all the street fighting, the using of women, and my general behaviour as a young man. At that point, I realised the problem was not the giant I'd thought I was. The real giant was the shame I was hanging on to. It was a dark shame, spanning many years, as I seemed to be built on it as life went on.

It was the real facade. I wasn't that ex-soldier who took out his anger on others and treated everyone with contempt. I felt the shame of a young life spent so aggressively and with that harm to others. But my deepest shame was pretending that wasn't me, just another time.

Amanda and then the boys had taught me there was another life, and they had given me something to change for. What I was now was down to them, for them, and about them. I had wasted so much time trying to find myself that I almost missed the fact that the real me was them. I fell to my knees on the ground. As I knelt there, I felt numb.

Then I smelt bad breath and cigarette smoke. A voice came quietly out of the dark, crackling like an old man's voice, a voice I knew well. 'All conditioned things are impermanent. When will you see this wisdom and turn away from suffering? Do not dwell on the past. Do not dream of the future. Concentrate your mind on the present moment.'

I whispered under my breath, 'You came just after the army. Before that, I never even saw the dark.'

Then I felt a flicker of realisation. I realised I had been suffering because of my behaviour as a young man. My unconscious mind must have created Doctor Dark to challenge me to realise where my suffering had originated, not, as I believed, to torment me. He wasn't pushing me into the dark; rather, he was showing me the dark, which allowed me to fight against it.

I heard Doctor Dark again. 'Peace comes from within. Mike, do not seek it without. You will come to realise that nothing is lacking. The whole world belongs to you.'

'How do I achieve this?' I asked. 'My mind is like a mad monkey swinging from tree to tree.'

The voice answered, 'Relax, Mike; all minds are. Nothing is under control. Everything is random. When thoughts arise, then all things arise. When thoughts vanish, then all things vanish. It's better to conquer yourself than to win a thousand battles. Then the victory is yours. It cannot be taken from you. Victory was never my goal, only wisdom.'

'I'm sorry,' was all I could say.

Doctor Dark responded, 'Every morning, we are born again. What we do today is what matters most. Just as a snake sheds its skin, we must shed our past over and over again. Peace comes from within. Do not seek it without, Mike.'

I said, 'It's been a long time. Where have you been? I thought you had gone.'

The answer came quickly. 'Nothing ever goes away until it has taught us what we need to know. You know some truth now, at least enough to let go.'

The dark wrapped around me, like a comfortable woollen blanket. Yet again, I felt like I was standing on a wall with the bricks of the wall just sliding out of place, forcing the wall to collapse. As before, I could feel them slide from underneath me as I fell. I saw myself in front of me, this time young and angry. That me did nothing to stop me and threw out no arms to catch me. So, I fell for another lifetime, as if the young me was committing suicide, knowing full well, when he reached the bottom, he would be gone. As I finally hit the bottom, all the horror of the past disappeared. A weight was lifted off me, and I could breathe easily again. It seemed like a lot, but in my early thirties, I had been hungry for knowledge and had secretly craved something to believe in. I had never found any belief, but I had found some peace from the past through meditation and mindfulness. My unconscious had manifested itself as Doctor Dark, whose mission, at first, seemed to be to get me to fight against the dark and then to get me to listen to what I had learnt from Zen.

For the last time, Doctor Dark spoke to me, in a gentle voice. 'You are exactly where you need to be.'

I looked up and found myself surrounded by the dark. However, it had no presence anymore—no more movement, no more veil-like properties. It was cold, but it was just the dark. Slowly, I stood up and looked ahead. And there he was, the little boy who wouldn't let go. I could see him now, and I could see what was holding him back. He was held by the arm of an action man, dressed like a soldier. I remembered that action man. It had been mine when I was a boy. I looked quickly at the boy's face, and it was the me as a child. At that point, I heard what he had been saying to me. 'This is just the way life is now.'

This is just the way life is now. He was right. The paralysis, the pain, the struggle to defecate, the second-class treatment by a government keen to use the disabled as a scapegoat for the country's debt, the loss of friends, the lack of access, the poorly designed toilets, the struggle for care, the helplessness to sue the NHS so that I could just live and afford care to strengthen myself to compensate for the loss of limbs—this was just the way life was now. The streets, the fighters, and the army uniform were gone, and I was just sitting there in my wheelchair, dressed normally.

The wind carried the voice of the stranger who visited me. 'This is not the end. It is the end of the beginning.' Every atom that made up my body tingled, and I knew holding on was useless.

Every morning, we are born again. What we do today is what matters most, not what happened or who we were in the past. Nothing is under control. Everything is random. I cannot go back to stop the meningitis. My body now is my body, and where I am now is exactly where I'm meant to be, which is a random place born out of random circumstances. What happens next is just the next thing that happens. I can't control it. Nothing is under control. My dreams were filled with the day I took control for the first time at Glastonbury Festival.

The festival had become a church to me in a way. However, nothing lasts forever. The last festival I attended was in 2013. It was a lovely sunny weekend, and I was with the friends of my brothers, who were all superb and great fun. Over 175,000 revellers attended the event, partying and enjoying great music. To top it all my, favourite band, the Rolling Stones played main stage, and they rocked it. Once the festival was over, we walked out carrying our backpacks, which seemed three times heavier than when we had come in. Exhausted, as I was falling asleep on my feet, an overwhelming feeling came over me, and for a second or two, I was walking the paths of the festival and the streets of the other world together. The sound of gunfire mingled with the shuffle of people walking back to their cars; the smell of burning flesh mixed with the smell of burger vans and filled the air. In front of me, Doctor Dark, covered in his dark veil, sat on an overturned dustbin, smiling and humming 'Paint It Black' by the Rolling Stones.

At that moment, fear became a living force that grabbed my insides while holding my brain captive. I shivered and shook off the experience. The suddenness of this vision pulled reality into sharp focus. And by the time we reached the carpark, I had the epiphany that, for some reason, this was my final Glastonbury. I was getting too old for it now, and I needed to grow up and deal with my responsibilities. I was a father, and if my kids caught a glimpse of me at Glastonbury, they would be horrified. I soon announced to the group, 'That's it! This year was a fantastic festival! Great weather, great people, and I saw the Rolling Stones. It's a good time to bring things to an end, so this is it, my last festival.'

Paul announced proudly, 'Not me. I'm coming back next year.' He has kept his word every year since. Paul had always been a free spirit, who took on life his way. At that time, he had been married twice and had five kids from the two marriages. He struggled the whole time between wanting a family life and being free and enjoying life his way and on his terms. He had been my companion all my life. I always saw him as a complete contradiction. But to me, the contradiction was the complete Paul. He was strongly independent. He did things when he wanted to and never danced to another's tune. He had his own hobbies and interests and wasn't that interested in sharing them. He enjoyed his own company and happily walked the festival by himself or went drinking downtown on his own. However, though he liked himself, he also despised himself. In contrast to his own ways, he was a disciplinarian with his kids, setting boundaries with everyone. He found time to take his kids to the park and worked hard to bring in money. He held two jobs—as a finance manager during the day and as a martial arts instructor during the night—so he was always working. Five years later, he met, married, and settled down with a lovely woman called Caroline. She was just like Paul, a free spirt who liked to party. He'd finally found his soulmate and happiness in this life, something that was of great joy for me.

We had enjoyed the Glastonbury vibe together and had walked what seemed like a thousand miles up and down the festival site. We had shared some amazing moments together. In my twenties, we had created merry hell in the night scene of Cheltenham, and we had always been together and been known for our antics. He wasn't just my companion. He was a great influence on my life. Every now and then, I found myself at loggerheads with his battle for two different lives, which resulted in some very standoffish and aggressive behaviour from him. It never mattered. I would walk through fire for Paul, and so would he for me. I could deal with the odd breakdown and forgive him for any harsh words uttered in the heat of his battle. However, after he met Caroline, this battle seemed to have been won, and I never heard a harsh word again, other than in jest. I may have changed since my Glastonbury days, but my willingness to walk through fire for Paul hasn't.

As I have said before, I also spent time with Rob, my cousin and friend. Since my thirties, I spent a lot more time with Rob. He was the other big influence on my life. Apart from being an ex-Glastonbury reveller, he was a psychotherapist and charity manager. He and I explored the nature of life and helped each other explore our own existence. Before my perceived rise to a senior management consultant, we became business partners and delivered a unique style of training together. Various businesses and public-sector organisations found our work useful, making it strangely popular. We had a great deal of fun along the way so that it hardly felt like work. Rob had a great deal to do with my change from an overcharged uncaring business executive to a calmer and more balanced individual.

The third great influence in my transformation has been and still is Amanda. A steady sailor in the rough seas of my existence, Amanda has always been there for me, regardless of whatever crazy new view of life I've had. Good or bad mood, she has stood by me. She laughs a lot, is open to people, and is very accepting but always on her guard. We had the kids in our early thirties, and she became a mother instantly to us all. She took on all the difficult work and decisions for the two boys and shielded me from the difficulties. Whenever I went too far in any direction, she would be there to steer me back to steadier waters. She opened my eyes to many things, most importantly, to my boys and their needs. I was never a natural father, but Amanda coached me and supported me, so the kids never saw my weaknesses.

Back when we were battling Amanda's cancer, I still had to work away from home and earn money for the family. I worked as a consultant, and that was the only way. During those hard times, I was repeatedly on the phone talking to those around her, making sure Amanda was all right and unfairly begging them to do more for her. Amanda and I talked on the phone every night, and I would have to suppress my urge to say everything would be all right, as she hated such optimism and wanted to face the possible dark future. I hid my anguish and tried to be as normal as ever. I lived with the constant feeling of anticipated grief, which made me scared. It felt like I was being slowly ripped apart as I fell into a black hole. I felt terrible about leaving her alone to fight the battle against cancer, even though being away helped me to deal with the pain. In my hotel room, which I called my fortress of solitude, I was able to deal with my fear and sadness and grieve in peace. This solitude helped me to explore who I really was and how I truly wanted to be.

Once Amanda survived cancer and started to get better, I felt I had changed enough to finally be worthy of all my friends and family's love, something I had never felt I deserved before. Ironically, this random universe wasn't finished with me yet. I was to undergo an even bigger change, and it came with a sudden and unexpected bang. In one fell swoop, I was injured, to a point where I would slowly waste away in hospital. My facade fell, my memory became fragmented and confused, and any hope of my recovery was hindered by an ABI. What seemed like reality and a real memory would stand in front of me one minute and fly away and become a distant vista the next. I have pieced together this story with the help of Amanda, my family, and my solicitor's medical report, all of which go towards helping to make the facts of this story right.

If I am to prove that I am real, then it has to be as close to the truth as I can get it. The names of some people in this story have been lost to the dark hazy fog of my mind, and I have created a name or two to fit. The odd name may be made up, but the part of the person is true. The dark forces that you've just encountered were as real to me as my family. My memory of these dark apparitions engendered the height of emotion, so I could not forget them, no matter how bad my ABI was or how hard I tried. You should be weary of them, as being injured brought on many hallucinations, and through them, many of my nightmares came alive. I'm not ruling out, though, that some things may have been real, just that I don't know.

As I awoke from the dark world, I was on my way back from corrective surgery. The surgery seemed to have done the trick. And soon after it, I went home. In their wisdom, the care agency sent a poor lad in his early twenties, without even telling him I'd just had brain surgery.

CHAPTER 17

THE GHOST AND THE GUN

Bearing in mind that this is how life is now and knowing there is now no control over what happens on a daily basis is not easy. I keep going through terrible bowel problems that last weeks, not days. The pain in my legs becomes unbearable at times and is a constant unwanted companion. We solved the house problem by moving to a large bungalow in the country. The move also cured the agency problem, as we shifted out of Swindon into Wiltshire. The carers have improved, as we have more say in what we want. Plus, the Wiltshire CHC and NHS team have made a massive effort, and I have been seen by every kind of health professional one can imagine. We have gone from zero to one hundred miles an hour in care. It's overwhelming and appreciated; in fact, it's life-changing. I'm sorry to say a postcode lottery exists on good health care. The NHS left me in a complex medical condition, which meant I couldn't work anymore. As much as I tried, I was constantly told by doctors that I would never work again. Ironically, even the NHS doctors who had examined me for the legal case said the same thing. I needed support, and suing the NHS was my only way of getting it. However, following the mistakes, the NHS had saved my life and brought me back to health. Now, I live in the right place for them to look after me.

My brain damage has reached a point where I struggle to keep track of conversation, where hallucinations and dreams seem very real, and where memories of the past are confused, and new memories are forgotten in an instance. I live in a constant state of fatigue and fall asleep two or three times a day. Though my dreams are full of unrest, I no longer see the darkness or feel the heart-gripping lung-stopping fear. The phantom is still here waiting for me to fail and turn to him for the answer, but I just try to ignore him now. However, I know that's not always possible. The struggle to stay alive, to stay sane, and to just get around makes life a challenge. But it's a challenge that keeps me going, I would even say that I like the struggle, as it reminds me that I'm still alive.

I am retired now, living in the country and spending my time writing or just staring at views and enjoying the present moment. Doctor Dark gave me a lot to think about, not that I remembered it all. But I decided that to live the words was better than to just remember them. I give myself an hour or two a day to let the mad monkey free in my mind so that I can think about what was said and shown to me, just in case I missed something. Every time I do, I find something new to learn about myself as I work through an unhinged mind trying to rehinge itself. I still haven't found meaning; it's more like the assembly instructions of flat-pack goods—difficult to understand, but the answers are there somewhere. Perhaps, the purpose of this book is to just help work through it all.

I know some very strong people who have a similar injury to me. Some fill their days with challenges, some struggle with their disability, and others just take one day at a time; all are trying to live life the best they can. All deal with pain, both physical and mental. In fact, I expect we all have unhinged minds of some form, as it's how we can live this life that we have no choice over. I mean, how can I do this without being unhinged in some way? It may be nightmares, it may be just waking up and feeling depressed, or it could be hallucinating like me. I would like to say my mind has become calm. Maybe it has, but it's still troubled. Though my meditation practice keeps the dark away, I still live with the feeling of the phantom breathing over my shoulder, and the phantom still hunts me.

Often, I feel trapped between the dark phantom and death, as if death feels cheated, and our handshake wasn't enough. The new phantom doesn't seem to have anything to teach me like Doctor Dark. How I got him wrong! Was it the dark he was trying to protect me from? Was he trying to open my eyes to a truth buried inside me? Who knows? He may have opened my eyes to enough wisdom to keep them both away. But one thing is for sure: No matter how many people love and surround me, I am still alone. I am still a ghost. Most of the time, I am upbeat, even content to sit and enjoy the view, write, and practise my meditation. I am even planning for a raised vegetable garden so that I can get outside more. I have stopped craving more and feel happy with my lot, no more blind ambition.

I dreamt the other night that I was back at work, with a boss telling me to stop swinging the lead and just to get up and get on with things. My unseen brain injury, my unseen mental state, and my presentation as a paraplegic when I was a tetraplegic—nothing was a problem in their eyes. The whole dream blocked me from the here and now, and it scared the hell out of me. It's strange that I have totally re-evaluated my life and that work, which was once my life, is now something I can't even contemplate anymore.

Dreams like that can knock me off my practice, letting the dark flood in. I'm not sure, but I would imagine I'm not the only disabled person who one minute is fine and the next is caught in the grip of depression. I can't imagine that anyone confined to a wheelchair by paralysis is free of dark thoughts. Some mornings I wake up, for no reason, feeling so down and depressed that I almost turn to the phantom and beg him to do his worst. Such thoughts can be de-escalated easily by thinking of those worse off than myself.

I once rolled out of a coffee shop and waited for Amanda to finish shopping. The coffee shop toilet was a joke, and trying to get around in there was a nightmare. As it was a cold day, my legs hurt. I sat in my chair, depressed, thinking of the phantom. Then, I saw someone in an electric chair, all crippled up, unable to move much but a couple of fingers to steer his chair. I instantly lost all my self-pity and just got on with it.

I believe that all of us who inhabit wheelchairs and suffer paralysis are just trying to get on with some kind of life. Somehow, we bury the hurt and resentment, hide the pain and ignore the ignorant. No matter how well we deal with our disability, lying just under the surface is unbelievable hurt and depression, which we all disguise in our own way. In my view, it's best to acknowledge the hurt and depression but keep it hidden and beyond harm. Some days, out of the blue, the depression hits us straight in the face. If we've been pretending that everything is fine, then this can be a bit of a shock. But if we can accept that hurt and depression exists, then we are more equipped to deal with it when it grabs us. It's as much a part of us now as our wheelchair.

I have learnt a great deal from my experiences in the last few years. My mind is mainly calmer and more focused, but the inner monkey still exists. I suspect the two facades, which I thought I saw die, are still about somewhere in my mind, perhaps waiting for me to summon them.

To explain my current state, I imagine I have a revolver, which I usually keep locked in my desk drawer, but now I have taken it out. The revolver represents my monkey thoughts, the power of my ego long forgotten. The phantom is out there and hovering around, but I'm not scared anymore. I may believe I have created a more balanced life, but I can't stop thinking of a quote by Buddha: 'However, many holy words you read, however many you speak, what good will they do you if you do not act on upon them?'

Some I act on; some I don't. Sometimes, I act on something; the next day, I don't. Each day is different, not only physically but also mentally. I don't think I'm acting on anything other than my own slow self-expiry. My family, my living joy, remains my reason for fighting, but they are no longer the reason for me not to cock the metaphoric revolver. I'm no longer afraid of death. In fact, it could be an escape, a way to rid myself of the pain, the indignity, and the ignorance of people.

Many without physical challenges can't see life through my eyes. Sometimes, people talk down to me like I am a child. Others ignore me, as they would rather I didn't invade their perception of life. People think I can do more for myself, and I am just overplaying things. The worst for me is when people know someone else in a wheelchair, and they think, *You are all the same. So why can't you do what my friend does?* You may want to tell them, 'We have different reasons for being in a chair, and we are not all the same.' But what's the point? They have their mental formation, and we need to fit into their world or not. But I say stuff them; they will not force me into their perception. I will create my own. The revolver represents my choice to live, to fight, and to carry on.

Not everyone thinks and behaves the same way. My close and extended family, along with my close friends, certainly do not, as they consider my access needs, ignore my chair, and concentrate on me. They're a breath of fresh air. But they all have their own lives, and they deserve to live them. So, I become a ghost slipping past people as they go through their day. It's hard to be anything but a ghost, even when you're with family and friends. It's not their fault. They ignore my disability, but I do not. I am fully aware of my brain injury, as each second of the day, I struggle to stay focused in this world. My bowel issues are ever present, and I feel as if I will lose control any moment. I'm glued to my wheelchair, and I need a seatbelt to hold me in. Then the pain reminds me I am not free like everyone else. All this makes me more of a ghost, so distorted from the real world that I can't possibly be part of it. And as others try hard to ignore my disability, I sadly cannot. Yet I still choose to be part of this world for as long as I can.

As I said before, don't pity me. I'm not looking for sympathy. I have merely attempted to explain things to you. I can't change them. I can't ignore them. But I can keep up the fight. And I do—not for those I love, not to prove Doctor Dark wrong, not to escape the phantom, but for myself. I don't view death anymore as a way of saving people from the burden or horror of being paralysed. I see it as a way of all this coming to an end—a full stop on the life of Michael Fisher. Though I fight this feeling every single day, I do go on, perhaps because each day is new—new bad sometimes, new good sometimes. I have let go of the past. The future no longer bothers me. I just take each day as it comes, each blow as it hits, and grab on to whatever happiness I can find that day. However, the phantom still has an effect on me. In my mind, my hand rests on the desk, the metaphorical revolver in hand. I slowly turn the bullet barrel, and with each click of the barrel comes a thought of dark intent.

Now, if you like, you can judge me.

AUTHOR'S THANKS AND ACKNOWLEDGEMENTS

I have a small army of people to thank: my wife and children; my mother and two brothers; Rob; Amanda's family; friends of all kinds, some with incredible generosity; and even strangers who turned up to raise money in a fun run for me. I thank every nurse, HSA, doctor, surgeon, consultant, case manager, physio, OT, paramedic, psychologist, therapist, CHC staff, carer, and Aneurin Bevan for creating the NHS, the greatest organisation on Earth.

The list above could go on forever. I have been overwhelmed by good souls out there wanting and willing to help. There are so many good people that it's hardly worth mentioning the small handful of people who abandoned us or treated us with contempt or how some professionals neglected their duty of care to the point that I was so badly hurt.

This story has told how I personally dealt with near death, paralysis, and pain in an emotional and psychological way. I was visited by phantoms, ghosts, and hallucinations—all of which explained how I felt, how I fought the dark, and even how I found hope. To have faith and hope, I needed to understand life fully. I'm not talking about religious concepts but that of everyday human perceptions. To do this, I found my reading of many authors, published or not, as the path to my ability to write this book. So, I thank every last author I've read over the years. I thank them for their insight and their integrity for their beliefs. I have, without a doubt, found my own truth. If I have learnt anything in life, it's never just be told; seek out the truth. For my perceived insight, I thank many people, friends, family, and even just people I met on my way.

I give special mention to the following list of writers who have also contributed to the belief of my truth. In some cases, these writers quote the words of philosophers long gone. Even though words were interpreted hundreds of years after their deaths, I have still named them in the list, as they have equally inspired me. I have quoted many of them in this book, as their words give me some insight and something inside of me made me think of them all.

Thank you, Sathya Sai Baba, Huang Po, Albert Einstein, Robert Chappell, Erich Fromm, Richard De Martino, Jiddu Krishnamurti, Siddhattha Gotama Buddha, Lao Tzu, Confucius, Niels Bohr, Bodhidharma, Jim Al-Khalili, Lagacé, Dogen, Pema Chödrön, D.T. Suzuki, Osho, Chuang Tzu, Leonard Susskind, Art Friedman, Aristotle, the Dhammapada, PyschologyToday.Com, Winston Churchill, Franklin Roosevelt, Sebastian Seung, Richard Feynman, and many more.